D 1 v

p 99
p 108
p 113
125
127
132
145—6
156
168
170 v2
171
174
176

The Debt We Owe

The Debt We Owe

*The Royal Air Force
Benevolent Fund 1919–1999*

Edward Bishop

Airlife
England

By the same author

THE WOODEN WONDER
MOSQUITO
THE BATTLE OF BRITAIN
THEIR FINEST HOUR
THE GUINEA PIG CLUB
BLOOD AND FIRE!
WELLINGTON BOMBER
EMMA, LADY HAMILTON
BETTER TO DIE
HURRICANE

Copyright © 2000 Edward Bishop

Fourth Edition first published in the UK in 2000
by Airlife Publishing Ltd

First Edition published in 1969

British Library Cataloguing-in-Publication Data
A catalogue record for this book
is available from the British Library

ISBN 1 84037 143 9

Typeset by Phoenix Typesetting, Ilkley, West Yorkshire
Printed by WBC Book Manufacturers, Bridgend, Glamorgan.

Airlife Publishing Ltd

101 Longden Road, Shrewsbury, SY3 9EB, England.
E-mail: airlife@airlifebooks.com
Website: www.airlifebooks.com

FOREWORD

by Sir Arthur Bryant CH, CBE, LLD, MA *(1969)*

Lecturing at the Royal Air Force Apprentices' School at Halton, before the war I made use of a phrase that was more true than I knew. I had been speaking of the close relation – one then forgotten by our leading intellectuals – between the historic British command of the seas and the development, preservation and expansion of our liberties. After outlining the naval occasions by virtue of which it had been won and maintained, I looked up from my notes and, on the spur of the moment, added, 'Gentlemen, it all now depends on you!' Three years later, in the Battle of Britain, the truth of my words was dramatically proved.

'For what we have received', I was taught to say after my meals as a little boy, 'the Lord make us truly thankful!' Every year, when the anniversary of the Battle of Britain comes round, we of our generation recall with thankfulness the men, living and dead, who by their courage, skill and devotion won for our country and the world that salvationary victory. In the epic autumn the Royal Air Force saved this country and, with it, the world's freedom. It did so again in those laborious years of preparation and endurance before the assault on Hitler's western wall, when night after night the crews of Bomber Command went out on their perilous missions, suffering losses in proportion to their strength unparalleled in any sustained successful operation known to history, yet winning by it that stranglehold on the aggressor's production-centres and communications without which D-Day would have been a shambles and a disaster, and London itself would have been slowly destroyed by German rockets and flying bombs.

We can never be sufficiently grateful. The Royal Air Force in its seventy-one years of life has won its place in the English heart beside the Royal Navy for the service it has done in preserving all we love and value. The strains of Walford Davies's noble Royal Air Force March arouse something of the same association and emotions as the noble air of 'Sunset' played by the Royal Marines band at the highest moment of naval ceremony. They remind us, with a sense of pride, pity and tenderness too deep for words, of the valour, sacrifice, unselfishness and imperishable glory of those who, transcending their own human needs and inclinations, laid down all they loved for their country and gave her existence continuance and her beliefs meaning. They commemorate all that was beautiful in those freely-given and dedicated lives, the love of their comrades and dear ones, the hours of life and happiness and preparation that had gone to make them what they were and, in doing so, to serve and save England. And they remind those who hear them that in the service of England there is no finality or discharge, that life for every one of us has a purpose, and that its highest achievement is sacrifice – the key that alone opens the door to the truest and enduring aspirations of men. For, if their sacrifice has meaning, it is that the end of life is not material satisfaction but mastery over self in the cause of something more satisfying and lasting than self.

Such spiritual greatness can only be achieved at a heavy price of intense human suffering, both material and mental, endured both by the giver of the initial sacrifice and by those who love and depend on him. The Royal Air Force Benevolent Fund exists to reduce so far as possible the extent of such unavoidable suffering and loss. Founded in 1919 by Marshal of the Royal Air Force Lord Trenchard, the man who more than any other was responsible for the creation of the service that saved England in 1940, it offers assistance to all Royal Air Force personnel and their dependants who stand in need of it. Anyone commissioned or enlisted in the Royal Air Force or Women's Royal Air Force in whatever capacity is qualified for consideration by the fact of his or her service, past or present.

The work that the Fund performs is of many kinds: grants or loans in time of sickness or convalescence or of great financial stringency, in providing tools and working equipment, in meeting maternity and similar expenses, in redeeming pawned articles and pressing debts incurred by virtue of past services, in the education of children and the provision of housing. The education work of the Fund is among its most important activities. It is the Fund's policy that children whose fathers were killed or died whilst serving should receive education of the standard they would have been given had they not been orphaned. This help is continued from earliest school-days to the university if the child shows promise.

In the last resort, all national security, active or passive, depends on the readiness of men to sacrifice themselves for the defence of their country. That readiness had been shown by the officers and men of the Royal Air Force ever since it came into existence in 1918. The confidence that their countrymen would look after their dependants in the event of their full sacrifice being accepted was, and still is, a most vital factor in the formation and preservation of the service's morale. The Royal Air Force Benevolent Fund is the permanent guarantee that that confidence shall never be misplaced.

Sir Arthur Bryant, the distinguished historian, has since died.

CONTENTS

The founder of the Royal Air Force Benevolent Fund, Marshal of the
Royal Air Force the Rt. Hon. The Viscount Trenchard, GCB, OM,
GCVO, DSO, DCL, LLD.

Chapter 1

Origins

I bore you on eagles' wings
And brought you unto myself   (Exodus 19:4)

Inscription on the Royal Air Force Memorial, Victoria Embankment

When The Royal Air Force Benevolent Fund was founded eighty years ago by Air Marshal Sir Hugh Trenchard, it was named The Royal Air Force Memorial Fund because one of its earliest objects was to raise a memorial to airmen who died in the First World War.

The memorial was completed in 1923. A simple monument in Portland stone, it is surmounted by a gilded eagle and on sunny mornings railway passengers arriving at London's Charing Cross terminal can glimpse it glinting in the sunlight from its riverside position on the Victoria Embankment.

The original intention was for Mr W. Reid Dick's sculpted eagle to face inwards to the embankment road traffic, but Sir Reginald Blomfield, the Fund's consultant architect, altered his design to allow the eagle to face across the river, symbolically to France.

In the summer of 1923 the memorial was unveiled by a youthful Prince of Wales who spoke prophetically, and heaven knows how when the Royal Air Force was so emaciated, of 'our cloud armies of the future'. When the flags fell away from the memorial a Royal Air Force guard of honour crashed into the 'present arms', and a carefully marshalled contingent of twenty-seven small boys lifted their caps. The boys had come from Vanbrugh Castle, where the Fund had already established a school at Blackheath in south-east London. They were the sons of airmen who had died in the Service.

The Thames embankment might not seem the most appropriate place for a flying men's memorial. This position was not the first choice of the Royal Air Force Memorial Fund. Discarding a proposal to join the Army and the Navy in building a memorial opposite Buckingham Palace, the Royal Air Force Memorial Fund had hoped to raise a Cross on the ground between Westminster Abbey and St Margaret's Church; a hope that the Dean of Westminster was unable to approve because he preferred not to consider a memorial for the Royal Air Force alone. In

The RAF Memorial at Victoria Embankment which was unveiled by the
Prince of Wales on 16 July 1923.

any event, as the Dean explained, the particular piece of ground
belonged to St Margaret's.

In the centuries preceding the Armistice of 1918, a year in which men
had sincerely believed that they had fought the war to end war, warfare
of the past had so sprinkled Britain with memorials that the selection of
places prominent enough to commemorate the dead, as well as to
symbolise the end of war, was limited. But sites were found and in village,
town and city, on the hills and in the valleys, the stonemasons chipped
away until the nation had remembered its dead, sailor for sailor, soldier
for soldier, and the new airmen too.

Thus when the Office of Woods and Forests offered the new Royal Air
Force a site at the head of the Whitehall Stairs on Victoria Embankment
about midway between Charing Cross and Westminster Bridge, the offer

was accepted thankfully, though only as a second best.

However, the passage of time has confounded any intention, if such it was, of keeping a somewhat junior Royal Air Force in its place. Seventy years on, and showing honourable scars from bombs in the Second World War, mere accident has placed this discreet monument neatly in view of the Air Force Board at the Ministry of Defence. It is tidy, too, that, as a result in 1956 of the placing of Lord Trenchard's statue in Whitehall Gardens below the windows of the present Ministry of Defence, the Royal Air Force Memorial stands in line of sight from the martial figure who conceived both the Royal Air Force and the Royal Air Force Memorial Fund. Here by the Thames, the man who started it all has, since May 1975, been joined by Marshal of the Royal Air Force Lord Portal, Chief of the Air Staff in the Second World War and Deputy Chairman of the Royal Air Force Benevolent Fund from December 1947 until his death on 22 April 1971.

The winter of 1919–20 provided a raw social and economic climate in which Trenchard, canvassing his Royal Air Force Memorial Fund, said, 'Lots of people will get into trouble and go looking for others to help them, but the finest men and women will not ask.' A pride in self-reliance and a readiness to meet privation and disability uncomplainingly were national characteristics as yet unwarped by social legislation. Such characteristics had dominated Trenchard's early career and he feared for the welfare of the 'finest men', his men of the Royal Air Force.

The armistice of 11 November 1918 had found the Royal Air Force, a wartime amalgamation under the Air Force Constitution Act 1917 of the Royal Flying Corps and the Royal Naval Air Service, not quite eight months of age. Lacking the long traditions of the Royal Navy and the Army, the Royal Air Force possessed no strong and influential lobby through which to preserve itself, no memorial by which to be remembered, and no existing charitable fund upon which to call and to build. Indeed, even some years later, it seemed possible that the Royal Air Force, 300,000 strong in war, might disappear altogether, and almost without trace.

But, if the outlook for the new service was bleak, the future welfare of its needy presented an almost hopeless picture. Disillusion was widespread among the demobilised, and particularly so among ex-servicemen of the Royal Air Force.

In war the aviators had been praised to the skies. 'The heavens are their battlefields,' the Prime Minister, Mr Lloyd George, had lyricised in the Commons. 'They are struggling there by day, yea, and by night – and amongst the multitude of heroes we must continually thank the Cavalry of the Air.' But the end of the war had brought the Cavalry of the Air very much down to earth, to bicycles and to buses, to competing with soldiers and sailors for work in the front line of civilian life, soldiers and sailors who held the advantage in that there were established service funds and societies to which they could turn in distress.

Outside such shared service charities as the Forces Help Society and Lord Roberts Workshops, the Soldiers' and Sailors' Families Association and other funds of the time, including the United Services and Flying Services fund, officers and men of the new flying services were unsupported. Neither the Royal Flying Corps, the Royal Naval Air Service, nor their successor, the Royal Air Force, had collected charitable funds of their *own* during the war. With peace their needs were soon apparent. They had suffered more than 16,000 casualties, leaving 2600 widows and dependants, and 7500 totally or badly incapacitated officers and men.

It was against this background that Trenchard conceived a charitable fund for the flying services.

Recruiting an executive committee of prominent and wealthy people, he persuaded Lord Hugh Cecil MP, who served in the Royal Flying Corps in 1915, to accept the chairmanship and to join the first Viscount Cowdray and himself as the founding trustees of the Royal Air Force Memorial Fund. The treasurer was Sir Charles McLeod and in November 1919 the presidency was accepted by Wing Commander the Duke of York (later to become King George VI). The Executive Committee held its first meeting on 23 October 1919 at 25 Victoria Street in the office of one of its members, Mr Frank E. Rosher.

Rosher had lost his twenty-two-year-old son, Flight Lieutenant Harold Rosher of the Royal Naval Air Service, in a flying accident at Dover. A pilot's death was, of course, a frequent sorrow in 1914–18, but Flight Lieutenant Rosher had earned what, even in the First World War, was an unusually chivalrous reputation. His prowess had been noticed personally by Mr Winston Churchill, recognition which Arnold Bennett, the author, recorded by way of introduction to a posthumously published collection of the pilot's letters home from Belgium and France. Rosher's name, therefore, was associated publicly with all that had been glorious in wartime flying. When Frank Rosher came to consider a memorial to his son he invited the new Fund to establish itself at his office, and it was this generous and farseeing act that got the Royal Air Force Memorial Fund off the ground.

Concisely, the early objects of the Fund were: to build a memorial, to establish boarding schools for the children of deceased airmen, to assist the education of deceased officers' children, and to relieve distress among officers and men and their dependants, particularly through the provision of medical treatment. Those eligible for commemoration or assistance were United Kingdom or Dominion service people who had served during wartime in the Royal Naval Air Service, the Royal Flying Corps, the Australian Flying Corps, the Royal Air Force and the Women's Royal Air Force.

It is noteworthy that Dame Helen Gwynne-Vaughan, the Commandant of the Women's Royal Air Force of 1918, was a member of the Executive Committee from its inception in 1920, and served the Fund continuously in committee and council until her retirement from the deputy chairmanship in 1947. At a council meeting in December 1947, Lord Riverdale, the Chairman at that time, paid tribute to the splendid work of Dame Helen, whose exceptional general knowledge had been of the greatest help in solving difficult problems. The Council unanimously approved her election as a vice-president in recognition of her long and invaluable service.

Dame Helen spent the evening of her life at the Royal Air Forces Association's home at Sussexdown, where she died on 26 August 1967. At a Service of Thanksgiving for her life and work in the Royal Air Force church of St Clement Danes on 2 November 1967, the Deputy Vice-Chancellor of the University of London, Professor C. T. Ingold, paid further tribute to this brilliant contemporary.

Another lady associated with the birth of the Fund was Mrs B. H. Barrington Kennett, a widow whose husband had served in the Grenadier Guards and the Royal Flying Corps. She attended the first meeting of the Committee in Mr Rosher's office on 23 October 1919, and remained on it until 23 October 1931. She was also an original member of the Vanbrugh Castle School Committee from its inception in 1921 until her retirement.

In 1921, under a resolution of the Executive Committee, benefits were 'to a strictly limited extent' opened to the post-war Royal Air Force in special cases of distress arising from sickness only, where the burden 'was not sufficiently met by the normal provision of medical attendance granted by the rules of the service'. At the time, service personnel in a service hospital were liable to 'hospital stoppages' from their pay.

At first the Executive Committee's main task was to raise money, and although it was well constituted for the purpose its early efforts held little promise of accumulating any very substantial sum. The total of £125,000 received in the first year fell far short of a target of £400,000, and of this sum £95,000 was from official sources, including £50,000 from the Air Council, being part of wartime canteen profits. It is interesting to compare this last figure with the generous sum of £636,000 from NAAFI profits during the Second World War.

When the first annual report was published at the end of 1920, Lord Hugh Cecil commented: 'If the objects of the Fund are to be properly supported the public must show greater liberality.' The fact was that the Royal Air Force Memorial Fund had set itself an ambitious programme for a new service charity of limited resources and an unpredictable future income.

Disappointment at public response was softened, however, by the knowledge that the message was spreading. The Fund had found friends almost everywhere and donations were received from forty different countries, including numerous contributions from places, authorities and individuals redolent of empire. Handsome donations were received from a number of India's ruling princes.

At home, some of the fortune makers of the early part of the century contributed generously, among them Trenchard and Cecil's fellow trustee Cowdray, and Northcliffe, the newspaper and periodical proprietor; while on its own account the Fund profited £550 from its first money-raising event, a ball held at the Ritz Hotel.

In the course of the ball the Fund's recently appointed Secretary, a young and badly wounded lieutenant in uniform, named McCulloch, was approached by the Colonel-in-Chief of the 16th Lancers who said he wished to make a personal donation. The Colonel-in-Chief, King Alfonso XIII of Spain, promptly disproved the belief that royalty never carry money, for he handed McCulloch a crackling five-pound note. The Secretary was not caught off balance by this unexpected generosity; he promptly asked King Alfonso to sign the fiver. The following morning the Secretary paid a substitute five-pound note into the Fund, intending to retain the royal autograph. But such was the general insecurity of the time that the lieutenant was soon obliged to settle an account with Alfonso's fiver, which, unless any reader of this story happens to know of its existence, has disappeared for all time.

In the winter of 1919, at the age of twenty-one, the Secretary shared a room with Rosher's Romanian clerk at 25 Victoria Street. Lieutenant Derek McCulloch, who was later to become widely loved as Uncle Mac of the British Broadcasting Corporation, was the first employee of the Royal Air Force Memorial Fund and was paid five pounds a week. He was still in uniform through the personal dispensation of Trenchard, who regarded McCulloch's battered appearance as a helpful advertisement.

Fighting at the age of eighteen as a private soldier on the Somme, McCulloch had lost his right eye in 1916 and that side of his face had been sewn up. He carried a bullet in a lung and eleven other wounds. Although released as unfit for further service he had talked himself back into the Army, receiving a commission in the Green Howards and obtaining a transfer to the Royal Flying Corps.

McCulloch's function was to knit together the voluntary work of members of the Fund's distinguished Executive Committee and at first he found it an unnerving experience. The Secretary's business with the Chairman was conducted at Lord Hugh Cecil's breakfast table at 21 Arlington Street, where McCulloch attended regularly with the Fund's papers. Although his broadcasting career was soon to separate him from the Fund's affairs, Derek McCulloch retained an affectionate and helpful interest in them until his death at the age of sixty-nine in May 1967.

Lord Hugh, who later became Lord Quickswood and retired as a Trustee of the Fund in 1944, would have totally disbelieved any prophecy that eighty years afterwards the struggling charity he was running from his breakfast table would own some £170 million of investment and be spending around £14 million a year on welfare.

CHAPTER 2

GETTING OFF THE GROUND

*'Their exploits and undoubted courage have established a tradition for the
new service which our cloud armies of the future, whether in peace or war,
will I feel sure follow with devoted pride.'*

His Royal Highness The Prince of Wales, 1923

In the very first year of the Fund's life two separate acts of generosity
opened the way for the beginning of its educational work. A Mrs M. E.
Salting who lived in Berkeley Square presented the Fund with two
unoccupied houses at Ascot, and Mr Alexander Duckham, who had
made a fortune in oil, offered his former London home, Vanbrugh Castle,
to the Fund.

Unfortunately, the Ascot houses were sold in poor market conditions.
But, producing a total of £9956 0s 5d after expenses, they enabled the
Fund to establish the first of many educational trust funds, the Salting
Benefaction.

Odd though it may seem at this distance in the light of Vanbrugh's
fine record and the establishment in 1976 of its successor, Duke of Kent
School in the Surrey Hills, Vanbrugh Castle was not accepted as
eagerly as was Mrs Salting's gift. After the war, when the house stood
empty, Duckham's brother-in-law, Wing Commander Vernon Brown,
had hinted, 'Trenchard could use Vanbrugh Castle'. Duckham talked
to Trenchard with the result that a special Memorial Fund Committee was formed to consider the offer. At first the Committee was
inclined to exchange Vanbrugh for cash, subject to Duckham's agreement, and this step would have been taken but for the vigorous
opposition of the Committee's two Royal Air Force members, Air
Commodore H. R. M. Brooke-Popham and Air Vice-Marshal Sir John
Salmond.

Brooke-Popham proposed and Salmond seconded the experimental
use of the house as a boys' home and his proposal was accepted by three
votes to two, four members of the committee abstaining. At about the
same time that Vanbrugh Castle's future was assured and the property
legally transferred to the Fund in 1921, the Air Council gave the fund
£50,000 from canteen profits.

In the light of Duke of Kent School's present role as a boarding school for the sons and daughters of deceased, and in some cases disabled, officers, warrant officers, non-commissioned officers, airmen and airwomen, as well as children of serving personnel, it is noteworthy that as far back as 1920 Vanbrugh Castle was conditionally tied to the education of airmen's children. In no circumstances were officers' children to benefit. But the world moves on and it will be seen how in the 1970s this stipulation was overcome.

To give is better than to receive and, since it is impossible to give if the charitable chest is empty, it is in the natural order of things that much of this account will be about the indispensable substance of money. The first Lord Attlee once said, 'Voluntary effort would always be necessary to humanise the state schemes.' Methods of obtaining money have altered considerably since the receipt of the earliest donation, a fact which reflects the redistribution of wealth and the great social changes which, cantering along between the wars, went into a gallop after 1945. As with the tax-burdened princes of private enterprise, the wealthy and generous potentates of Britain's imperial past no longer proliferate, and minor royalty has either disappeared or finds itself in sadly reduced circumstances. The Emperor of Ethiopia addressed a bag of gold to the Fund during the Second World War, but King Alfonso's fiver was a once-and-for-all.

Within the Fund, the arts of appeal have accorded with prevailing conditions over the years, the exceptions being the constant appeal for legacies and the concept of the Air Display.

The first Royal Air Force air display, or aerial pageant as it was described, took place at Hendon on 3 July 1920. Flight Lieutenant E. B. C. Betts and Air Commodore B. C. H. Drew acted as the secretaries. It was a big success, *Flight* commenting that it put pre-war aerial race meetings 'in the shade'. The Fund reported:

> For the first time on record the British public were able to witness an exhibition of almost every phase of modern aerial warfare . . . a sausage kite balloon was brought down in flames, trenches were bombed from the air and aerial duels between British and captured Boche machines were displayed.

Mr Heath Robinson's aeroplane, 'smoke belching from the funnel, nearly took the air'.

The occasion was charmingly period. The 50,000 spectators who witnessed Miss Sylvia Boyden's parachute descent from a Handley-Page machine accepted it as the courageous highlight of a most daring afternoon.

At the end of the day, the Fund's gate amounted to more than £6700, a sum large enough to present Air Vice-Marshal Sir John Salmond, who had supervised the pageant, with the immediate problem of what to do with the money.

But Salmond, whose imaginative mind was to benefit the Fund for so many years, provided a characteristically unorthodox solution. Summoning six officers to his tent, he asked them to fetch their wives. Shortly afterwards, the astonished ladies were despatched to their homes, each with more than £1000 in her custody. 'Put the money under your pillows,' Sir John instructed them, 'until I find out what to do with it.'

If Salmond's overnight banking ruse was splendidly unorthodox, the Fund's general finance and legal arrangements were, of course, professionally advised. The Fund's bankers and solicitors, Barclays, Cox's and King's, and Charles Russell and Co., had been appointed at the outset. The auditors were Blackburns, Barton, Mayhew and Co. With the alteration that Barclays now bank for the Insurance Advisory Service and Lloyds Bank, incorporating Cox's and King's, for the Fund generally, these founding arrangements remain.

From the beginning, the chartered accountants, lawyers and bankers have been employed as the paid professional servants of the Fund. All decision has rested with members of the Fund's honorary committees which, by the year 1922, were the Executive Committee, the Vanbrugh Castle Sub-committee, and the Grants Sub-committee.

In 1922 the Grants Sub-committee was authorised to spend up to £4800 at the monthly rate of £400. Any proceeds from the annual pageant were received as 'corn in Egypt' and spent as available. Practically, this brought the Fund's spending power to £9000 for the year, an infinitesimal sum by contrast with the £7.5 million which was spent on relief in the seventieth anniversary year.

Looking back from the present when relief lies largely in the realm of home purchase loans for widows and disabled; loans for property maintenance; the resolution of indebtedness that has arisen from circumstances beyond an individual's control; the private education of orphaned or needy service children, and the provision of the smaller comforts and extras which brighten the lives of the disabled and the elderly, some of the Fund's early rates and forms of relief were of necessity comparatively modest. But society has changed. When a man had no boots in which to seek work, or lacked the elementary tools of his trade, such possessions as a home of his own, a car if he was disabled, were beyond all contemplation.

In 1922, benefits, which included sixty-three grants for clothing, twenty cases of redeeming pawned goods, and fifty-six grants for hawker's licences, were necessarily minimal, but on the whole rather better than assistance available from other war charities.

Individual calls for assistance in the 1920s were small and uncomplicated. Small awards were as little as a shilling for a night's lodging at the Young Men's Christian Association huts at Waterloo or Victoria, and such small grants alleviated the distress of large numbers of men out of work or stranded in London. 'Seven days Soldiers' Home', or twenty-one shillings a week, and threepence a day pocket money at the Soldiers' Home was an everyday decision.

Modest though such measures were, together with the larger issues of educational assistance and the commemorative centrepiece, the Royal Air Force Memorial, they consumed money. But the Fund was in no mind to preserve capital while distress existed, as is still the case today. In 1922 the Executive Committee was of the opinion that 'the need for assistance in the present bad state of trade and the country's finances generally' was far more acute than it was likely to be in the future. It was considered 'wiser and better to spend now in relieving distress among the deserving who had helped to win the Great War, rather than accumulate capital for posterity'.

The early part of that resolution sounds a familiar note and, as will be seen, subsequent experiences of a 'bad state of trade and the country's finances generally' were to tax the Fund's resources.

But after the 1914–18 War the natural mood and desire was to assist all officers and men who had fought in the flying services, and to raise a memorial to the dead, a place at which to pause, to pray and to remember now that the war belonged to the past. However, as memories of the war receded, the mood began to change, and change introduced concern for the future needs of ex-service people and the immediate troubles of serving officers and airmen or their dependants.

As it happened, the completion and unveiling of the memorial in 1923 separated the two moods as an inscribed stone might mark the boundary between adjoining towns. The Prince of Wales presaged the future course of the Fund when he unveiled the memorial on 16 July 1923. Speaking of the dead, he said:

> Their exploits and undoubted courage have established a tradition for the new service which our cloud armies of the future, whether in peace or war, will I feel sure follow with devoted pride; and the nation on whose behalf I am asked to accept this Memorial, and to whom I am to dedicate it, will ever thankfully remember the gallant lives and great deeds it commemorates.

The possibility of war again was publicly accepted. Four months after the ceremony, the Executive Committee of the Royal Air Force Memorial Fund resolved to assist the next of kin of serving officers or airmen, bearing in mind that the hazards of peacetime flying caused casualties during training flights.

The raising of the memorial, and the attendant publicity, had played its public relations role in helping to perpetuate the Royal Air Force. Now, it was clear to the Fund that its resources ought to be available to the men who were losing their lives, their limbs and their livelihoods in peacetime service. Henceforth, Air Ministry Weekly Orders announced at the end of 1923, the Fund would offer immediate financial assistance to the next of kin of officers or airmen killed on active service, or who died from accident or disease while serving. The object was to bridge the gap between death and the issue of a pension of gratuity.

The Fund's resolution to accept responsibility for serving families was an important milestone on its journey, even though the resources to support it were limited. Relief expenditure had risen from £919 in 1920 to £9861 in 1923; and, with 1923 donations tailing off to £1554, income from all sources totalled £17,783. But the milestone marked rather more than the broadening of the Fund's scope. It indicated a dawning appreciation of the Fund's potential value as a first-rate morale factor throughout the Royal Air Force.

For the moment, however, the outlook was gloomy. In 1924 the maximum grant of £100 was suspended and in the following year public donations fell to £2043. Without the aerial pageant which had become an annual event, and subsequently the Royal Tournament, the Fund would have been in peril of collapse. Memories of the flying services' wartime exploits were fading and, apart from a momentary interest in the pageant and the Royal Tournament and the publicity given to record-breaking flights, crashes and casualties, the public was largely unaware of the mostly distant and little publicised day-to-day activities of the Royal Air Force.

It was a critical period for the nation's future as an air power, a period in which the Royal Air Force Memorial Fund had its contribution to make by staying the course with the Royal Air Force and the fledgling aircraft industry.

Losing support from such exotic quarters of the Empire as the princely states of India and the white citizens of Swaziland, the Fund grew more conscious of the potential value of such modest contributors as the struggling aircraft companies, and the Royal Air Force stations themselves: Biggin Hill in 1926, ten shillings. An airfield's mite, but it reflected an awakening concern within the Service and such contributions were to place the Fund's subscriptions' account on a more durable basis for the future. Fourteen years separated Biggin Hill from the Battle of Britain and 1926 found the Royal Air Force, the aircraft manufacturers and the Fund stumbling forward under the most frustrating conditions. Fortunately, the Royal Air Force and the British aircraft industry persevered and donations flowed into the Fund in thanksgiving during and after the touch-and-go events of 1940.

Organisationally, the Fund was developing in the mid-1920s. There was now very much more paperwork than could be shuffled at breakfast, while the Secretary and the staff of four had outgrown the shared room with Frank Rosher's clerk. The Fund occupied three rooms at Iddesleigh House, Westminster, where Lieutenant-Colonel W. S. Burch had succeeded Lieutenant Derek McCulloch. There were also an Assistant Secretary, Mr J. P. Cunninghame, who remained a Fund Helper and

Education Adviser for many years, and two shorthand typists, one of whom, Mrs Grace Inglis, was promoted to Relief Secretary and spent forty years with the Fund, retiring in 1965. She was awarded the MBE for her long and devoted service.

The small staff worked long hours and on Saturday mornings. Administrative expenditure was kept to a minimum. Such economy was only possible because of the Fund's inspired founding principle of co-operation with other interservice organisations such as the Forces Help Society and Lord Roberts Workshops, the Soldiers', Sailors' and Airmen's Families Association, and the British Legion, a principle that has remained fundamental to the Fund's relief work for seventy years. In 1921, for example, the Fund reimbursed the Officers' Association £200 per month for its work with ex-Royal Air Force officers and such an arrangement continued by which the Officers' Association accepted responsibility for veterans of the First World War, with no service after August 1921, subject to an upper limit, until the Royal Air Force Benevolent Fund took over responsibility. Nowadays the Fund also works very closely with the Royal Air Forces Association.

Early co-operation with other organisations for the investigation of cases, and financial sharing in the work of sympathetic societies, reduced outgoings and fostered many connections for the future. Aided from the outset by the Executive Committee's self-adjuration to beware 'mis-chievous overlapping', this process was greatly advanced when Earl Haig invited two of that committee's members, Lieutenant-Commander H. E. Perrin and Mrs L. M. K. Pratt-Barlow, to join his Services Funds Advisory Council.

CHAPTER 3

BETWEEN THE
TWO WORLD WARS

*'After church they lectured us in the cinema on savings certificates, telling us
we'd be glad of the money when we left the service and faced civil life.'*

Aircraftman T. E. Shaw (Lawrence of Arabia)

From the 1920s to the early 1930s the Royal Air Force was busy justi-
fying its post-war reprieve in the developing role of an airborne
imperial constabulary. Whitehall had learned the economy of
patrolling troublesome people from the air, and Royal Air Force
squadrons were replacing the marching, ambushed, waterless columns of
imperial experience.

Trenchard, supported by Colonel T. E. Lawrence at the 1922 Cairo
conference, had first urged this new role upon the Colonial Secretary, Mr
Winston Churchill. It was accepted and the Royal Air Force was stationed
thinly across the British Empire, far removed from the headquarters of
the Royal Air Force Memorial Fund, but by no means out of mind.

In 1924 the Fund paid £200 to the Air Ministry to enable commanding
officers in Malta, Palestine, India and the Middle East, excluding Iraq, to
give immediate help to families distressed by the death of an officer or
an airman. Iraq was excluded because Royal Air Force families were not
then permitted in that country. Happily, though, the restriction did
not deter units stationed in Iraq from supporting the Fund. Indeed, they
could scarcely do otherwise. The Air Officer Commanding was Sir John
Salmond, who had vacated the chair of the Vanbrugh Castle Sub-
committee upon appointment.

In its formative years the Fund was fortunate that members of the
immediate generation of Royal Air Force leaders had involved themselves with its ideals and aspirations from the start. The Air Officers
Commanding carried their enthusiasm for the Fund to their commands
overseas with encouraging results, the Salmond brothers being exceptionally successful. Sir John and Sir Geoffrey Salmond pulled off an
excellent family double in 1927. While Sir John collected 10,000 rupees
at an aerial pageant in Delhi, Sir Geoffrey raised £8006 4s 7d on his
brother's old pitch at Hendon.

The interchange of the Salmonds' appointments suited the Fund admirably, and for their part the brothers enjoyed competing with one another to raise money. It was in the nature of things, therefore, that after Sir Geoffrey's return from Egypt in 1921 he should have succeeded his brother as Chairman of the Vanbrugh Castle Sub-committee.

The Fund's acceptance of responsibility towards serving members of the Air Force applied at Vanbrugh too, and in 1926 the castle gates were opened to the sons of serving airmen, in addition to the sons of men who died in the service, but the fatherless boys were still given priority. The addition of a new dormitory for twelve boys increased Vanbrugh's numbers from twenty-seven boys between the ages of five and school-leaving age in 1923 to thirty-nine boys in 1926.

Although Vanbrugh was already known as Vanbrugh Castle School, no teaching took place there except of the very youngest boys. During Vanbrugh's earliest months the boys attended a local elementary school. But from the summer of 1922 the Fund had paid grammar school fees for boys able to pass the entrance examination.

From the outset the Fund held that 'the future of the boys lies to a large extent with themselves and is greatly dependent upon their own abilities'. The reality of this raw opportunity amounted to a roof, a bed, and the institutional care of a superintendent and a matron, Captain and Mrs G. A. R. Slimming.

Vanbrugh boys were not obliged to enter the Royal Air Force but the Fund hoped that, partly by environment and partly by training, the boys might desire to join their fathers' service, thus 'furnishing', as the Fund phrased it, 'the service with a supply of men whose upbringing from boyhood has been in the very closest touch with its best traditions'. In 1926 the entry of two boys as aircraft apprentices at the Royal Air Force School of Technical Training, Halton – their fathers had died in the war – launched a tradition through which many Vanbrugh boys have volunteered for a service career.

 In that year too, Mrs F. Vesey Holt, a young Royal Air Force bride, joined the Grants Committee and Appeals Committee. She was also on the Council. Not retiring until 1973, she was the longest-serving committee member of the Fund in her day.

In its early life the Royal Air Force Benevolent Fund made poor financial progress. When Sir Charles McLeod, the Honorary Treasurer, succeeded Lord Hugh Cecil as Chairman in 1929, only £195,000 of the target £400,000 had been reached. The very conditions which demanded the Fund's existence drained its resources and conflicted with its chances of support.

It was recognised that of the total income the excellent proceeds from the Air Display and the Royal Tournament were unhealthily top-heavy items, but economic conditions seemed to defy the attainment of a balance between these receipts and other donations. For example, in 1926 £6905 6s 4d and £1700 were received in respect of the display and the Royal Tournament against £2599 8s 7d from all other sources.

Unfortunately, for all Biggin Hill's ten shillings in 1926, the Fund lacked any consistent subscription support from the Royal Air Force, where it was widely, if erroneously, held that the Fund possessed ample means.

There was, however, one serving airman who knew this was not so. He was better informed about the Fund than most of his fellows because he happened to know Trenchard personally. He also had the disconcerting practice of calling at Iddesleigh House to inquire for himself how things were going. But this supporter extraordinary was serving in India when the Fund learned that he had arranged (with later supplements) a £20,000 trust known as the Anonymous Educational Fund, to provide an income for the education of the children of deceased or disabled officers.

If the facts have not already disclosed this airman's identity, then possibly a quotation will unmask him: 'Our hut is a microcosm of un-employed England, not of unemployable England for the strict Royal Air Force standards refuse the last levels of the social structure.'

No serving member of the Royal Air Force could have been more conscious at this time of the value of the Fund to the service than Lawrence of Arabia. Colonel Lawrence, who had re-entered the Royal Air Force in 1925 as Aircraftman T. E. Shaw following the discovery of his identity as A. C. John Hume Ross, and a brief intervening spell in the Army, observed the distress in others at first hand and brought cases personally to the notice of Colonel Burch. He wrote, too, of cases known to him in and out of barracks. Two of his letters have survived the Fund's periodical disposal of waste paper:

August 25, 1932

A. C. Shaw, Myrtle Cottage,
Hythe, Southampton

Dear Colonel Burch,

This is a private letter to ask you to be good enough to advise on pro-cedure. Some friends of the late Flt. Lt. J . . . of Tangmere (he died at Halton this year, of cancer, after twenty-two years service) have asked me how his widow can be helped in the matter of educating her daughter. Her son goes to Halton as an aircraft apprentice this next entry. The girl is seventeen and apt for a business career, if she can receive some preliminary training. I suppose a single grant of some forty or fifty pounds would cover the whole affair, and this you can probably easily arrange, when approached on the proper lines. For an airman applications are made through* . . . last C.O., I believe. How about widows of officers: Mrs J's . . . address is . . . She does not know about . . . I expect, and I hope she won't.

---

* Breaks indicate where letter torn and illegible.

Will you deal either direct with Mrs J . . . if proper, or tell me to my address how the . . . should be presented? I am very sorry for troubling . . . In writing will you let me know if . . . income tax problem upon your education fund . . . solved yet? I am holding up the . . . of a lump sum to provide instalments for Mrs H . . . our Mountbatten sergeant's widow, until I hear that the tax question is settled: and meanwhile the station is paying her £5 a quarter, which is not easy for so small a strength to raise.

Yours sincerely,

6.IX.32

338171 A. C. Shaw
Royal Air Force,
Mountbatten,
Plymouth.

Dear Colonel Burch,

You will note that I am returning to my Plymouth address in a day or two. Please forget the Hythe one.

Mrs J . . . is definitely not interested in the interview arranged by a lady offering help with D. H. Evans for her daughter. The girl is described as intelligent and bookish, far more cut out for secretarial work than for the sales department. Only her father's death has taken the family by surprise, and so she is untrained. Her mother's means is only about a pound a week, insufficient to maintain them while her daughter is being trained, and to pay the training fees into the bargain. So it is clearly a case in which a grant for commercial-educational-training should be applied for. Will you please let Mrs J . . . know (your AMS 1061) how she is to apply for this grant? Her friends are quite definite in their statements to me, after having seen your letter and discussed it with the widow.

Lawrence had earned the money with his pen. His story of his wartime exploits, *Revolt in the Desert*, was a best-seller; Bernard Shaw had named it a masterpiece and its author a genius. But the author was earning airmen's pay in India when he completed his astonishing act of self-denial. As 338171, A. C. Shaw endured the prickly heat and Noël Coward addressed him, 'Dear 338171, may I call you 338?' Lawrence laboured in the knowledge that he was educating ten or more children of Royal Air Force officers.

When Lawrence died in 1935 his trust had paid £4142 towards school fees and he was educating thirteen children in that year. He was buried in the Dorset village of Moreton on 22 May 1935 in the presence of a small private group of mourners. Amid them stooped the tall figure of Marshal of the Royal Air Force Sir John Salmond who felt simply that 'someone from the top ought to be there'. Mr and Mrs Winston Churchill were present too.

Perhaps the oddest turn in this strange episode was Lawrence's decision to benefit only officers' children at a time when he knew that airmen, falling prey to their natural suspicions, believed the Fund was mainly concerned with the relief of officers and their families.

Communication between the Fund and the barrack room was almost non-existent. Airmen did not generally appreciate that in its formative years the Fund had consistently striven to keep a fair balance between officers and airmen. Because of the high ratio of officers to airmen, and because flying was mostly carried out by officers, casualties among officers were disproportionately large and the Fund was closely exercised to achieve fairness. Of course there was always the possibility that at any moment disaster might tip the balance, and this happened at Quetta in 1935.

Out of 358 British servicemen in No. 3 (Indian) Wing, fifty-five were killed and 130 injured in that historic earthquake. 'The Royal Air Force Station, Quetta, looks like Ypres in 1917,' the Wing Commander wrote to Group Captain G. I. Carmichael, who had recently succeeded Colonel Burch as secretary. The Wing Commander reported that fifty-two of the fifty-five men killed were Royal Air Force non-commissioned officers and airmen, adding, 'Some of my own records are still buried and I have not a complete list.' A baptism, indeed, in Benevolent Fund affairs for Wing Commander J. C. Slessor, who was to serve with such distinction during the Second World War and who, in the rank of Marshal of the Royal Air Force, was to maintain his association with the Fund as a vice-president, until his death on 12 July 1979.

Quetta gave rise to forty-nine cases in Britain, twenty of which required financial assistance. There was, for instance, the case of the airman with nine years' service who was killed at Quetta, leaving a wife and two children. As it happened the Fund was already in touch with the family because of illness and medical expenses. After the earthquake the widow was helped to take her children to Australia, where she had been offered a home and a job. It was, incidentally, an example of co-operation with other organisations, the Fund paying the emigration expenses in conjunction with the Royal Patriotic Fund, the Salvation Army and the Society for the Overseas Settlement of British Women.

Quetta had come at the tail end of an exceptionally difficult period. The trouble was that the national economic depression had so increased requests for assistance and so lowered the Fund's income that in 1933, for example, expenditure had exceeded income by £455. Even those financial buttresses, the Air Display and the Royal Tournament, were shadows of their former glory.

In this worrying situation the Fund stated its duty clearly:

> To take money out of capital might be thought to afford a temporary solution of the problem but would be definitely wrong because the Fund does not exist to tide over the temporary problem of helping wartime cases. It must continue to work for all time for the benefit of the post-war Royal Air

Force. The Fund must not be allowed to die out through the expenditure of capital, but must be preserved and indeed the capital increased. The Council, therefore, have reluctantly decided that until there is a greater response to the needs of the Fund, both from the service and the public, there is no alternative but to reduce grants.

On the Benevolent Fund of the Service that fights in the air, the needs of the disabled and the dependants of those killed flying must always be a first charge, and a large measure of the help available must be directed towards the assistance of widows and the education of their children.

Other casualties, disability, sickness, and general distress will continue to present many cases and the Fund will meet, as far as means permit, appeals not only from those who left the service years ago, but from those who are leaving in present times and from serving personnel whose needs are beyond station resources.

Thus, fifteen years after the Armistice and in the year as it happened that Hitler and his National Socialist Party came to power in Germany, the Fund readjusted its sights. Several years were to elapse before the Fund was in a position, during the 1939–45 War to change to the policy, which it has followed ever since, of using capital whenever income is insufficient.

Since inception to 5 December 1933 the Royal Air Force Memorial Fund had made 18,608 grants involving, with the £30,000 maintenance of Vanbrugh Castle, an expenditure of £150,000. The Memorial phase was over and, now that 'benevolent' was thought to be more descriptive of its purpose and qualified it for tax relief, the Fund in December 1933 restyled itself the Royal Air Force Benevolent Fund, an alteration of name that was followed by a change of Chairman. Sir Charles McLeod, Honorary Treasurer since the Fund's inception and Chairman since 1928, resigned at the end of 1934. He was succeeded as Treasurer by Mr Walter S. Field, also a founder member of the 1919 Executive Committee and Chairman of the Grants Committee. The new Chairman was Lord Wakefield.

At this time of change Lord Wakefield brought the Royal Air Force Benevolent Fund precisely what it needed: a wealthy friend who had the right connections and his heart in the Service.

Welcomed to the Fund as 'the man to whom British aviation owes so much', Wakefield, who was seventy-four, soon demonstrated that when a man's heart and enthusiasm are spiritedly engaged, neither his age nor his period will restrain him. Some of Wakefield's contemporaries, born around the time of the Indian Mutiny and already in their forties at the beginning of the century, were content in the depressed and dangerous 1930s to grumble themselves to the grave. But not so C. C. Wakefield. Son of a Liverpool customs official, he had seized upon the combination of the new motor car and of castor oil as a means to a fortune, giving birth to and marketing from this clever marriage the internationally renowned lubricant, Castrol.

After making his money on the roads, Wakefield spent it liberally in the air, coaxing, encouraging the development of speed, comfort and design in the manufacture of aircraft and the growth of skill among the pioneer aviators of the 1920s and 1930s.

One of his earlier actions as Chairman of the Royal Air Force Benevolent Fund was to establish the Viscount Wakefield Benefaction with a gift of £10,000. Since 1936 the income from this trust has provided for the academic or technical training of young officers or airmen who have left the service, and paid for the further education of Royal Air Force children after leaving school.

At this time of change the Royal Air Force Benevolent Fund also restyled and reorganised its executive structure. Detail was removed from the Executive Committee to a freshly constituted Finance and General Purposes Committee, while the Executive Committee raised itself to the status of a policy-making council. The significance of this reform, however, lay not so much in style as in the reconstruction of the Council which followed. Hitherto, membership of the Executive Committee had evolved as a mixture of business and service leaders with additional members able to bring humanitarian and common-sense judgement to its meetings. On the whole this had been satisfactory but, now that the Royal Air Force Benevolent Fund was as permanent as the Royal Air Force itself, there was a need to regularise its composition and in particular service and ex-service representation. Late in 1934 eligibility for membership of the Council was defined to include:

The Air Officer Commanding-in-Chief, Air Defence of Great Britain; the Air Member for Personnel; the Air Officer Commanding Coastal Area; two members, not serving personnel, nominated by the Air Council; representatives of the Comrades of the Royal Air Forces Association and any other similar air bodies approved by the Air Council, six members nominated by the Council of the Fund.

An early and important result of the reformation was the appointment to the Council of Air Marshal Sir Hugh Dowding in his capacity as Air Officer Commanding-in-Chief Fighter Command. Dowding, of course, in his efforts to prepare the fighter defence of the realm was engaged elsewhere on more urgent work, but he quickly saw how badly the Fund needed money and what ought to be done to get it. Joining the Council, he was dismayed to find some members much in favour of launching a major public appeal. It was not that he was against a future appeal in principle but that he thought it was wrong to seek help outside before asking and getting the Royal Air Force to do more for itself. He said: 'It is right and proper that serving personnel should be the principal contributors and they can do very much more than they are now doing.' He was supported by Air Vice-Marshal Sir Philip Game, who suggested that regular annual subscriptions, as in the Royal Artillery, would be felt by no one.

The time was approaching, too, as Dowding well knew, when the Fund would lose the income from the annual Air Display for the reason that new aircraft types were outgrowing the small Hendon airfield.

Thus in the early spring of 1936 Dowding and Game had set the Council thinking about an idea which was eventually to transform the Fund's financial prospect. But it was not to happen yet because the Air Council was neither prepared to back an appeal to the public, nor to ask the Royal Air Force for increased support. It was, however, no unusual experience for Dowding to plant ideas which were slow to take root and more than a year passed before his proposal began to gather support.

It was only postponement of better times but it was a delay the Fund could little afford. Certainly the improved trade conditions of 1936 had resulted in a reduction of minor cases of distress but the Fund was feeling the cumulative effect of casualties in the service and among ex-members of the Royal Air Force in civil aviation.

Relief expenditure in 1936 was £18,825, of which post-war casualties among serving and reserve personnel accounted for £3607. Education absorbed £7335, including the maintenance of Vanbrugh Castle where there were now forty-two boys in residence.

By 1936, of the boys who had passed through Vanbrugh receiving their education at local schools, notably the Roan Grammar School, nineteen boys had entered the Royal Air Force Apprentice Training Establishments at Halton and Cranwell.

The successes of Vanbrugh boys who had volunteered for the service greatly pleased Lord Wakefield, who enlarged the school by presenting an adjacent house at a cost of some £3000. This Wakefield Wing accommodated twenty-five boys and raised Vanbrugh's capacity from forty-two to sixty-seven boys. The wing was ceremonially opened in May 1939 by Lady Newall, wife of the Chief of the Air Staff.

In Council in the summer of 1937 the Commanders-in-Chief of Bomber and Coastal Commands, Air Chief Marshal Sir John Steel and Air Marshal Sir Philip Joubert, returned warmly to the subject of voluntary subscription from the service. Sir John urged: 'The situation whereby the Royal Air Force practically lives on outside charity with only a very small contribution by Royal Air Force personnel should not be allowed to continue.' It was the Air Marshal's opinion that the Royal Air Force ought to put its house in order before there was any question of going to the public. But still the Council remained chary of committing itself to a general service appeal.

However, when the Fund finally introduced the half-a-day's-pay-a-year scheme late in 1938 it was an immediate success, reaping £11,111 through unit pay ledgers and officers' mess bills. At one stroke Dowding's idea had eliminated the old reliance on the Royal Tournament and the

Air Display. It was as well, because in 1938, as Dowding had warned, the Air Display was withdrawn.

Aerial pageantry had paid much of the Fund's way for nearly twenty years. When it passed into history, Hendon, and from 1934 the annual Empire Air Day, had produced almost £200,000 between them. But every penny of this sum had been spent on the relief of distress, leaving the capital outlook as bleak as ever.

War, it was assumed, would break the Fund and war was coming. The pilots and crews of the Royal Air Force, the Auxiliary Air Force and the Royal Air Force Volunteer Reserve were training for war and the Fund now covered them all.

As Germany invaded Poland the Fund's secretary, Group Captain G. I. Carmichael, insisted upon returning to active service, leaving his assistant, Squadron Leader V. S. Erskine-Lindop, in charge. Required to evacuate London, Erskine-Lindop packed his wife, three female clerks and a parcel of current files into his car and drove down to the coast.

CHAPTER 4

THE SECOND WORLD WAR

*'Never in the field of human conflict was
so much owed by so many to so few.'*

Winston Churchill, 1940

War came again on 3 September 1939, and on the very day of its declaration the air-raid sirens sounded on the roof tops below the Royal Air Force balloons which were already flying over London. Any 'cloud armies' forecast by the Prince of Wales at the unveiling of the Royal Air Force Memorial sixteen years earlier were on the airfields of the enemy.

If, however, the Royal Air Force was inadequately equipped and undermanned, the very existence of the Royal Air Force Benevolent Fund, however meagre its resources, placed its families at an advantage over their predecessors of the First World War. Yet warfare had changed radically since the building of the Thames-side memorial. The Council, only too aware that this was going to be an air war, anxiously considered the prospect of massive need.

For the moment, though, the Royal Air Force Benevolent Fund could do little more than issue a calm reminder of intent before, as the Council expected, the crisis came. The Annual Report for the year 1939 seemed the right place to do this and there the Fund repeated its creed:

> The general policy of the Fund is controlled by the Council and put into effect through the Grants, the Vanbrugh Castle School and the Finance Committees. There are no hard and fast rules as to the kind of cases which may be helped or as to the amount of financial assistance which may be given. The only limitations are those prescribed by the dictates of commonsense and by the money available. Within these limits the aim of the Fund is to provide relief quickly and to provide adequate relief. In short the Fund endeavours to enable dependants to carry on in some semblance of the life to which they have been accustomed, and to help children into the careers that their fathers might reasonably have expected them to follow. The Fund being a service fund must take into account not only the human side but service given. Casualty cases are normally more lasting and if adequate relief is to be given it must be

more expensive than those of temporary distress through sickness or unemployment.

The 'phoney war' of the winter of 1939–40 postponed the awaited avalanche. Equally, it was not dramatic enough to stir public generosity.

Although obsolescent twin-engined aircraft of Bomber Command were attacking enemy rival naval installations in daylight and sustaining heavy losses, such raids coupled with the leaflet 'attacks' failed to stimulate any more donations than the meagre sums received between the wars. It helped, all the same, that Lord Wakefield diverted his £1500 prize money for the cancelled King's Cup air races to the Fund and that the Duke of Bedford sent a cheque for £1000 in token of the unsuccessful search by the Royal Air Force for his wife after the celebrated flying duchess had disappeared on a solo flight.

Among the Fund's old friends there were those who, remembering 1914–18, feared that the lull would not last, and foremost among the old friends stood Alexander Duckham, whose gift of Vanbrugh Castle had so greatly assisted the Fund's education efforts for eighteen years. For the second time in his life Alexander Duckham offered his home for the use of Royal Air Force children. Duckham was now living at Rooks Hill House, a country mansion high in the Weald of Kent near Sevenoaks and surrounded by 200 acres of land. Moving to a cottage in the grounds, Mr Duckham made a gift of Rooks Hill to the Fund together with a settlement of £1000 a year towards upkeep and maintenance of the estate.

It was Duckham's wish that Rooks Hill should shelter the very young children of officer and non-commissioned pilots killed in action or in flying accidents, and for the greater part of 1940 fifteen boys and girls between the ages of two and seven were accommodated as his guests. But Sevenoaks lay amid the fighter defences of south-east England and along the bomber lane to London. At the end of August 1940, at the height of the Battle of Britain, Rooks Hill was closed and the children were returned to their families.

Because of its proximity to London's dockland, Vanbrugh Castle had been closed too. Both Rooks Hill and Vanbrugh were damaged by enemy action and neither school was to reopen until the end of the war. Vanbrugh boys who had been attending the Roan Grammar School locally were evacuated with that school to the country.

For all its reluctance to appeal to the public or even to the Royal Air Force, the main reason why the Fund was so short of capital between the wars is traceable to its late start in 1919. Had the Fund been introduced while Lloyd George was praising the 'Cavalry of the Air', while London was threatened by Zeppelin attack and the Royal Flying Corps and the Royal Naval Air Service were producing a new breed of hero, public response must surely have created a good round sum of capital. But as Churchill later remarked: 'We are a nation of short memories.'

Between 1914 and 1918 this chance had been missed and as the 'phoney war' passed from 1939 into 1940 it began to look as if the new war might fail to produce a second opportunity. Then, after the spring *blitzkrieg* of 1940 had placed Germany on the Channel coast, the Battle of Britain, which altered so much, completely changed the comparatively unimportant fortunes of the Royal Air Force Benevolent Fund.

It is rare that a battle's place in the full perspective of history can be seen while it is still being fought, but such was the case of the Battle of Britain.

Wakefield, the motor-oil opportunist of the early century, whose encouragement of weekend flying was now being justified in many a dogfight overhead, was not the Chairman to let this chance slip.

On 30 August 1940, as the Battle of Britain was fought over southern England, he wrote to *The Times*:

> The wonderful achievements of the Royal Air Force in these critical weeks of the second Great War of our time have naturally led to various suggestions being made as to the best way in which we can give expression to our gratitude. In the deepest sense, there is no way in which the heroism and sacrifices of our airmen can be assessed or our debt to them in any way liquidated.
>
> As there is, nevertheless, the desire to express the nation's thanks in tangible form, let it be devoted in part to some constructive aim, some cause that can be shown to be solely and entirely for the permanent benefit of all ranks and their dependants. I venture to submit as the most appropriate object of our generosity, The Royal Air Force Benevolent Fund, which exactly fulfils these conditions.
>
> This Fund, founded in 1919 by Viscount Trenchard, in addition to assisting airmen in various circumstances of special need and difficulty undertakes the education of children of Royal Air Force parentage and helps to establish them in careers that their fathers would be proud for them to follow.
>
> Up to now the funds of the Royal Air Force Benevolent Fund have been raised without any public appeal, largely by contributions from members of the Royal Air Force. It is only too sadly obvious that in the near future there must be heavy calls upon the Fund, to an extent not at present calculable. With the gallant heroism of officers and men of the Royal Air Force before us day by day, I am confident that as a tribute to their ceaseless fight for the cause of freedom, many will wish to support their cause.
>
> Contributions will be gladly acknowledged if sent to me at Eaton House, Eaton Road, Hove, Sussex.

Public response to Wakefield's appeal was more generous than Erskine-Lindop and his small staff, by then established in the former Air

Training Corps headquarters at Hove, had dared to hope. They were overwhelmed, donations being received in every mail and mounting magnificently to a total of £354,530 10s 0d.

Among the many who had been stirred by Wakefield's letter was Lord Nuffield, who let it be known that he wished to support the appeal. This was enough for Wakefield who, at eighty years of age, called immediately on Nuffield, the pioneer Morris motor manufacturer, leaving with a cheque for £250,000 in his pocket. Normally a Morris might be said to depend considerably on Castrol, but in this neat reversal of form Lord Nuffield had given Castrol good cause to be thankful for Morris.

Shortly after Wakefield's letter had appeared in *The Times*, the founder of the Fund, Lord Trenchard, relaxed his self-imposed rule of radio silence and spoke to the nation. He said:

> This is the first time I have ever broadcast. I had intended never to broadcast, but when it was pointed out to me that it was on behalf of the Royal Air Force Benevolent Fund, and all that that means, I felt it was a duty – and indeed an honour – and I hope, therefore you will bear with me.
>
> Many years ago, at the end of the last war, it was my privilege to start the Royal Air Force Benevolent Fund in 1919 for all the dependants of those wonderful Air Force men of the 1914–18 War – those great men who had covered themselves with glory and thought of nothing except to work for others. Many were lost in those days and it was our duty to help their relations. It is tragic to think that, twenty years later, the Royal Air Force would again be in the forefront of a still greater war and this time surely we can never pay a better tribute than was paid to them by our Prime Minister: 'Never in the field of human conflict was so much owed by so many to so few.' How true this is. They kept off the German hordes at a very critical time of the history of the fight. They won their fight – and have won many – and they will win many more . . .
>
> It is now time to ask this country, as I feel the whole British Empire recognises all that the Royal Air Force has done, to put the Fund on a firm basis. A very large sum will be required for us to carry out our obligations to the airmen, their wives, children and dependants, so that these men may go into battle, feeling that the future of their immediate relations will, anyhow, be secured from want.
>
> Sometime ago we thought of appealing to the public, but we all considered it was not right to broadcast an appeal for this Fund only, until the Royal Air Force could feel that such great causes as the Air Raid Distress Fund and others were in a better position financially. A short appeal, however, by our chairman, Lord Wakefield, which appeared in *The Times* a few months ago, showed that the public would like to help and that very few people had realised that this Fund was in existence.

Trenchard's broadcast reaped a record £53,342. It was a high figure for a broadcast appeal in wartime Britain.

Perhaps the Fund *had* been too quiet about its existence for all those years, but if this was so, then it was a fault that reacted in the Fund's favour when finally it decided to drop its general disapproval of appeal. The Fund became appeal-minded at precisely the right moment. Departed were the drowsy summer days of aerial pageantry, of dogfight make-believe, and in their place the *Luftwaffe* had provided an air display for almost any day of the great weeks of the Battle of Britain. It was not exactly Hendon, but it was quite a show; and when the enemy was defeated, as of course he always was in the mock dogfights of pre-war air displays, the public showered money on the Fund, a free-will 'gate' given out of sheer gratitude for the national deliverance.

Wakefield had seen the opportunity in 1940 and he had acted. Shortly after the Battle of Britain had enforced enemy abandonment of Operation *Sealion*, the invasion of Britain, he died. As the Council of the Royal Air Force Benevolent Fund understated in its message of sympathy to Lady Wakefield, the Chairman had given 'a wise lead in the extension of the Fund in war'.

CHAPTER 5

ROYAL PATRONAGE

'Wings for Victory now and good homes and
employment in peace time are inseparable.'

Her Royal Highness The Duchess of Kent, 1943

From inception in 1919 and the unveiling of the Memorial by the Prince of Wales in 1923 the Fund had engaged the active and sympathetic interest of the Royal Family. King George VI, Patron from 1936, had previously followed the Fund's fortunes closely since, as Wing Commander the Duke of York, a serving officer, he had accepted the Presidency in 1919, while at the time of Wakefield's death the King's brother, the Duke of Gloucester, was President. However, as was customary, neither the King nor his brother exercised any executive

The Royal Patrons of the Fund: King George VI (right), who as Prince Albert, Duke of York, had been President of the Fund since its inception in October 1919, conferred Royal Patronage on the Fund in May 1936. He is with his father King George V and his brother King Edward VIII.

authority in their appointments and it would have been inappropriate for the Council to invite a royal duke to accept the chairmanship.

It was only after a short list had been prepared of prospective chairmen to succeed Lord Wakefield that the Council learned with surprise and delight of Air Commodore the Duke of Kent's offer to take the chair. The list was scrapped and the Duke became Chairman of the Royal Air Force Benevolent Fund in April 1941. Unhappily, the Duke was not spared to lead the Fund through the war and into peace. He was killed on active service in August 1942 when an operational Sunderland of No. 228 Squadron, flying from Scotland to Iceland, crashed into a Scottish hillside, killing all but the tail gunner.

Thus, little more than a year after her husband's election as Chairman, the Duchess of Kent was herself a Royal Air Force widow. She asked immediately what she might do to preserve the family connection with the Fund and in March 1943 the Duchess accepted the Presidency of the Royal Air Force Benevolent Fund. Princess Marina, who served the Fund for twenty-five years until her death in 1968, never failed to attend an annual meeting of the Council. In the Fund's eightieth anniversary year the family tradition continues through the Presidency of the Duke of Kent, who succeeded his mother.

Making her inaugural address, the Duchess said:

> I consider it a very great honour to become President of the Royal Air Force Benevolent Fund, as my husband, who was Chairman, was so deeply interested in it. From him I learnt something of your excellent work. The least we can do is to look after the welfare of the men of the Royal Air Force and women of the Auxiliary Air Force, and their families, if they need help. They do not ask for more than this, and by subscribing to the Fund, all people can pay their tribute to them. I shall follow closely the work of the Council, and feel sure that it will never lack the means to carry out its important work. Much has already been done, but there will be still more to do in the future, on which all have set their hopes. Let us, for our part, see that they are not disappointed.

The Duke's death had rendered the chair vacant for the second time in two years and the Fund was faced again with the election of a leader. Now there was an obvious choice in Lord Riverdale, who had joined the Fund as Vice-Chairman in January 1941 and was Chairman of the recently formed Appeals Committee.

Arthur Balfour, first Baron Riverdale, Sheffield industrialist, past Master Cutler, had already made an enormous success of appeals. Honoured by the Air Council with the appointment as Honorary Air Commodore of No. 601 (County of London) Squadron, Riverdale enjoyed an altogether very special relationship with the Royal Air Force, having negotiated the Empire Air Training Scheme in which most wartime aircrew were trained in the safe and clear skies of Canada,

Australia, Rhodesia, South Africa, New Zealand and the British West Indies. Vastly successful in the steel industry, Riverdale was a particularly good picker of men and a great deal of his success as Chairman of the Appeals Committee and of the Fund can be ascribed to his part in the recruitment of a certain Bertram Rumble.

During the Second World War, when Air Vice-Marshal Sir John Cordingley was in charge of Manning, he lived at the Royal Thames Yacht Club and Rumble lived there also from Monday to Friday. Rumble, during the early stages of the war, repeatedly said he wanted to serve in some capacity but he was being turned down all the time on account of age. When Riverdale and Cordingley decided that the Fund required an individual of a particular type to run the appeals, Riverdale invited Rumble to dinner. That night Rumble received the run of Riverdale's cellar. 'It drinks well, yes, it certainly drinks well – yes, I'll do it providing you arrange things so I don't get paid.' Riverdale had recognised his man, corralled him in the cellar and won his acceptance of the all-important post of Appeals Secretary. Bertram Rumble refused a salary and established himself at the invitation of Barclays Bank in rooms above its premises at 1 Sloane Street.

Setting themselves to maintain Wakefield's impetus, Riverdale and Rumble had raised £1,250,000 within two years and had greatly broadened the Fund's scope of appeal, an achievement much aided by their inexhaustible ally Alexander Duckham. Beyond his gift of Rooks Hill, Duckham personally raised £100,000 from industry.

Riverdale, Rumble and Duckham were a magnificent team, and with their ranging business interests and connections they were ideally suited for the task which, in Trenchard's words, was that of putting the Fund on a firm basis. Of the trio, Duckham did not live to see victory although when he died in 1944 it was clear that was assured. He knew too that out of fifty-six Vanbrugh old boys, forty-nine were in the armed forces, of whom forty-four had followed their fathers into the Royal Air Force, four serving as commissioned officers, four as flight sergeants, ten as sergeants, twelve as corporals, nine as leading aircraftmen and five as aircraftmen.

Meanwhile, the Fund's appeal activities were attracting the notice of some of the great institutions which, in gratitude for the deliverance of 1940, had been making charitable collections of their own. In particular there were the initiatives of the Auctioneers' and Estate Agents' Institute – subsequently 'Chartered' – and of Lloyd's of London.

In 1943 the Auctioneers' and Estate Agents' Institute entered a long association with the Royal Air Force Benevolent Fund, instigated by Mr S. Linney and Mr F. C. Hawkes, their President and Secretary, as a result of which the Fund benefited directly with £221,084 to create the Pilots and Crews Fund, to be expended within twenty-five years. In addition the Fund benefited indirectly from the use of Headley Court, Epsom, originally given to the Secretary of State for Air as a rehabilitation centre for aircrew and now a Royal Air Force medical rehabilitation unit for the armed services and civilians. The Fund also benefited from a wealth of professional advice, especially that of Mr W. Wallace Withers who joined the Grants Committee in 1943, was elected to the Council and Finance and General Purposes Committee in 1948, and whose firm, Debenham, Tewson and Chinnocks, advises the Fund on property matters to this day.

It was in 1943, also, that the Corporation and Members of Lloyd's made the Fund a gift of £50,000. Loyal to its sea traditions, Lloyd's accepted the Fund's suggestion to devote the money to officers and airmen of Coastal Command and to the dependants of the large number who lost their lives in that Command.

As with the property men's gifts, the Lloyd's gesture has meant more than money to the Fund. It introduced, among many new friends, Mr Ernest de Rougemont who became Lloyd's representative on the Council and a member of the Finance and General Purposes Committee from 1958 to 1975, and also a member of the Christ's Hospital Selection Committee.

'Wings for victory now and good homes and employment in peacetime are inseparable.' With this expressive phrase the Duchess of Kent, as President, identified the central theme of the Fund's mid-war philosophy; and it was open to all to subscribe to this philosophy in a very modest way because the Ministry of Aircraft Production decided that two-fifths of every donation to the Spitfire Fund should be allotted to the Royal Air Force Benevolent Fund.

Few people, however, were wealthy and generous enough to be troubled by the choice between buying a complete fighter or bomber or presenting the equivalent purchase price to the Fund. Lady Rosalind Davidson of Huntly paid £20,000 for four Spitfires between November 1940 and September 1941, and was then undecided as to a bomber or the Benevolent Fund. As an interim gesture she offered her *estancia* in Argentina to the Minister of Aircraft Production, who passed her offer on to the Fund. But wartime administrative, legal and communication difficulties decided the Fund against property development down South America way and Lady Rosalind, dropping her plan to buy a bomber, made the Fund a gift of £30,000.

At about this time too, the daily postbag was as exciting as a lucky dip and Lord Riverdale received an extraordinary package. It contained 100 ounces of gold from Emperor Haile Selassie of Ethiopia. A later message said: 'His Imperial Majesty greatly appreciates the formidable task that the Royal Air Force had to put up in the great fight, and it is hoped that the war will soon be won with complete victory for the allies.' The Emperor's gift had arrived unsolicited but the Council was fully alive to the need to attract donations while the public memory of Royal Air Force exploits remained fresh. For instance, there was the story of the

East End of London publican for whom a Lancaster crew had signed the label of a bottle of whisky. When the bomber failed to return from operations, the publican presented the bottle to the Fund and it was auctioned in the Isle of Man for £100.

Generally, however, it was unnecessary to guide the protected or the defended towards an acknowledgement of their debt. One such instance was perhaps unique in that it related to a specific air action during which the defended made a collection for the dependants of those who were at that very moment losing their lives.

This splendid gesture was made by United States troops on passage eastwards through the Mediterranean in HMT *Karoa*. When the troop-ship came under attack two Royal Air Force officers died in her defence, but as it happened neither family wished to accept financial help. Very well, please pass the collection to the dependants as a gift, Royal Air Force Middle East instructed the Fund. There being no question of distress the Fund could only act as an unofficial intermediary and divided nearly £900 between the families.

Complying with the *Karoa* request was a comparatively simple matter for the Fund's hard-pressed wartime staff and it was but one of shoals of weekly requests that poured into Erskine-Lindop's seaside headquarters at Hove.

When the staff of four had left London for Sussex-by-the-sea in 1939 the Fund's total annual expenditure on relief was £22,921. Between 1940 and 1943 it had risen from £27,766 to £89,495, involving 12,824 cases in 1943, the administrative details of every one of which had been handled at Hove.

Certainly the Appeals Department and, from early 1943, a newly created Disablement Branch under Air Commodore E. Digby-Johnson, were self-contained at 1 Sloane Street and relieved some of the pressure. But liaison with the bereaved and the preparation of cases for presentation to the Grants Committee were usually more exacting and time-consuming by their nature.

Although wartime meetings of the Council, of the Finance and General Purposes Committee and of the Grants Committee took place at the Air Ministry in London, the volume of work being handled at Hove did not pass unrecognised. After visiting headquarters early in 1943 with Bertram Rumble, Lord Riverdale paid a warm tribute to Erskine-Lindop, his wartime joint secretary, Group Captain C. G. Murray, their retired officer assistants and the locally recruited staff of young girls, one of whom, Miss Jean Ashton, long since appointed MBE, served the Fund until 1988 when she retired as Deputy Director Welfare, after nearly forty-four years of devoted service. The Chairman said in Council, 'I met all members of the staff and found them all working like a happy family. I examined the books and their methods of dealing with cases and I am glad to say that the organisation is perfect and quite as good as any industrial concern I am connected with.'

The President, Princess Marina, personally recognised Erskine-Lindop's great devotion and dedication when she presented him with her late husband's cuff-links; a gift deeply appreciated by the Squadron Leader, who retained a keen interest in the Fund's progress until his death in April 1978 denied his hopes of participating in the Diamond Jubilee celebrations twenty years ago.

CHAPTER 6

GRANTS POLICY AFTER THE SECOND WORLD WAR

'I'd like to feel that no one who is, or has been in the Service need ever be without someone to turn to if they have bad luck.'

Marshal of the Royal Air Force Viscount Portal, 1945

T
he avalanche which had been expected in 1939, and had not fallen, landed on Erskine-Lindop and Murray and their staff in mid-war. As fighter sweeps began to prepare the way for a return to France and the Low Countries, as Bomber and Coastal Command operations intensified against Germany and in the Atlantic respectively, and as the Royal Air Force helped to hold the Mediterranean and supported the armies in North Africa and Burma, so casualties mounted and lights burned late behind the Benevolent Fund's blackout – to midnight and beyond.

In figures, grants made and cases assisted ran:

   1943   £89,495 covering 12,824 cases
   1944   £163,679 covering 17,780 cases
   1945   £326,697 covering 28,591 cases

Sir Arthur Bryant, writing in the *Illustrated London News*, described the heroism and sacrifice which gave rise to so much need:

It is the Fund's policy that children whose fathers were killed or died whilst serving with the Royal Air Force should receive education of the standard they would have been given had they not been orphaned.

   This help is continued from earliest schooldays to the university if the child shows real promise. Among those benefiting from it at the present time – and I see him every term – is a boy whose father, formerly an apprentice at the great Royal Air Force Apprentices' School at Halton, to which he had gone, like some many of its members, from a fine provincial Grammar School, fought as a sergeant-pilot in the Battle of Britain and won the Distinguished Flying Medal in its course.

   Later this gallant young pilot was commissioned, rose to the rank of Flight Lieutenant and won the Distinguished Flying Cross. He was killed towards the end of the war flying Mosquitos.

He left behind a widow and two children, a boy and a girl, as well as a devoted mother and father whose only son he was – the latter himself a most faithful servant of England who had served in all three Services, as a Regular soldier before 1914, as a Naval Chief Petty Officer during and after the First World War, and, at an advanced age, as a technical Sergeant Instructor in the Royal Air Force during part of the late war.

During the Battle of Britain the hero of this story – one of many similar ones which together helped to change the course of human destiny – was shot down in flames and left unconscious, covered in oil, near his aircraft.

He was subsequently retrieved and found to be suffering from severe shock and bruises but not, by some miracle, seriously wounded. In the stress of that time, instead of being taken to hospital, he was sent to his parents on convalescent leave to recover. After twenty-four hours at home, deeply grateful for the peace and rest and love by which he found himself surrounded, he quietly told his father and mother that his comrades were fighting the Battle of Britain without him and that he must return.

Next day, though anything but fit, he reported for duty and insisted on resuming operational flying. It is to repay some small part of the debt we owe to such men that the Royal Air Force Benevolent Fund exists, and that its support is a permanent duty of all who love their country.

And there were many smaller grants, comparatively minor in monetary terms but totally disproportionate in value to the relief they brought. A sergeant with sixteen years' service had a wife whose leg had to be amputated. All his savings had gone in paying for her medical treatment. The Fund stepped in and bought the artificial limb. A squadron leader and his wife were returning from India. The ship was torpedoed and sunk and the husband drowned. The Fund maintained the widow, reclothed her and returned the financial value of her lost belongings.

But what, it will be reasonably asked, was the State doing? Certainly not as much as more recent legislation enables it to do. War pensions were not on a generous scale.

The Fund explained in a wartime appeal letter:

Nowadays the State has a very large number of citizens of this country to look after. Few, if any, nations of the world have a better system of social legislation and social insurance than Great Britain, but government funds are not unlimited. What money it has the State divides to the best of its ability. It seeks to provide the dry bread without which continued existence is impossible. But no one can live on bread alone and it is funds such as the Royal Air Force Benevolent Fund which exist to find the butter, and if possible, the jam.

However, this considerate approach to the ever-present problem of the demarcation between government and charitable responsibility should not be taken to imply that the Fund was not prepared to press for at least a scraping of margarine where it believed the government was failing in its duty.

Throughout its eighty years the Fund has kept careful watch on this wobbly line of demarcation and there have been numerous occasions when Grants Committees had remonstrated vigorously that the government was attempting to evade its responsibilities. There have been occasions when the Fund has been compelled to render a beneficiary ineligible for State help in order to bring the beneficiary to a standard which the Fund regards as a minimum.

Generally this question arises from the much disputed interpretation of the all-disclaiming tag of 'non-attributable', a tag which, as may be imagined, ignited some especially heated comment in a wartime atmosphere, as in 1943 when Air Vice-Marshal Sir Charles Longcroft raised the matter in Council.

Sir Charles said that the Grants Committee of which he was Chairman felt very strongly that some 'non-attributable' cases were not a fair burden on the Fund and should be the responsibility of the government. Such cases, Sir Charles explained, were typified by that of a flying officer killed in a car accident in Canada and leaving a widow and two children, aged two-and-a-half and one-and-a-half. In another case an airman had been killed in a cycling accident, leaving three children and a widow. Neither of these men would have been at the scene of the accidents had not their service taken them there.

Nevertheless, successive governments have consistently refused to accept responsibility in such cases and to this day the often disputable suffix 'non-attributable' appears all too frequently after the cause of death and involves the Fund in considerable expense.

Morally the Fund has always felt obliged to assist such cases and it has always done so subject to Grants Committee acceptance of distress.

Of all the Fund's seemingly limitless wartime responsibilities there was one which in mid-war assumed an important priority: the assistance of disabled men and in particular of aircrew. Here, the Disablement Branch established early in 1943 soon came into its own and from 1943 onwards service people were assisted right through their hospital life and whenever necessary into new or suitable civil careers, often with the co-operation and advice of the Resettlement Branch of the Air Ministry.

A number of parents who had lost sons in air operations against the enemy offered to help individuals so far as they could, and among these generous, sad-hearted actions that of Mr Charles P. Ackers is especially noteworthy. Ackers arranged a forestry training scheme for ex-officers and airmen on his Gloucestershire estate, helping the scheme with a £1000-a-year deed of covenant in memory of his son, Flying Officer Robert David Ackers, who had been killed over Normandy shortly after D-Day.

Had the Royal Air Force Benevolent Fund glanced momentarily into a mirror at this time, as the war in Europe turned into the home stretch, it might have perceived a prosperous if weary countenance, and smiled wanly as it remembered that lean and hungry look of 1939.

To 1944, £397,823 had been distributed in wartime relief and capital stood at £4,807,673. The Fund could afford to smile and congratulate itself. But there was at least one member of the Council and the Finance and General Purposes Committee and Grants Committee who was convinced that the Fund's most testing time lay in the years ahead.

As Royal Air Force Director-General of Manning throughout the war, Air Vice-Marshal Sir John Cordingley was apprehensive about the future welfare of some one-and-three-quarter million men, women and their families. He therefore proposed to Lord Riverdale that the Fund should prepare carefully for the problems of peace and appoint a general Controller of administrative ability and standing. In October 1944 Air Vice-Marshal Sir Hazelton Nicholl, who had flown as a bomber pilot in the First World War and had been in charge of administration at Fighter Command during the Battle of Britain, became the first Controller of the Royal Air Force Benevolent Fund.

The appointment was of material assistance to Squadron Leader Erskine-Lindop, who had then reached the stage when his head was just beginning to appear above the avalanche. Erskine-Lindop continued to

Air Vice-Marshal Sir Hazelton Nicholl,
Controller 1944–47.

serve as Secretary until his retirement in 1958. At that year's Annual Council Meeting the Air Member for Personnel, Air Marshal Sir John Whitley, expressed the Air Council's particular thanks to Squadron Leader Erskine-Lindop for his outstanding services to the Fund.

It was evident, even before the war ended with victory over Japan in September 1945, that money might again become the problem it had been between the two world wars. The wartime scale of generosity was drying up. In the last year of hostilities the Fund received £948,959, of which £250,000 was accounted for by a final wartime windfall.

A gift from the people of South Africa, the cheque for £250,000 was received in October 1945, by the Duchess of Kent from the hands of Mrs Jean Hamilton in the presence of the High Commissioner for South Africa, Mr G. Heaton Nicholls. This generous gift owed much to Field Marshal Jan C. Smuts's interest in the Royal Air Force and to the Fund's untiring and voluntary representative in South Africa, Mrs A. C. Haswell, who had lost her son in the air.

In a letter to the President, Field Marshal Smuts, South Africa's Prime Minister – whose recommendation to the British Cabinet in 1917 had resulted in the creation of the Royal Air Force as a separate service – wrote:

> The people of South Africa are sending in the person of Mrs Jean Hamilton, a mission which you have graciously consented to receive.
>
> It is a small tangible expression of South Africa's recognition of the immense debt which our nation, amongst others of the United Nations, owes to the men of the Royal Air Force, who during the Battle of Britain itself, saved the whole civilised world and later played so magnificent a part in achieving victory. It is a tribute of gratitude, of admiration and of pride.
>
> We in South Africa have had the privilege and the pleasure of having as our guests during training many of the gallant young men who have upheld the prestige of the Royal Air Force in the greatest human trial in history, and it is the measure of the affection we have felt for them that, when we came to provide funds for assisting our men of the South African Air Force, it was decided to appeal also for the men of the Royal Air Force, and to send more than half the total collection for the relief of distress among dependants of the latter service.
>
> In asking you graciously to accept on behalf of the Royal Air Force Benevolent Fund this gift from the people of South Africa, I would ask your Royal Highness to convey to the men of the Royal Air Force this expression of South Africa's thanks and admiration.

Smuts' message belongs already to that other age when the British Commonwealth was an Empire, before the wind of change began to blow through Africa. Today it is a message that seems as archaic as Lloyd George's exaltation of the 'Cavalry of the Air' in the First World War.

Yet it was delivered as the Royal Air Force was basking in the admiration of the Allied world, just as in its own time the Royal Flying Corps had been praised to the skies.

Now, as in 1918–19, the airmen were due to come down to earth with a bump, to the necessity of facing the problems of civilian life in peacetime austerity: to finding somewhere to live, to learning a job and getting it, and to educating children.

Widows were left to face it all – alone.

Making a timely broadcast in the early autumn of 1945, Lord Portal, then Sir Charles, put the Royal Air Force Benevolent Fund's seal on the war. The wartime Chief of the Air Staff said:

> Exactly six years ago, on this first Sunday in September 1939, 126 young men took off in Wellingtons and Hampdens to strike at the German Fleet. This was the first offensive operation of the Royal Air Force in this war. And now, thank God, they've done their last, and it's all over, and we've won.
>
> Well, it's been a long story, much too long to go over it all, but one mustn't forget the beginning of it, how our squadrons fought to help France and the Low Countries and Norway. They did all they could, but it was impossible to achieve anything much except glory.
>
> You remember too the desperate days of Dunkirk and the Battle of Britain: almost miracles they seemed at the time. Then Greece and Burma and Singapore – impossible odds again. They never had a hope, but they went down fighting for the honour of our country.
>
> Then slowly we began to grow stronger and the Americans – bless them – began to come over in strength. We had North Africa and Malta and all the time that grim Battle of the Atlantic. And so from Alamein on to Berlin and now at last to full victory over Japan . . .
>
> Perhaps we owe the biggest debt of all to our bomber crews. Night after night and night after night again hammering away at Germany; and those long journeys home over the North Sea – for the lucky ones. Do you know our Bomber Command alone won 19,000 decorations for gallantry, and lost 47,000 killed.
>
> The war's over, but I'm afraid this Fund's got years of urgent work ahead of it.
>
> Now, I know some people think that this sort of thing shouldn't be necessary. Well, I'm here to assure you it *is*. The government does all it can, but there's still an urgent need for personal help. That's the great thing. The Fund's personal; it's quick to act; it doesn't wait to be asked. I wouldn't ask for your support if I didn't feel strongly about it. *I'd like to feel that no one who is, or has been, in the service need ever be without someone to turn to if they have bad luck . . .*
>
> May I read you a bit of a letter from the wife of an airman. This is what she says, 'If it hadn't been for the Fund I often wonder what would have happened to us. My baby was only three days old when my husband died.

Sir, may I say you have done the best thing that could be done with the money.'

By God's grace we've won a great victory and tonight I ask you to give thanks by helping this Fund and so helping those of my Service for whom the end of the war may not be the end of suffering or distress.

The broadcast brought in £12,890, but the future implications of Portal's message were every bit as important as the flow of money which resulted from it.

Chapter 7

Management and Relief

*'For a time I didn't even want to live. That is what despair does. The
Royal Air Force Benevolent Fund convinced me that I could start again in
a life of my own choosing and assisted me with means to do it.'*

Battle of Britain Hurricane Pilot

In the autumn of 1945, the Fund moved back to London where a
973-year lease had been acquired on very favourable terms of
a period building at 67 Portland Place. Removed from its Hove villa,
the Royal Air Force Benevolent Fund was wholly unrecognisable from
the evacuee which Erskine-Lindop had packed into his car in 1940.

Relief expenditure had risen from £22,919 in 1939 to £323,233 in
1945. Total relief expenditure in the war years had amounted to
£724,520 and the Fund entered peace and Portland Place with capital of
£5,542,616.

On paper and behind its imposing façade the Fund appeared well
breeched to meet the demands of peace. Certainly it understood the re-
action of the man who, intending to arrange a £2000 legacy, turned on
his heel in Portland Place and wrote instead, 'You don't need my money'.
But the Royal Air Force Benevolent Fund has never been persuaded by
that particular comment, or by any similar criticism to conceal itself in the
suburbs.

For some fifty-five years the accessibility of 67 Portland Place has facilitated Council and Committee work, simplified liaison with the Royal Air
Force and the Air Ministry or the Ministry of Defence, and provided
reasonable working conditions for staff, honorary representatives and
visitors. Another, if incidental, gain has been the lease itself. Purchased
for £35,000 at a ground rental of £500 a year, generously reduced to
£200 by the ground landlord, Lord Howard de Walden, it has proved
an excellent investment.

Re-established in London, the Royal Air Force Benevolent Fund bore
no outward resemblance to its pre-war self in four rooms at Iddesleigh
House, Westminster, and the end of the war found it a world apart from
the modest start in 1919.

Now a memorial existed, standing out into the Thames on the Victoria
Embankment and awaiting the addition of a 1939–45 inscription on its

bomb-scarred surface. Now, demobilised air and groundcrew could return to civil life supported by a charitable accumulation mountainous by comparison with 1919.

Whereas in that year Trenchard had feared for his new airmen, 'the finest men', because unlike soldiers or sailors they had no fund of their own, 1945 found the circumstances reversed. The Royal Air Force Benevolent Fund had outpaced all comparable service charitable organisations. The generosity with which the world had responded to the exploits of the Royal Air Force in war had placed the Fund in this enviable condition and left it pondering its future responsibilities.

Clearly, therefore, now that Sir Hazelton Nicholl was contemplating retirement, the future executive direction of the Royal Air Force Benevolent Fund would call for an exceptional man possessing an almost impossible combination of qualities: a good heart, an inflexible purpose, a record of administrative achievement, a close appreciation of human nature, a flair for publicity and a working knowledge both of the Fund and of the Royal Air Force.

Extraordinarily, there happened to be at hand a paragon of these virtues, and of many others besides. Air Vice-Marshal Sir John Cordingley, who had served the Fund in Council or Committee for more than ten years, assumed salaried office as Controller of the Royal Air Force Benevolent Fund on 1 May 1947.

Air Vice-Marshal Sir John W. Cordingley,
Controller 1947–62.

A few days later the Duchess of Kent addressed the Council. The President said:

> Though we are still in a position to meet all demands and money continues to come in, the peak of subscriptions and donations may be said to have been reached and passed.
>
> In these very difficult and disturbing days one cannot expect people to be so lavish with their gifts as formerly, though in the public eye the Royal Air Force Benevolent Fund holds a unique position, and we continue to be by far the largest service benevolent fund.

The President's allusion to future income inspired one of Cordingley's earliest actions as Controller. No one was more aware than the wartime Director-General of Manning of the Royal Air Force that, while the balance sheet looked fairly healthy, the future promised unprecedented demand upon the Fund's resources. He knew that several million men and women and members of their families were privileged to call upon the Fund should need arise. If the peak of public subscriptions and donations had been reached then action must be taken to improve support from within the service. Consequently, one of Sir John's first moves was to sharpen up the half-a-day's-pay-a-year voluntary subscription scheme, particularly among officers.

The introduction of this scheme in 1938 had restored the Fund's fortunes most effectively after the withdrawal of the Hendon Air Display, and between 1938 and 1946 the Fund received £562,350 from this source. Learning in 1947 that only fifty per cent of serving officers were contributors, the Controller began to sell the scheme more aggressively. He adopted mail order tactics.

With the co-operation of the Air Ministry, the Controller wrote personally to every newly commissioned officer. Where this failed, and in the cases of previously commissioned officers who were not subscribing, he arranged to send a reminder letter at every promotion in an officer's career. It should also be acknowledged that the co-operation of the Royal Air Force Agents, Lloyds, Cox's and King's and Glyn Mills, in agreeing to collect subscriptions from officers, and of the Royal Air Force itself in permitting the men's subscriptions to be paid through the pay ledgers, contributed greatly to the success of the half-a-day's-pay scheme. These mail shots met with increasing success and, when the Controller retired in 1962, over ninety per cent of serving officers and airmen were subscribers.

Another matter to which the Fund gave priority early in 1947–48 was the implementation of decisions recently taken towards constitutional reform. Arrangements which had developed out of such early and rudimentary decisions as may have been taken at Lord Hugh Cecil's breakfast table were no longer suitable for the Royal Air Force

Benevolent Fund in its altogether changed and better circumstances. Certain financial formalities had, for example, become operationally impractical, as Lord Trenchard knew only too well. 'We're getting old and being chased by paper,' the founder had commented on the chores of the Trustees.

One problem was that the signatures of Trenchard and his fellow trustee, Lord Weir, were required on every stock market transaction in the post-war £5–6 million investment portfolio.

Therefore a scheme was needed which would vest any funds or property of the Charity in the hands of a custodian trustee, allowing the Royal Air Force Benevolent Fund managerial control of monies required from time to time for the relief of distress and for administration.

Such a scheme was prepared under the guidance of Mr John Fletcher, a senior partner of the Fund's solicitors, Charles Russell and Co., and approved by Mr Justice Harman in the High Court on 21 July 1948. In effect the Deed of Trust appointing Lloyds Bank as the Custodian Trustee rendered the Royal Air Force Benevolent Fund answerable only to the law officers of the Crown. It conferred powers wider than usual, either before or after the execution. Indeed, the new constitution anticipated by twelve years the general legislation which was to unshackle charities from their traditional low-yield investment obligations.

The new trust became operative on 1 January 1949, allowing the retirement of Trenchard and Weir, who had served as trustees since 1920 and 1929 respectively.

Constitutionally fit, potentially free under the new trust deed to invest more adventurously, the Fund embarked in the late 1940s and early 1950s on a varied and costly programme of relief.

Grants to resettle or establish a man or woman in civil life, help over education and housing – these were the chief calls the Fund had to meet.

Inevitably, since a large charitable capital was involved, there were criticisms that the Fund was either spending too much or too little. To which the Controller replied, 'Not a penny too much, not a penny too little. The Fund is constituted to relieve distress. Why give half the help really needed and then fail to relieve the distress?'

In fact the Fund was not only giving but lending. The making of loans as distinct from grants held advantages when so many 1939–45 service people were young enough to start or return to civilian careers and repay loans in part or in full. Loans in suitable cases can completely relieve distress and in certain instances preserve self-respect.

In 1946, 1947 and 1948, a total of £166,666 was paid out in business grants and loans, assistance that was amply justified when repayments began to provide money for recirculation. Sometimes there were profits, as in the example of the flying officer who received a loan on his release leave to buy and stock a cycle, electrical and toy shop. After repaying the loan in monthly instalments the beneficiary wrote four years later:

May I thank you from the bottom of my heart for the help you so generously gave me when I was released from the Royal Air Force . . . Without
that help I could not have started up in business; yet because of it the small
business I bought then is today worth several thousands of pounds . . . I
have confirmed the cancellation of the Banker's Order after next month's
payment as your loan to me, being free of interest, is then repaid in full. I
would, however, wish you to send me a further Banker's Order form, as it
is my wish as a token of appreciation of your help, to make a donation of
£10 each Christmas Eve for as long as I live, or if hard times should come,
for as long as I can afford it!

Although Grants Committees considered carefully whether a man was
capable of building his own business, if there was doubt they inclined
to the generous view. Not every post-war business the Fund helped to
finance was as successful as the flying officer's cycle shop, but for every
failure there were many success stories, and the Fund remains thankful
that in the high streets and industrial estates of Britain there are numerous
undertakings which owe everything to an initial interest-free push from
67 Portland Place.

The successful outcome of many of these business loans was attributable to the practical assistance received from established businessmen.
One such was Mr A. E. Scotcher, who offered to arrange for applications
for assistance to establish small businesses to be investigated by an experienced representative whose advice and recommendation were
available to the Grants Committee when they considered each individual
request.

So many businesses were launched in this period that it would be
repetitive to quote further examples, but just occasionally there was a
loan with a difference, and such a loan was that made to a badly burned
Battle of Britain pilot who needed capital to establish himself as headmaster of a preparatory school for boys. The Fund, always as opportunist
as any individual venturer it has helped, made the fighter pilot a loan
under a mutually advantageous agreement. In repayment the Royal Air
Force Benevolent Fund obtained the board and education of three boys
at any one time, and at eighty per cent of the headmaster's current school
fees.

Some years later this arrangement produced a richly rewarding sequel
when the headmaster collected a £10,000 postbag following his Battle of
Britain Sunday broadcast appeal on behalf of the Fund. He said:

Fifteen years ago I was in hospital. My Hurricane had crashed in flames a
few days before. Now my job is teaching. I am not giving you my name as
the Royal Air Force Benevolent Fund will not make public the names of
those it has helped.

It is the link across those fifteen years – from a Hurricane cockpit to a
classroom – that I want to talk about tonight. That link – it was more of

a lifeline – brought me through a period of my life that I could not have faced alone. For I am one of the many thousands helped back to worth-while life by the Fund.

You may think that is not so remarkable: perhaps you are wondering why I am broadcasting rather than some famous person. Well – as one of 'The Few' – I am speaking not only for myself, but for more than a quarter of a million others, men, women and children – all having reason to be grateful to this wonderful Fund.

Forgive just a few words about myself. The Battle of Britain meant my facing the fact that I should never use my hands again, that I was burned and scarred for life. For a time I didn't even want to live. That is what despair does. The Royal Air Force Benevolent Fund convinced me that I could start again in a life of my own choosing and assisted me with means to do it. So I am speaking with first-hand knowledge.

Of course, as you know, the State gives assistance to the disabled and dependants, but there are a hundred-and-one ways in which the Fund is helping over and above this. When my friends and I realise what it has done, and will do for the widows and children of those who were killed, we don't hesitate to seek support for it.

What of the future? Will the Fund carry on? It will and it must. The Royal Air Force Fund's work will undoubtedly increase. Men who fought in the Battle of Britain and afterwards will need assistance in their old age. Many will meet bad luck and trouble for the first time.

Casualties happen in peacetime too, and for younger men still flying it is wonderful to know that, if anything should go wrong, their dependants will be looked after, and their children educated in the same way as they had planned.

It was Sir Archibald McIndoe, the great plastic surgeon, who in the 1940s drew the Fund's attention to the needs of badly burned members of aircrew – his Guinea Pigs, as the Consultant in Plastic Surgery to the Royal Air Force called them. A special Grants Sub-committee including Archie McIndoe's widow, Connie, was set up, and still meets regularly, to consider assistance for ageing Guinea Pigs. Was it really so long ago that Archie asked: 'When their bodies are whole again we also rebuild something of their lives?'

The Fund is also fortunate in having Honorary Consultants to whom it can refer other complicated or difficult medical cases for advice and guidance.

After business loans and grants, housing and furniture accounted for the next highest expenditure on relief, totalling £298,713 in the im-mediate post-war years of 1946, 1947 and 1948. While the greater part of this sum was distributed among individual applicants the Fund also maintained its practice of co-operating with other organisations, provided Royal Air Force families were guaranteed to benefit. The following are examples:

Under an agreement with the Housing Association for Officers' Families, £24,000 was provided to build twelve houses at Morden named Trenchard Court in honour of the founder. A similar arrangement was made with the British Legion Haig Homes to build eighteen houses for airmen's families on their estates at Morden, named Rhodes-Moorhouse Court in honour of the first VC of the air; also to build houses at Leicester and Cardiff at an estimated £29,000, and at Leckhampton £19,000.

The sum of £1800 was given to the Thistle Foundation for a Royal Air Force house. In addition, £10,000 was contributed towards the Officers' Association's purchase and equipment of Frimley Park House, Camberley, now removed to Huntly, Bishopsteignton, Devon, as a home for aged and infirm officers of the three services; the Fund agreed to pay £1000 a year towards upkeep for fifteen years, twenty-five per cent of the accommodation being reserved for RAF officers; £3700 was given to provide two Royal Air Force houses on the Haig Homes Seacroft Estate, Leeds; £9000 towards two British Legion country houses for aged and incapacitated ex-servicemen; £2800 for two houses at the Scottish Veterans Garden City . . . some examples from one year's list, and representative of the Fund's annual participation in ex-service projects throughout Britain.

CHAPTER 8

EDUCATION AFTER THE WAR

'The Council of the Fund realised many years ago that money spent on the education of children is one of the most valuable and fruitful investments that the Fund can make.'

Lord Wolfenden, 1954

As VJ Day receded, the Fund's resettlement liabilities gradually declined. Housing remained a perennial problem, but by 1949 education at £86,597 had emerged as the most costly item on the books.

In this broad and varied field the Fund needed advice and in 1949, on the recommendation of the Education Advisory Committee, which had been set up two years earlier, a national panel of educational advisers was appointed, known as the Education Advisory Panel. Together, the new panel and the Education Advisory Committee presented a formidable front line of learning. But it was necessarily so if the Fund was to continue to fulfil its fundamental promise to provide the children of deceased and disabled officers or airmen with the education the fathers had wished for their sons and daughters.

In the post-war competition for places in preparatory and public schools and in the universities, the Fund needed all the specialist advice and liaison it could muster by employing the knowledge and connections of members of the Education Advisory Committee. The Honorary Secretary of the Education Advisory Committee from its inception in 1947 and for many years was Mr Peter du Sautoy, who served in the Royal Air Force during the Second World War and subsequently became the Chairman of Faber & Faber, the publishers.

The function of each member of the Education Advisory Panel at the time was that of personal adviser to parent or guardian. There were some two hundred panelists geographically distributed to give guidance wherever an education case occurred, it being an adviser's delicate task to suggest an education suitable to each child's individual need. Lord Wolfenden who sat on the Education Advisory Committee summed up the panel's value in human terms:

One of the first and deepest anxieties of a widow is the education of her children. Sheer information and advice are often the first need. And this the Fund takes great care to supply. For it sometimes happens that a widow, simply not knowing what is best for her children in this rather specialised sphere, and not knowing what opportunities are available, embarks on a course which turns out to be mistaken, misleading and unduly expensive.

The education opportunities available through the Royal Air Force Benevolent Fund are numerous and varied enough to exercise the most knowledgeable educationist. A parent or guardian, unescorted by a member of the Education Advisory Panel, might become inextricably lost in the maze of educational opportunity, although it has not been constructed, of course, to bewilder the uninitiated. The success of the Scheme owes everything to the Fund's long-established principle of co-operating with outside bodies rather than running its own establishment.

Vanbrugh Castle School and Rooks Hill House Nursery School near Sevenoaks were exceptions to this general policy because they had been presented to the Fund by Mr Alexander Duckham for specific purposes. Rooks Hill had to be closed during the Battle of Britain but reopened in May 1946 with twenty aircrew children of from two to seven years of age. It was run by a committee of well-wishers, mostly with Royal Air Force connections, who lived nearby. For many years the Chairman was Lady Babington, the wife of Air Marshal Sir Philip Babington, a former Air Member for Personnel and subsequently Chairman of the Fund's Grants Committee. She was succeeded as Chairman by Squadron Leader Harold Pound.

The Nursery School was closed in July 1957, partly because the demand had decreased since the advent of safer jet aircraft and partly because it was difficult to staff on account of its inaccessibility in the country.

Vanbrugh Castle School, its war damage repaired, reopened in April 1947, with twenty-five boys between the ages of seven and fourteen years and able to accommodate fifty boys. Shortly after reopening the school fell under the Controller's scrutiny. In accordance with pre-war practice the boys were attending the local schools, including the Roan Grammar School, Charlton Secondary and Royal Hill Elementary Schools, with the difference that Roan was no longer fee-paying, entrance depending upon examination, report and selection. The Controller was much impressed by the fact that at each outside school Vanbrugh boys were distinctly identifiable by their smart appearance, a tribute to the lasting influence of the late matron, Mrs Slimming, and to the discipline of her husband, Captain G. A. R. Slimming who, excepting wartime employment at Hove, had been in charge at the School since 1921. Nevertheless, for all the good order and discipline at Vanbrugh itself, there had been complaints from some mothers about the manners and behaviour of their sons during the holidays. It was plain, therefore, that there was a risk that certain boys might deteriorate in character, possibly as a result of some of the company they kept outside the Castle.

It deeply concerned the Controller that, as the sons of deceased airmen, Vanbrugh boys were entitled morally and financially to the Fund's protection. When he visited the outside schools with Wing Commander J. F. Burnet MA, a member of the Education Advisory Committee and Bursar of Magdalene College, Cambridge, they were disturbed by conditions generally and the size of classes. There was the point, too, that in no sense did the Fund wish to fall short of its cherished promise to provide Royal Air Force children with those same opportunities they might have enjoyed if their fathers had lived.

In April 1950, rather than accept this risk, the Fund transformed Vanbrugh into a boarding school for boys between the ages of seven and eleven, while older boys up to the age of eighteen continued to attend local schools.

That year, as it happened, Captain Slimming was due to retire after thirty years' service and Mr J. W. Webb-Jones MA was appointed headmaster. Previously headmaster of St George's School, Windsor, Webb-Jones had served in the Royal Air Force during the war as an Education Officer.

Thus when the Duchess of Kent visited Vanbrugh Castle in 1951 she found the embryo of a boys' preparatory school. Although Vanbrugh Castle School was recognised by the Ministry of Education as an efficient Primary School in 1950, it did not attain the status of a recognised boarding preparatory school for boys between the ages of eight and thirteen until the early 1960s.

Some schools welcome Royal Air Force children at reduced fees, others receive them on varying terms because of past and present Air Ministry or Royal Air Force Benevolent Fund support. There are also numerous scholarships and endowments arising out of two world wars. Coming under the heading of bursaries, foundations, nominations, presentations and scholarships, they commemorate individual or corporate acts of sacrifice and bravery and, in one instance, perhaps the most celebrated bomber operation in Royal Air Force history.

The story of the Dam Busters is one of the best known single Royal Air Force operations of the Second World War. The Lancaster bomber crews and the inventor who figure in it have been immortalised in Paul Brickhill's book and in a film. But the breaching of the Mohne and Eder dams in 1943 by a force of Lancasters of No. 617 Squadron, led by Wing Commander Guy Gibson, using the bouncing 'ducks and drakes' bombs devised by Dr Barnes Wallis, had a sequel which is not so widely known.

After the war when the government was making awards to inventors whose genius had contributed so vitally towards victory, a grateful nation gave £10,000 to Dr Barnes Neville Wallis, who was knighted in 1968. It so happened that when Wallis received his award the Controller was trying to charm Christ's Hospital, the Bluecoat School, into accepting boys nominated from the Fund. As Sir John Cordingley explained, 'few boys had been put down for public schools by their fathers and I was scratching around for nominations at schools at prices one felt were reasonable'. The Fund was particularly attracted to Christ's Hospital by its magnificent record and because it had places for boys *and* girls.

Mr Ernest de Rougemont, a member of the Fund Council and an Almoner of Christ's Hospital, had placed at the disposal of the Fund his Donation Governorship, normally covering in succession the education of three children. Air Marshal Sir Aubrey Ellwood had done likewise in memory of his son, Flying Officer A. J. A. Ellwood, who was killed flying, and Mrs Gregory, the widow of Air Commodore A. L. Gregory, had offered the Fund two presentations.

In 1949 the Fund purchased a single Donation Governor's Presentation at Christ's Hospital. For many years the Governor was Mr Paul Cutting, Secretary (Administration), who exchanged letters every month with the child he had nominated on behalf of the Fund. Having got one presentation, the Controller recalled, 'I said: please could we have some more, but was told that would be most unusual as Christ's Hospital didn't really do this for corporate bodies.' When he persisted, 'The Fund would like nineteen more', his request was refused as contrary to policy.

It was at this stage that Barnes Wallis, who had been educated at Christ's Hospital and was then a member of the Court of Almoners, approached the Fund. Dr Wallis told the Controller that he knew the Fund had been refused presentations and would like to help. The upshot was the creation between Dr Wallis and the Royal Air Force Benevolent Fund in 1951 of a £20,000 Royal Air Force Foundationers Trust at Christ's Hospital, the Fund to match Wallis's £10,000 inventor's award with £10,000, plus a contribution of one-third of the cost of Foundationers whose fathers were dead or disabled. Five years later the Trust was increased by nearly £11,000, consisting of £911 3s 1d from the Associated British Picture Corporation's première of *The Dam Busters* and £10,000 from the Royal Air Forces Association, being part of cinema foyer collections made by Royal Air Forces Association branches during the showing of the film.

The Royal Air Force Foundationers Trust provides annual studentships at Christ's Hospital in perpetuity – on average three for boys and one for a girl – for the education, maintenance and clothing of boys and girls whose fathers of any rank, and whether or not they have since died, are serving or have served in the Royal Air Force, the Royal Auxiliary Air Force or the Royal Air Force Reserves, and who need help in educating their children.

The following extracts from the Trust Deed record in Sir Barnes Wallis's own words his wishes concerning the selection of candidates:

> In no case should selection be made by means of a competitive examina-
> tion. That is to say, I earnestly desire selection to be based on the service
> record of the father, as being a man who has shown himself in the words

of Cecil Rhodes, to be a man of 'truth, courage, devotion to duty and sympathy for and protection of the weak', and secondly one who has exhibited during his service days 'moral force of character and an instinct to lead and to take an interest in other men . . .' In addition, the character of the child should of course be taken into account, in that he or she must be of a type that will, as far as can be judged by experienced people, benefit in an outstanding manner by a public school education, and one who has shown, as far as a child of tender years can be expected to show, a desire to serve others rather than themselves.

Some of the Foundationers have since shown signs of emulating the noble character of their fathers and on completion of their education at Christ's Hospital have joined the Royal Air Force, the other armed services, the Police Force, and teachers' training colleges, and most of them have gone to university.

Lord Wolfenden, in an article in *The Times Educational Supplement* on 18 June 1954 wrote:

> The Council of the Fund realised many years ago that money spent on the education of children is one of the most valuable and fruitful investments that the Fund can make. And throughout the whole range of possible ages and possible types of school this policy is faithfully pursued by the committee and staff.
>
> The essence of the policy can be simply stated. It is that when a member of the Royal Air Force is killed his children should be able to have the kind of education which he could reasonably have hoped to provide for them if he had lived. It is no part of the Fund's duty to provide, automatically or capriciously, an education more expensive or more prolonged than would have been provided by a father who had continued to serve in the Royal Air Force. Nor is it part of the Fund's practice to expend money in such a way as will relieve public funds. The statutory provision made by the Ministry of Pensions, by local authorities, or by other grant-aiding bodies is mobilised in the first instance often as a result of advice proffered by the officials of the Fund itself.
>
> At several schools, notably Christ's Hospital and Wellington College, there are Royal Air Force foundationerships, established either by private generosity or by gifts from the Royal Air Force Central Fund or the Royal Air Force Prize Fund.

Other schools, including the Royal Wolverhampton, Reed's School, the Royal Alexandra and Albert School, and the Gordon Boys School (now Gordon's School), have given tremendous assistance to the Fund since the Second World War by educating hundreds of Royal Air Force children under the most favourable terms. Another school, St Edward's, Oxford, produced a large number of gallant men for the Royal Air Force, so much so that the Air Ministry endowed the Guy Gibson Scholarship at the school and paid for a commemorative library window. In addition, both the Fund and the Royal Air Forces Association donated bursaries at this school for sons of deceased and disabled officers and airmen.

From the end of the Second World War to 31 December 1968, some thirty-six thousand educational awards were made and expenditure, including the Fund's own schools at Vanbrugh Castle and Rooks Hill House, amounted to £3,435,702.

The following letter from the orphan son of a fighter pilot summarises the usefulness of the Fund's assistance with education:

I recently [1963] read in the Press that the Royal Air Force Benevolent Fund is having to spend well over half-a-million pounds each year to relieve distress amongst past and present members of the Royal Air Force and their families, widows and orphans.

As one who has benefited immeasurably from this Fund, I feel that merely to see this sum of £500,000 printed in cold black and white does not give any indication of the constructiveness of the help given to myself and many others.

My father was a fighter pilot in the Royal Air Force during the Second World War. Both he and my mother were killed during the war when I was less than a year old. It was left to my grandparents to bring me up. Soon after I started going to school my grandfather was taken ill and was bed-ridden for five years, until he died. All our family's income went on giving him proper medical care and treatment.

But thanks to this Fund I was still able to receive the first-class education my father would have given me. Because of my grandfather's state of health it was vital that I should go to a boarding school and the Fund helped to finance this. Not only did I receive this aid, but the Fund also helped me to live as normal a life as possible by sending clothing grants, so that I was not obliged to wear my school uniform all the time, and even money to help with holidays.

Nor did I ever feel that the Fund consisted of a bunch of impersonal 'do-gooders'. A keen interest was always taken in everything I did (and still is) and I never found any unwillingness to try to help with every sort of problem. But I am sure that the most important thing I received from this organisation was a sense, throughout the days of my childhood and adolescence, of being quite secure. I honestly feel that as a result of the work of this Fund I had as happy and useful a childhood as any child with parents.

Of one thing I am quite certain. Without this help I should never have been able to gain a University education, as I have done, and the whole course of my life would have been radically different.

May I close by saying that I hope, and indeed I am sure, that other applicants are as grateful to the Royal Air Force Benevolent Fund as I am myself.

CHAPTER 9

THE CONSCIENCE
OF THE NATION

*'The Royal Air Force Benevolent Fund is part of the conscience of the
British nation. A nation without a conscience is a nation without a soul. A
nation without a soul is a nation that cannot live.'*

Winston Churchill, 1951

'Not a penny too much, not a penny too little.' The Fund had
worked faithfully to the Controller's creed and weakened its
capital position in the process. Relief expenditure rose steeply to
£668,656 in 1948 and to £711,829 in 1949. There were reasons. In many
cases wartime savings, gratuities or terminal benefits had been spent.
Children were growing up and reaching the expensive age for clothing,
maintenance and education. True, recent social legislation, in particular
the welfare state and education acts, had partially relieved the pressure
but the Fund existed to provide Royal Air Force families with a better
future than government assistance alone could offer them.

There was the case, for instance, in which a flying officer had been
killed in the First World War before he was able to marry the mother of
his child. Between the wars the mother became a teacher, refusing to
allow the father's family to educate her son. The boy went to college,
passed out as an outstanding young Royal Air Force officer and was killed
in 1940 during the Battle of Britain. As the mother became elderly, the
Fund heard that she needed assistance and accepted responsibility for her
future care.

One case, picked at random. But which cases are to be quoted out of
the many thousands of buff folders which pack the basements at Portland
Place? Perhaps this one. A Royal Air Force reserve officer died ferrying
aircraft in 1945 in the Air Transport Auxiliary. His daughter, after taking
a scholarship to university with the object of graduating as a teacher,
contracted polio and was paralysed from the neck downwards. She spent
six months in an iron lung. Later, assisted by the Fund, she entered a
specialist's private nursing home and after that a residence for polio
victims. Gradually the girl's health improved as a result of all this private
and costly care, and in time her scholarship was restored. Yet, in order

to make use of it, she needed the attendance of a trained nurse companion, whose salary was paid for by the Fund. Thus assisted, the pilot's daughter took her degree and became a teacher – a happy ending to a sad story, and it had been achieved as a result of great personal courage on the part of the beneficiary and a considerable sum from the Fund.

However, the cumulative relief of such individual cases was by no means the only cause of the post-war rise of expenditure. At this time, and it merits repetition, substantial sums were paid to outside organisations in accordance with the Fund's old and proven policy of co-operating with kindred bodies. This form of investment was costly at the outset but the annual dividends in educational openings and opportunities, hospital beds, front-door keys, convalescent and many other facilities have amply rewarded each act of faith.

Some further examples, other than the £10,000 contribution towards the Royal Air Force foundationerships at Christ's Hospital, are: £34,000 for the Royal Star and Garter Home at Richmond for disabled sailors, soldiers, and airmen, endowing six Air Force beds; £60,000 for endowing six beds at the Royal Air Forces Association Home at Sussexdown and contributing towards modernisation of the building; £2600 to the Papworth Village Settlement to build two houses for pulmonary tuberculosis patients; £3000 to King Edward VII's Hospital for Officers – Sister Agnes's – to endow a Royal Air Force bed and contribute towards their extension.

In addition, regular donations have been made to such organisations as the Royal Hospital and Home for Incurables, Putney; the Queen Elizabeth Foundation for the Disabled at Exeter; the Queen Alexandra Hospital Home, Gifford House, Worthing; Chaseley Home for the seriously paralysed at Eastbourne; the Ex-Services Mental Welfare Society; the Thistle Foundation, Edinburgh; the Scottish National Institution for the War Blinded; and many others.

Nor were those men forgotten who had travelled from overseas to fight for Britain in the Royal Air Force. Throughout the war men had arrived from many countries to join the Royal Air Force, and after the war the Fund acted to keep open the lines of communication to these men in their home lands.

Within the United Kingdom a Scottish branch had functioned since 1947. For twenty-one years until his retirement in August 1978, Air Marshal Sir Brian Baker, who won the DSO, the AFC and the MC in the First World War, had been the Branch Secretary and as well as supervising the welfare work had been instrumental in raising large donations in Scotland. But the Fund was concerned that neither in Northern Ireland nor in the Republic of Ireland was the Fund directly represented. In the war, with the approval of their governments, 10,000 men had joined the Royal Air Force from Northern Ireland, including many who had crossed the border from Eire to enlist; a further 16,000 men had entered

the service from Eire. The Controller visited Northern Ireland and the
Republic of Ireland in 1948. Finding that 'pawning clothing on Monday
and redeeming it on Saturday was a custom, and money-lending was rife',
the Fund swiftly established branches in Belfast and Dublin, with the
approval of the governments in Northern Ireland and Eire. Sir Basil
Goulding was Chairman of the Republic of Ireland Branch at its inception. In later years as need diminished the branch closed.

But, if resettlement was rough for the Irish, the state of the 4600
Jamaicans and 900 other British West Indians who had served in the
Royal Air Force was grievous. The Controller visited Jamaica in 1950
and was appalled by the poverty and living conditions of many of those
who had served in the war. So the Fund raised a Committee at Kingston,
which was to prove very active under the Chairmanship of Squadron
Leader (later Major) H. G. Vyse, to carry on the excellent work of Flight
Lieutenant C. S. Williams, who had personally represented the Fund
while commanding a small wartime administration unit there.

Between 1948 and 1967 the sum of £38,638 had been spent on all
forms of relief in Jamaica but conditions are so wholly different in the
West Indies from those in Britain that the Fund makes no claim to
dispense relief on equal terms. In the course of his travels the Controller
also visited the United States, where he thanked Mrs Edward Antony of
New York for the great volume of welfare work she had devoted to the
Royal Air Force aircrew trainees whilst in the United States during the
war. He also conferred with the organisers of the Air Force Aid Society,
the Royal Air Force Benevolent Fund's equivalent organisation, which
had been formed during the war after consultation with Riverdale and
Cordingley. The Fund was glad in this modest way to be of further service
to the Air Force Aid Society of the nation which established a Royal Air
Force Benevolent Fund (USA) Inc. in 1940 and contributed generously
to the Fund before the United States' entry into the war.

In South Africa Mrs A. C. Haswell, a former Chairman of the South
African Air Force Fund, was appointed the Fund's Honorary
Representative in 1949. Applications from ex-members of the Royal Air
Force resident in South Africa were referred to her in the first place. For
many years Mrs Haswell held an imprest account on behalf of the Royal
Air Force Benevolent Fund and as well as dealing with disbursement of
assistance she also received loan repayments in that country. Air Vice-
Marshal Sir Matthew Frew and Wing Commander W. H. Moyles, who
retired from the Royal Air Force and settled in Johannesburg, were also
appointed Fund Representatives.

No more branches were established outside Britain but imprest
accounts were opened in various localities so that eligible ex-servicemen
and women might be assisted in time of need everywhere in the world,
except behind the Iron Curtain where investigation was not possible. So
great were the outgoings at home and abroad that in 1949 expenditure
of £776,942 exceeded the income by £308,855 and resulted in a sale of

investments totalling £365,055. Spanning 1948–50 the Fund's expenditure exceeded income by £548,559. The sale of investments was not the happiest of decisions and the Fund had to brace itself to spend capital as well as income. It would have to seek a peacetime income, as it had between the wars, but with the difference that this time it was more experienced and better equipped to do so.

Thus, the burden would ordinarily have fallen squarely on the shoulders of Sir Bertram Rumble, who had been knighted in 1947. Rumble, while retaining his Appeals Secretaryship, and still unpaid, was also Honorary Treasurer, having succeeded Air Commodore B. C. H. Drew in that appointment in 1944. But, sadly, Sir Bertram did not live long enough to meet this new challenge. When he died in 1948 it was calculated that £6 million had been raised during his seven years as Appeals Secretary.

Sir Bertram's successor as Honorary Treasurer was an ex-Air Minister, Sir Archibald Sinclair – later Lord Thurso – who had served the Churchill Government in that office throughout the war. Lord Thurso was the Honorary Treasurer of the Fund from 1949 to 1969. Before his death in 1970 he helped to reshape the financial policy of the Fund. Viscount Ward of Witley, a former Secretary of State for Air, succeeded him. He served until 1987 and died in 1988 after serving the Fund since 1958 when he was appointed a vice-president.

After the end of the Second World War Group Captain J. E. Redding, before becoming a member of the Grants Committee, had given talks about the Fund at every Royal Air Force station at home and abroad. Some years later a film about the Fund had been shown twice at six-monthly intervals on an equally wide circuit within the Service. But the Service was contracting rapidly and some other source of income was required.

Though Royal Air Force voluntary subscriptions were improving now that sixty-two per cent of serving officers and fifty-four per cent of serving airmen and airwomen were in the scheme, the Finance and General Purposes Committee was soon faced with the prospect of a further and substantial loss of capital. This was temporarily averted by a windfall.

The Royal Air Force is not normally associated with prize money, the traditional perquisite of the Royal Navy, but under the Prize Act of 1948 the Royal Air Force received £1,250,000, a share which was largely due to Coastal Command air operations over the sea.

In naval practice prize money is distributed among officers and ratings, but the Air Ministry, having a smaller sum to divide, established the Royal Air Force Prize Fund for charitable and similar purposes. It was the Air Council's gift of £200,000 from this fund that prevented another sale of Royal Air Force Benevolent Fund investments in 1950. In 1951 a further £100,000 from the Prize Fund was received, to be held in trust for the education of children of deceased service people killed on duty or whose death was attributable to service; a final gift from this source of £14,630 19s 10d being received in 1959.

In the red as the Royal Air Force Benevolent Fund was, where expenditure over income was concerned, the Fund was especially aggrieved in 1948 to be criticised by *The People* Sunday newspaper.

Hesitantly, the Fund had recently engaged the public relations consultancy of F. J. Lyons and was sunning itself in the comforting rays of frequent publication of complimentary news items and feature articles. But now it was to learn the lesson of any publicity seeker: that the retention of good public relations counsel does not indemnify against a critical press. On Sunday 23 May 1948 *The People*, opening a series of articles on service charities, accused the Army Benevolent Fund of hoarding and promised future disclosures about 'the equally amazing state of affairs inside the Royal Air Force Benevolent Fund'.

The phrasing of this trailer came as a thunderclap, but when the article appeared a week later it was clear that the newspaper had assembled a carefully documented argument even if the Fund could not accept its basic premise: that ex-Royal Air Force families went in distress while the Royal Air Force Benevolent Fund sat on its millions.

The newspaper alleged that 30,000 ex-Royal Air Force service people had been helped in 1947 while the appeals of another 30,000 were turned down: 'Every other man or woman who appealed for help was refused, yet there is still nearly £6 million to be spent.'

The Controller's explanation was quoted:

> It is our policy to conserve our Fund. If we answered every call that is made upon us without exercising some sense of responsibility we would very soon run out of money. We have to think of the future . . . In ten years' time there may be another slump like the one we knew in 1931. There are four and a half million people liable to call upon our funds if there is such a slump and we have got to be ready for it. After all it will not be much use making new appeals for war heroes in 1948. The people have too short a memory.

It was emphasised that the Fund had to plan many years ahead for education, especially university education. But in the euphoric atmosphere of post-war welfare and education measures *The People* disputed the need for such prudence. In retrospect it can be fairly observed that the Council's determination to preserve the Fund has been justified many times over since 1948, especially in the late 1950s and the 1960s. But in 1948 when the war had been over for only three years there was a natural demand among some donors and recipients for the immediate use of money that had been given while the enemy was overhead.

The Fund understood this and told *The People*, 'Send us any cases of airmen in need and we will see that they are investigated and every possible help given.'

On 5 December 1948 *The People* announced that it had sent 650 cases to the Fund, of which 367 had never before applied for assistance and 204 had been assisted previously. Readers' letters had resulted in 418 grants totalling £11,925 18s 9d. After this announcement 537 more letters were received, resulting in 332 cases of assistance.

The thunderclap had fallen and had cleared the air with gain to all concerned. The Fund was delighted that the publicity had produced so many new cases – forty-four per cent from ex-servicemen and women or dependants who were apparently unaware the Fund existed – and *The People* could, and did, congratulate itself on a successful campaign.

A few years after *The People* episode another publicity opportunity arose, this time to beat that highly respectable and much sought after broadcast appeal drum, known the world over as the British Broadcasting Corporation's weekly charity appeal broadcast. Competition is keen among charities for acceptance in this Sunday night 'commercial' and the Fund was obliged to wait six years before receiving its third call to Broadcasting House.

Viscount Trenchard had made the first radio appeal in 1940, and there had been no further broadcast since Viscount Portal's on Battle of Britain Sunday in 1945. The Fund had sought a Week's Good Cause opportunity for some while. When, at last, the Fund was offered Battle of Britain Sunday, 16 September 1951, the Controller knew that there was only one man he wanted for the broadcast. There were problems, however; Winston Churchill, aged seventy-six, was out of office and as Leader of the Opposition was more free to accept an invitation, but the British Broadcasting Corporation warned, 'You'll never get him.' Churchill had made only one previous broadcast appeal, for another charity before the war.

He would have to be won over by strategy and the Controller took up the challenge. There were four factors which had to be considered – Churchill's reputation for personal loyalty, his sense of duty, his impulsive character, and his sense of the fitness of occasion:

1. Loyalty: Well, the Chairman, the Deputy Chairman and the Honorary Treasurer of the Fund had each served handsomely in the war. Riverdale had negotiated the Empire Air Training Scheme; Portal had run the Air Force as Chief of The Air Staff under Churchill's minister, Sir Archibald Sinclair.
2. Duty: The Fund felt that a man who can say 'Never in the field of human conflict was so much owed by so many to so few' must carry some responsibility for saying it.
3. Impulse: The request must be submitted in such a way and at such a moment as to elicit an impulsive 'yes'.
4. Occasion: Imperative for getting that decisive 'yes'. Must be warm and congenial, preferably connected with wartime memories and in wartime company.

Sir Winston Churchill, whose BBC appeal on the theme of 'The Debt
We Owe', broadcast on Battle of Britain Sunday in September 1951,
suggested the title of this book. He was a vice-president from 1919 until
he died in 1965. This portrait of the wartime Prime Minister, wearing
the uniform of Air Commodore, hangs in the Council chamber.

The Controller went to work and at the appropriate time he had arranged for Churchill to receive a written invitation to make the broadcast under the signatures of Riverdale, Portal and Sinclair. Moreover, he had the letter delivered on the very day on which Churchill happened to be entertaining the Portals at a family lunch.

Unbeknown to anyone, Princess Marina had also played her part in securing Churchill's agreement to make this broadcast. On 20 July 1951 the Princess wrote privately to Churchill, who was an old friend of hers, to ask for his help in this way; on 26 July he replied as follows:

> I thank Your Royal Highness for your letter of the 20 July about the broadcast appeal for the Royal Air Force Benevolent Fund on 'Battle of Britain' Sunday. I am shortly going to be abroad, but I expect to be back in time for this event and will be glad to make this broadcast for the Fund. I am indeed complimented that Your Royal Highness should wish me to do so.

The broadcast took place on Battle of Britain Sunday in September 1951, and, over and above the unique advantage Churchill's name and voice brought to the appeal, the recording provided the nation with a remarkable radio archive. It was the first time that the war leader's immortal tribute to 'The Few' had been heard in public. Much published though the tribute was, it had been spoken in the House of Commons in 1940. Opening his broadcast, Churchill said:

> 'Never in the field of human conflict was so much owed by so many to so few.'
>
> With those words in 1940 – our darkest and yet our finest hour – I reported to the House of Commons on the progress of the Battle of Britain, whose eleventh anniversary we now celebrate. I repeat my words tonight with pride and gratitude. They spring from our hearts as keenly at this moment as on the day I uttered them. Time dims our memories of many events which, while they are happening, seem tremendous. But the fame of the pilots – a thin blue line indeed – who broke the aerial might of the enemy and saved their native land shines ever more brightly.
>
> Our debt is now not only to 'The Few'. As the Royal Air Force grew larger and larger and the hard years of war unrolled, many thousands of their comrades died so that our Island might live, free and inviolate. By 1945, alas, as our casualty lists told the tale, 'The Few' had become 'The Many'. Had it not been for those young men whose daring and devotion cast a glittering shield between us and our foe, we should none of us be sitting at rest in our homes this Sunday evening, as members of an unconquered – and, as we believe, unconquerable – Nation. Let us all welcome this chance to pay a small measure of *the debt we owe* to the paladins of the Royal Air Force. And I will tell you one thing we can do, and do now.
>
> I am appealing to you tonight on behalf of the Royal Air Force

Benevolent Fund. This Fund exists solely to help members of the Royal Air Force – men and women – in time of need, and their families or dependants when they are in trouble. More than two million pounds has been spent in this cause during the last three years alone. The money which has been spent by the Royal Air Force Benevolent Fund has gone beyond the Fund's ordinary income by nearly £600,000. A renewed effort must be made if the future is not to be overclouded.

My friends, I am certain we are all together on this and that we are all agreed upon our purpose. We all rejoice that there is a Royal Air Force Benevolent Fund to give help to the dependants of those undaunted men who lost their lives in the war or have died since, leaving their record behind them. This fine organisation, for which I now appeal, has fortunately up to the present always been able to give at least a measure of aid.

It is our duty now to make sure that the Fund will be able to go on helping, and will not fail as the survivors of the war grow old and feeble. Only thus can the Fund maintain its claim and reputation that no genuine case of distress is ever turned away. The Royal Air Force Benevolent Fund is part of the conscience of the British Nation. A nation without a conscience is a nation without a soul. A nation without a soul is a nation that cannot live.

Please send whatever you can to Winston Churchill, Royal Air Force Benevolent Fund, 1 Sloane Street, London SW1.

I thank you for listening to me. Goodnight.

Donations ranging from 6d to £1000 arrived from all over Britain and the world. At the final count £26,460 had been received, including the remainder of the rifled contents of a mail bag recovered from the dark waters of the Serpentine, where it had been tossed by a gang of thieves.

Shortly after the broadcast the Controller was at home one Saturday morning when Winston Churchill came on the line. 'Sir John, how is the appeal? I was going to send you my cheque but I've got a better idea. A film has been made of me. I'll give you that film to show all over the country if you'll give me a quick decision. Korda has the film. Go and see it.'

The Controller went to Sir Alexander Korda's home and saw *The Robin Gets Its Wings*, a charming reel, starring a robin coming closer and closer to Churchill until it fed out of his hand. Cordingley saw at once that the Fund could capitalise on that robin.

By this time Churchill's interest in the idea had been thoroughly aroused. With the assistance of the documentary film producer, Mr Castleton Knight, of the Rank Organisation, a short film was made about the Fund, using the robin sequence as the centrepiece. When the film was ready Churchill, now back in office as Prime Minister, was on his way to the United States and insisted upon seeing it there. Back across the Atlantic came some suggested modifications and the instructions that whatever else was done to the film the robin sequence must remain intact.

The commentary of the completed film was supplied by Churchill's appeal broadcast.

With the cheerful co-operation of the cinema industry the film was widely exhibited and, although unfortunately for the Fund it clashed during its run with a King George VI memorial film and the Lord Mayor of London's Flood Relief Fund for the East Coast flood victims, it produced £54,300. Together, Churchill's appeal broadcast and film benefited the Fund by a total of £80,760.

While, thanks to the co-operation of Sir John Davis of the Rank Organisation and Sir Philip Warter of the Associated British Picture Corporation, Churchill and his robin provided the Fund's most spectacular screen result in this period, the Fund is indebted to film producers and cinema exhibitors for their friendship over many years, and after the Churchill film a reception was held at the Ministry of Defence, Whitehall, attended by Princess Marina, members of the Air Council and leaders of the cinema industry.

A flair for quality showmanship, whether in the foyer or on the airfield, had long been one of the Fund's appeal attributes. It was, therefore, not surprising that five years after the war the Fund returned to the air display as a source of income. In 1950 the Fund accepted the Air Council's invitation to make all arrangements, outside the flying programme, for the Royal Air Force's first post-war air display at Farnborough. It took place on 7 and 8 July. Obviously, the revival of the full Royal Air Force air display as a form of appeal raised many problems, including the negotiation of insurance cover against accident. Nevertheless, the Fund, after consultation with the Air Ministry, decided to be its own 'showman' and to organise the display in return for any profits.

With this object, the Royal Air Force Benevolent Fund Development Trust was formed to finance the promotion and presentation of air displays. Approving a grant of £30,000 from the Royal Air Force Central Fund, the Air Council gave this new and separate trust a start in life. At one stage of the preparations the Fund was committed to an expenditure of more than £30,000. Because a weather insurance policy had been rejected on grounds of expense, a bad weather forecast was initially depressing. But the clouds cleared and the two-day event at Farnborough was a great success. The occasion was graced by the presence of King George VI, the Queen, Princess Margaret and Princess Marina. A total of 130,000 people were admitted to the display and the Fund profited by £8995.

The resumption of the traditional air display, the great coup represented by the Churchill broadcast appeal and the general improvements under Sir John Cordingley's administration are to be especially numbered among the Fund's achievements in the closing days of Lord Riverdale's chairmanship. During his twelve years in office he had done a great amount of entertaining on behalf of the Fund at his own expense. He had introduced, with the concurrence of the National

Provincial Bank of which he was a director, Mr Francis Wilkins, the head of the Bank's Stock and Investment Department, whose advice on investments was of enormous value to the Fund. Riverdale's directorship of the Halifax Building Society had also been most useful when the Fund started to finance mortgages for the beneficiaries. Although often away from London, he kept in close touch, by telephone, with all its affairs.

It should not pass unrecorded that Riverdale's family, like so many he had worked to help, had suffered its loss in war too. Lord Riverdale's son-in-law, Group Captain E. J. L. Hope, had been killed in air operations in 1941, and his memory was perpetuated by Lady Riverdale's £200-a-year Jack Hope Scholarship at Wellington College.

Riverdale was in his eightieth year when in 1952 he announced his wish to retire, and when this became effective on 31 December 1952 he received the following letter from the Private Secretary to The Queen:

> Buckingham Palace
> 12 January 1953
>
> My Dear Lord Riverdale,
>
> I have laid your letter before The Queen.
>
> Her Majesty is indeed sorry to hear that you feel obliged to give up the Chairmanship of the Royal Air Force Benevolent Fund, for she well knows what an incalculable benefit to it your long and devoted service as the Head of its Council has been. It must be a great satisfaction to you to leave the Fund in so flourishing a condition as it now is, and to look back on all the good results it has achieved throughout your twelve years' association with it.
>
> I am to send you The Queen's best wishes for an improvement in your health.
>
> Yours sincerely,
> A. Lascelles.

CHAPTER 10

POLICY REAPPRAISAL

*'No matter what provision we make there will always be a place for
voluntary organisations. For only by voluntary organisation are you able to
touch the bottomless reservoir of kindness, humanity and self-sacrifice.'*

Aneurin Bevan, 1950

Lord Knollys succeeded Lord Riverdale as Chairman of the Royal
Air Force Benevolent Fund in the new year of 1953, Marshal
of the Royal Air Force Lord Portal continuing as Deputy
Chairman. At Knollys's election Portal reminded the Council:
'We consider that the practice hitherto that the Chairman should be
a civilian with wide experience of business life outside the service,
and not a retired Royal Air Force officer, is an extremely sound one and
should be adhered to.'

Although Lord Portal did not refer to it on this occasion, another practice in the making of the Council's chief appointments is the appointment
of a retired senior regular Royal Air Force officer as Chairman of the
Grants Committee. The holder of the office was Air Chief Marshal Sir
Francis J. Fogarty, a former Air Member for Personnel, who in 1957
succeeded Air Chief Marshal Sir James Robb.

While most of Lord Knollys's working experience had been outside
the service – he was a banker by early training – he had been connected
with military or civil aviation for much of his life. From the 16th London
Regiment in the First World War, he had joined the Royal Flying Corps
and had won the Distinguished Flying Cross. Appointed Chairman of
British Airways Overseas Corporation in 1943, he had led Britain's overseas airline through the transition from war to peace and in 1956 he was
to become, in addition to chairman of a great insurance corporation,
chairman of Vickers, an appointment which kept him in touch with the
Royal Air Force. In every respect Knollys fulfilled the Fund's preference
for a Chairman of 'wide experience of business and life outside the
service'. His experience of public service included the Governorship
of Bermuda and a senior appointment at the British Embassy in
Washington.

Although, as will be recalled, the new constitution approved by Mr
Justice Harman in 1948 had sanctioned a more adventurous investment

policy than the majority of charities were permitted before the passing of the Trustee Investments Act of 1961, general conditions had frustrated advantage being taken of this remarkable opportunity until shortly before Lord Knollys's arrival.

It was not that the Controller with his bright eye to the opportunity had not keenly sounded the Fund's honorary investment and property advisers, Wilkins of the National Provincial Bank and Wallace Withers of Debenham, Tewson and Chinnocks, but that under Riverdale's leadership the Fund had of necessity picked its way cautiously towards a change. Looking back, no praise can be too high for these two investment consultants who advised the Fund on its first equity and property investments, which nowadays form a substantial and profitable part of the Fund's investment portfolio. Thanks are also due to Sir Ronald Thornton, a vice-chairman of Barclays Bank and later a director of the Bank of England, for his helpful advice.

Nevertheless, at the end of 1951 the Controller, who had been growing increasingly apprehensive about many opportunities that were slipping by, had decided to sound the Chairman, suggesting that the Fund ought perhaps to provide itself with a greater margin of safety against the falling purchasing power of the pound by transferring some of its assets to real estate, property and equity shares. Lord Riverdale's response was not enthusiastic. The Chairman, who had guided the Fund's investments and financial affairs for so long, expressed himself as naturally cautious about any change 'which might leave us open, however slightly, to an allegation that there is a speculative element in our investment policy'. He did agree, however, that the Controller should discuss the matter with Lord Portal in his separate capacities as Deputy Chairman of the Royal Air Force Benevolent Fund and on the Boards of Barclays Bank and Barclays DCO.

It was now very apparent that, if the Fund was to arrest the decline in the book value of its assets and to improve its capital position under peacetime conditions, a somewhat drastic alteration of its investment policy would be required.

By the following May, many soundings had been taken of the investment and property worlds as a result of the Chairman's amber light; and the council learned that the Finance and General Purposes Committee had decided, after searching investigation, to consider suitable properties with first-class covenants for investment within a current limit of £250,000 and to invest in carefully selected ordinary stocks and shares to the same limit.

The Chairman was unable to attend this meeting but in his absence it was reported:

> Lord Riverdale considers that the change in the investment policy is necessary in the light of the economic and financial position. He commends it as being in the best interests of the Fund, bearing in mind that inflation

affects the Fund in two ways: firstly, by reducing the purchasing value of income and, secondly, by increasing the rate of assistance we have to give.

At the outset of Lord Knollys's Chairmanship, the Fund's appeal side came under scrutiny. Already those of late middle age when the Royal Air Force fought the Battle of Britain were approaching the end of their lives. Memories of the war were fading too.

Inevitably the question arose; where could the Fund look for future support outside such routine sources as the service personnel voluntary subscriptions scheme, Battle of Britain week 'At Homes' at Royal Air Force stations, the Royal Air Forces Association, and other intermittent or incidental appeal activities?

The answer lay in the general public, and a need to strike a balance between reminding the public of its past debt to the Royal Air Force and emphasising that the inheritors of the Air Force's wartime tradition were still occupationally liable to death or disablement.

But the Fund was closely exercised as to the best approach now that the direct, and in retrospect somewhat brash, appeal of wartime could no longer be employed. For in the 1950s it seemed hardly credible that the Fund had actually touched off a big response by mailing this sentiment:

> If it were not for the men of the Royal Air Force, Hitler would be now in Buckingham Palace and Goering swigging Ribbentrop's champagne in the Savoy. You and I and our children would be dead or slaves. Men who have saved us and who are daily saving us from such a fate deserve something more than State help and State support for those whom they love when they fall on evil days.

Very true, but it simply would not do in 1952!

It was plain that what was required was a steady flow of factual publicity. The Controller therefore encouraged F. J. Lyons, its public relations consultant, to increase his firm's activities. For more than thirty years Peter Taylor, a former RAF public relations officer, at first a senior partner of F. J. Lyons and subsequently a private consultant, notified newspapers throughout the country of the quarterly and annual relief expenditure of the Fund in every county and most principal cities of the United Kingdom. Approved news of gifts and legacies, and of the money-raising activities of the Charity were prominent in Taylor's output of feature articles and news stories about the Fund. Paid advertising was placed through Dorland Advertising for many years until it switched to Social Services advertising, since re-titled Donation Development Consultants.

The Fund is often remembered in donors' wills, and just occasionally a wealthy man's estate will reveal a windfall, as happened in the magnificent benefaction of the Hattersley bequest. It was puzzling because, in contrast for example with a former colliery-owner, Mr H. Watson-Smith, who left the Fund £30,000 and endowed a scholarship in memory of a son killed in the Royal Air Force, Mr R. E. Hattersley, an industrialist, appeared to have no association with the Royal Air Force.

Hattersley, who died on 2 May 1949, left the residue of his estate to the Fund following the death of his wife. She died on 8 January 1952. This placed almost the entire ordinary share capital of his company, Hattersley (Ormskirk) Limited – since merged with Peglers (Holdings) Limited – in the Trust of the Royal Air Force Benevolent Fund; his total bequest, with other investments, provided the Fund with approximately £320,000 at probate valuation. Subsequently, the Hattersley shares were increased by bonus issues and sales of shares have produced £428,405.

It is known that Hattersley considered that but for the Royal Air Force he would have had nothing to leave and that the Royal Air Force Benevolent Fund was the soundest service charity he could find. It seems fair, therefore, to surmise that the publicised memories of Royal Air Force exploits and post-war publicity of the Fund's activities may have inspired this outstanding legacy, as no doubt they have inspired others.

While, in general, legacies large or small are as uncomplicated as the Hattersley bequest, the Fund is occasionally disappointed where a will has been incorrectly drawn. To take one very substantial example, it had appeared from the will of Mr Philip Hill, a financier, that he had intended to benefit the Fund to the extent of several hundred thousand pounds after his widow's death, but the Courts ruled that the Fund had no claim. However, the Fund was much comforted to learn later that Mr Hill's widow had instructed her trustee to give it especial consideration after her death.

A number of gifts have been directly linked with Royal Air Force exploits. For example, when *Herr* Barge Moltke-Leth handed the Fund £4000 in Copenhagen the gift represented the Danish resistance movement's acknowledgement of the bombing by the Royal Air Force of *Gestapo* headquarters in Denmark. Presenting the cheque, *Herr* Moltke-Leth explained that, after the liberation, the Royal Air Force had flown a number of air displays to benefit Danish families which had suffered from their action. After receiving the gift, the Fund transferred £1000 to the Royal Australian Air Force in respect of two Flying Officers of the Royal Australian Air Force who were killed while taking part in the attack.

Another gift which revived wartime memories came from former British officers, mostly Royal Air Force, who made contributions from their pay to finance escapes and to assist those in need. Under the lead of Group Captain H. M. A. Day, the senior British officer in the Stalag Luft camp, the escapees at the end of the war had a large surplus in Reichsmarks against which the Treasury made available £11,000. The Escaping Society, after advertising their intention, entrusted their savings to the Fund, stipulating that the money must help Royal Air Force officers or airmen ex-prisoners-of-war in Europe, or their dependants, with the provision that any capital remaining after twenty-five years be absorbed in the general fund of the charity. The money was finally expended during 1961 after 127 awards had been made.

In 1961 the Executive Committee of the Royal Air Force Church, St Clement Danes, Strand, London, presented an oak table to the church to mark the Royal Air Force Benevolent Fund's work for the Service.

Besides seeking publicity for bequests and its general activities, the Fund has initiated social functions in recent years, some of which have brought the double advantage of income and publicity. But, with a few exceptions, balls, dances and entertainments in London other than film premières generously offered by the cinema industry have been eschewed.

There are more profitable methods of raising money and the Appeals Department has always endeavoured to keep up with the expenditure of the Grants Committee. Neither did Sir John Cordingley spare his own back, because he had no objection to repeating a published description of himself as 'the unbeaten champion beggar of the world, 1956–60'. This tag was in some ways a disservice to his scrupulous ideals but its creator, Air Chief Marshal Sir Hubert Patch, had a point. To encounter the Controller on his social round was a revelation. Lord Mayors with charitable funds at their disposal, great companies of charitable disposition, millionaires, all were assailed. There was the occasion, for instance, when he encountered the late Lord Marks at a St James's Palace party to celebrate the fortieth birthday of the Royal Air Force Benevolent Fund, and Lord Marks promised a donation of £5000. A cheque for £7000 was received. Making his retirement address to the council in 1962, Sir John reflected: 'Sometimes I blush to think of the extent to which I have bothered some of those people but when begging is one of the principal functions one has to have an element of toughness in the make-up.'

The Controller's approach was equally direct when he broached the highly successful unwanted foreign coins scheme. Lunching opposite Sir Anthony Milward of British European Airways, Sir John Cordingley asked, 'Do you know that your show, when you bend anything, is very expensive to us? Because so many of your aircrew are ex-Air Force the burden falls more heavily on us than it does on you.' The Fund was seeking – and obtained – a page dealing with the unwanted coins scheme in the British European Airways booklet, *About Your Flight*. Between 1955 and 1967 this scheme, through which returning air travellers were invited to drop their 'chicken-feed' coins into airport boxes collected £20,238. Boxes are provided at airports and Channel crossing ports.

On one occasion an American visitor dropped in a silver dollar by mistake. Reporting that he attached great sentimental value to the coin, the American asked for its return. Thomas Cook's found the coin and the Fund was delighted to receive a donation of far greater value from Mr

Amory Houghton, former United States Ambassador to France and head of Corning Glass. Foreign currency remains an annual source of revenue through the diligence of Squadron Leader T. Bas Golightly.

The Controller, recalling the origin of this enterprising idea, said:

> At the outset we noticed a letter in *The Times* suggesting that charities were missing a good opportunity by not collecting unwanted foreign coins. I sent a letter to *The Times* stating that we were not quite as bad as that because we had explored this means of raising money and were informed that we could not do it as we were not licensed to act as bankers. Mr E. W. Berry, the Foreign Exchange Manager in Thomas Cook's office, rang me and said that Cook's were licensed as bankers and would gladly do the exchanging and banking part of the business, if we organised the collection of the coins. That is how the scheme started and when British Railways refused us permission to install the boxes at the seaports Thomas Cook's came along and said, 'We have a kiosk. You can hang your box on the outside' – which we did.

Another income-producing idea introduced by Rumble was the 'take a little, give a little' lighter fuel scheme, with which almost every smoker in the land will have been familiar. Launched in 1949, the scheme had produced more than £50,000 after payment of all expenses when it was discontinued in its original form in 1964, partly because of the spread of gas lighters.

From time to time the Fund was challenged that its eagerness to put its name to foyer, lighter fuel or foreign coin collections was at variance with its policy not to participate in flag days. In reply the Fund said that there was a distinction between collecting money for a flag and accepting money after giving a service such as the famous Churchill robin film, a drop of lighter fuel, or even relieving the weary traveller of his 'chicken-feed' coins.

Naturally, Battle of Britain week over the years has offered the Fund its best opportunities for publicity, such as the Chairman's annual letter to the press and the gift from Rolls-Royce of the front cover of *Flight*, and to 'earn' money when Royal Air Force stations are 'At Home' to the public. Proceeds from car parking and sideshows are shared with the Royal Air Forces Association, there being no entrance fees. 'At Homes' are the modern counterparts of the Hendon and Empire Air Displays.

Here the Fund has been exceptionally adventurous, producing, originally at the suggestion of the Air Ministry, its own *Battle of Britain Souvenir Book* and co-operating with the Royal Air Forces Association and the Ministry of Defence over its sale and distribution. The *Souvenir Book*, now the *Royal Air Force Yearbook*, has been published annually by the Fund since 1960.

On Battle of Britain Sunday each year at Westminster Abbey, and in many churches throughout the country, there are special services at which the collections are allotted to the Fund, with the foreknowledge and support of the heads of those churches, who every year draw the attention of their clergy to this observance.

Battle of Britain Week is an annual occurrence but there is one permanent exhibition of benefit to the Fund and this is to be found at Salisbury Hall near St Albans, formerly the home of Mr W. J. Goldsmith, where W 4050, the prototype de Havilland Mosquito, is the centrepiece of the Mosquito Memorial Museum, which houses a wide selection of historic de Havilland aircraft and their engines. This moated pocket manor house, where Nell Gwyn once lived and where Winston Churchill visited and fished as a boy, has become a place of pilgrimage for followers of the Stuarts and lovers of historic aircraft. But with respect to Nell, it is the aircraft that attract the crowds and the money for the Fund.

Visitors learn of the unusual and romantic circumstances in which the first Mosquito was designed in the manor house, assembled alongside the moat and flown from an adjacent field.

For many years the Fund's most glittering annual event was a concert. Beginning in 1956 and repeated each April on a night as near as possible

Princess Margaret, Guest of Honour at the fifth concert by massed bands of the Royal Air Force in the Royal Albert Hall in October 1988, presented, on behalf of the Fund, a *poignard* to Wing Commander Eric Banks, the RAF's Principal Director of Music, in recognition of his contribution to the success of so many fund-raising concerts.

to the anniversary of the birth of the Royal Air Force on 1 April 1918, a Royal Festival Hall audience enjoyed the RAF Anniversary Concert. The concerts were the joint inspiration of Sir John Barbirolli and of the late Kenneth Crickmore, who as Secretary and Director of the Hallé Concerts Society asked the Air Council if it might associate itself publicly with the Royal Air Force for the benefit of the service. Appreciative of the gesture, the Air Council suggested that the Fund should be the beneficiary and be responsible for arrangements.

The opening concert at the Royal Albert Hall on 7 April 1956 was attended by the Queen and the Duke of Edinburgh, who also attended the tenth anniversary concert in 1965 at the Royal Festival Hall. Other members of the Royal Family who have attended the concerts include Princess Margaret, Princess Anne, the late Princess Royal, the late Princess Marina, the Duke of Kent, Princess Alexandra and Princess Alice, Countess of Athlone. In 1961 the Queen Mother attended a concert at the Royal Festival Hall in commemoration of the twenty-first anniversary of the Battle of Britain, and returned in April 1978 for the Royal Air Force Diamond Jubilee Concert.

The concert in the Royal Festival Hall on 5 April 1968 in the presence of Princess Marina was given to celebrate the Golden Jubilee of the Royal Air Force.

Since the introduction of concerts in 1956 the orchestras have performed together with the Central Band of the Royal Air Force. Many conductors and soloists have given their services without fee. Conductors who have thus benefited the Fund include Sir John Barbirolli, Sir Arthur Bliss, Sir Charles Groves, Wing Commander A. E. Sims, Wing Commander J. L. Wallace, Wing Commander R. E. C. Davies, Wing Commander J. Martindale and Wing Commander E. Banks. The soloists have included Agustin Anievas, Gina Bachauer, Peter Frankl, Dame Myra Hess, Jose Iturbi, Eileen Joyce, Julius Katchen, Peter Katin, Malcuzynski, Denis Matthews, Yehudi Menuhin, Henryk Szeryng, Constance Shacklock, Fou Ts'ong, Tamas Vasary and several others.

Anniversaries that call for an unadorned and simple act of remembrance are observed at the Royal Air Force Memorial, Victoria Embankment, for which the Fund is responsible. Each year on Battle of Britain Sunday the Chief of the Air Staff places a wreath there on his way to the Thanksgiving Service at Westminster Abbey. On Remembrance Day a very large wreath in the shape of a pilot's brevet with a twelve-foot wingspan is attached to the Memorial at dawn. Some years ago it was found that if a strong breeze happened to be blowing along the Thames the wreath was inclined to take off. The Fund sought suggestions from its friends and the Royal Air Forces Association proposed attaching a symbolic propeller to the Memorial to hold the wreath in place. But the architect disagreed. 'The Memorial', he commented, 'embodies something better than a mere portrayal of the arms and mechanism with which the Royal Flying Corps and Royal Air Force accomplished their noble achievements.' He advised the fitting of inconspicuous lugs faced with the Royal Air Force Badge to which wreaths might be secured and his advice was accepted.

Lord Trenchard, to whose inspiration the Memorial and Fund are due, died on 10 February 1956, a week after his eighty-third birthday. Although towards the end of his life the founder had lost his sight, he insisted on hearing news of the Fund and the Annual Report was read to him. He continued also to promote the Fund, writing to the press, shortly before he died, 'I wonder how many of your readers realise what an important date 1 April is in the history of our Nation. It is the birthday of the Royal Air Force as we know it, for on that day in 1918 the service came into being by Act of Parliament . . .' Trenchard's letter went on to remind the public about the existence and work of the Fund.

Freshly commissioned Cranwell officers, undertaking to subscribe to the Fund under the half-a-day's-pay-a-year voluntary subscriptions

Marshal of the Royal Air Force Lord Trenchard's statue, appropriately situated in Whitehall Gardens between the Ministry of Defence and the RAF Memorial on the Embankment, is another venue of commemoration, as when Lord Catto, Chairman of the Council, laid a pilot's brevet wreath there in the Fund's Diamond Jubilee year.

scheme, will find interest in one of Trenchard's favourite observations when Chief of the Air Staff. 'This Air Force', he said, 'will never be complete until a Cranwell cadet sits in my chair.' That wish was fulfilled in the year of Trenchard's death when Air Chief Marshal Sir Dermot

An annual memorial service for Marshal of the Royal Air Force The Viscount Trenchard is held in the RAF Chapel at Westminster Abbey. In February 1989, the occasion also marked the dedication of the memorial to six wartime leaders of the RAF. The Queen Mother attended and kept a short silence after she had placed a wreath on the tablet marking the tomb of the Founder of the Royal Air Force Benevolent Fund.

Boyle became Chief of the Air Staff. The Marshal of the Royal Air Force is a Vice-President and former Deputy Chairman of the Council of the Fund.

There was also much news from the Fund to cheer Lord Trenchard in his last years, and notably the news of Vanbrugh Castle. There, in 1955, Mr John Corner from King's School, Canterbury, had succeeded Mr Webb-Jones, upon the latter's appointment as headmaster of Wells Cathedral Junior School. Suitable boys were now being coached for entry to the Royal Air Force as cadets as well as apprentices, and Trenchard could, allowably, visualise a former Vanbrugh boy sitting in the Chief of Air Staff's chair.

Two years after Lord Trenchard died the Nation raised his statue in Whitehall Gardens, immediately below the windows of the present Ministry of Defence and in sight of the Royal Air Force Memorial. It is not here, however, that the Fund pays its annual respects to the memory of the founder. Each year he is remembered in the Royal Air Force Chapel at Westminster Abbey. The chapel provides a symbolic setting for this simple act of remembrance and respect, which is held on or around the anniversary of Trenchard's death. Above the company the famous Battle of Britain window incorporates the memorial badges of the sixty-three fighter squadrons which fought and the flags of the nations to which the pilots and aircrew belonged. The stained and painted window by Hugh Easton is dedicated to the memory of 1495 pilots and aircrew who gave their lives during the summer and autumn weeks of 1940, when the Battle of Britain decided the future of the world. The new window has replaced stained glass shattered by the bomb which destroyed the House of Commons, but a hole made by a bomb just beneath the window in the north corner of the chapel has been allowed to remain, filled by a few square inches of plain glass.

Below the window the Dean of Westminster takes the service in the presence of members of the Trenchard family, the Chief of the Air Staff, Air Force Board and Royal Air Force Benevolent Fund representatives and a thinning company of elderly men who knew and worked with the founder of the Fund. Mr Sidney G. Kemp, General Trenchard's driver in the First World War, and for many years Sir John Cordingley's chauffeur at 67 Portland Place, was a regular attender.

Before the service ends, a Marshal of the Royal Air Force who has been Chief of the Air Staff, the rank and final appointment of Lord Trenchard, places a wreath of Haig poppies in the shape of Royal Air Force pilot's wings on Trenchard's memorial tablet. The company stands in respectful silence and those who know remember that the entire chapel and the great window dominating the scene were made possible by a joint appeal from Trenchard, 'Father of the Royal Air Force', and Dowding, 'Leader of the Few'. Hugely oversubscribed, the appeal produced a surplus £50,000, which Trenchard and Dowding and their Committee presented to the Royal Air Force Benevolent Fund.

Lord Trenchard's death was followed by that of Lord Riverdale, who died in July 1957, at the age of eight-four – Riverdale, who, succeeding the Duke of Kent as Chairman in 1942, had confidently declared: 'I intend to go on until the financial position of the Fund has been so strengthened as to be able to meet every likely contingency in the future.'

During the first ten years of Riverdale's chairmanship from 1942 to 1952, the Fund had increased its assets from £680,000 to more than £5 million, notwithstanding an expenditure of £4,869,000 on all forms of relief.

The success of the Riverdale-Rumble money-finding partnership of the past and of Riverdale's guidance of the Fund's investment policy have been noted. His death left a serious void. Thus, shortly afterwards, the Controller negotiated a new arrangement to safeguard and, as it transpired, to strengthen further the financial position in which Riverdale, carrying out his promise, had placed the Fund. He persuaded Sir George Erskine, a partner at Morgan Grenfell, the city bankers, to join the Fund's Finance and General Purposes Committee and, subsequently, Sir George obtained the services of Morgan Grenfell as financial consultants – services which were remunerated nominally as the volume of work increased.

The Fund's portfolio of investments is constantly under review by the Finance and General Purposes Committee and the Controller and Director Finance. In the notoriously difficult investment year of 1966, the Royal Air Force Benevolent Fund, advised by Morgan Grenfell, managed to obtain a stock market yield of 5.7 per cent. With the inclusion of property investments the overall yield reached 6.9 per cent, thanks to the advice which the Fund has received from Mr K. Martyn Sanders of Debenham, Tewson and Chinnocks since the death of Mr Wallace Withers in 1958. Sanders also joined the Grants Committee and served until his retirement in 1989.

When Sir George Erskine retired as Honorary Investment Consultant in 1968, the Fund continued to benefit from his interest as a member of the Council. Meanwhile, the close working relationship with Morgan Grenfell continued through its chairman, Lord Catto, a Mosquito photographic reconnaissance pilot in the Royal Air Force from 1943 to 1947. After the death of Sir Harald Peake in May 1978, Lord Catto accepted the Council's invitation to succeed Sir Harald.

Of all the outside and linked organisations, and all the many thousands of individuals with good cause to be thankful for the financial wisdom and expertise which inspire the Fund's investment decisions, perhaps none holds the Royal Air Force Benevolent Fund in greater veneration than the Guinea Pig Club.

To the end of 1967 the Fund had disbursed more than £70,000 for the resettlement and relief of 367 individual members of this wartime association of badly burned aircrew. Further assistance in the past thirty years underlines that although the Fund does not and cannot have favourites, the Guinea Pigs, after the children of men killed in the service, are in the front line of welfare.

The Guinea Pig Club was founded over a bottle of sherry in 1941 by a small group of badly burned pilots in Ward III, a wooden hut at the rear of East Grinstead's Queen Victoria Cottage Hospital. Thereafter the Club was fostered by Sir Archibald McIndoe who, as consultant in plastic surgery to the Royal Air Force, had hundreds of wartime Guinea Pigs in his care.

With peace, McIndoe, 'the Maestro', as his Pigs called him, was nagged by the question, 'When their bodies are whole again can we also rebuild something from their shattered lives?' In Battle of Britain week, 1958, McIndoe broadcast the BBC's Week's Good Cause and answered that question. He said:

> We could and we did. But we did it only with the help of what I firmly believe to be Britain's most wonderful remedy in time of trouble; the Royal Air Force Benevolent Fund. You know, Sir Winston Churchill called it part of the conscience of the British Nation.
>
> One of my Guinea Pigs was Flight Lieutenant Richard Hillary, who flew again after we had healed his terrible wounds. Later he was to meet his last enemy, death, but before he died he wrote these words, 'I looked down at my hands, and not seeing them, I realised that I had gone blind. So I was going to die. It came to me like that – I was going to die and I was not afraid.'
>
> What is there to say about courage like that? There are no words noble enough to honour such heroism, not enough tears to shed for such a loss.
>
> That gallantry was typical of the young aircrew who gained air supremacy in many theatres of war for six years, and they are still doing it. Some are flying tonight, watching over the western world's uneasy peace.
>
> How can we right the balance of payment? We can't do it personally – the job is too big. But the Royal Air Force Benevolent Fund will do it for us, if you will help.

More than £5000 was received.

In 1947 the close liaison which had been long kept between the 'Ben Fund', as the Guinea Pigs affectionately call their 'bank', and the Guinea Pig Club was further improved by a co-ordinating committee to keep all burns cases under review. The Controller takes the chair and the Committee has included Sir Archibald McIndoe, until his death in 1962; the Chief Guinea Pig, Group Captain T. P. Gleave; the 'Maestro's' widow, Lady McIndoe, who was also on the Grants Committee; 'Blackie', Mr J. E. Blacksell, the Guinea Pig Club's Welfare Officer until his death in 1988; and Dr Russell M. Davies.

The courage displayed by young aircrew, which was so greatly admired by Sir Archibald McIndoe, is exemplified in the following letter published in *The Times* on 18 June 1940 and a copy of which was framed and hangs in the Royal Air Force Club.

April 1940

An Airman's Letter to His Mother

Dear Mother,

Though I feel no premonition at all, events are moving rapidly, and I have instructed that this letter be forwarded to you should I fail to return from one of the raids which we shall shortly be called upon to undertake. You must hope on for a month, but at the end of that time you must accept the fact that I have handed my task over to the extremely capable hands of my comrades of the Royal Air Force, as so many splendid fellows have already done.

First, it will comfort you to know that my role in this war has been of the greatest importance. Our patrols far out over the North Sea have helped to keep the trade routes clear for our convoys and supply ships and on one occasion our information was instrumental in saving the lives of the men in a crippled lighthouse relief ship. Though it will be difficult for you, you will disappoint me if you do not at least try to accept the facts dispassionately, for I shall have done my duty to the utmost of my ability. No man can do more, and no one calling himself a man could do less.

I have always admired your amazing courage in the face of continual setbacks in the way you have given me as good an education and background as anyone in the country; and always kept up appearances without ever losing faith in the future. My death would not mean that your struggle has been in vain, far from it; it means that your sacrifice is as great as mine. Those who serve England must expect nothing from her, we debase ourselves if we regard our country as merely a place in which to eat and sleep.

History resounds with illustrious names who have given all, yet their sacrifice has resulted in the British Empire, where there is a measure of peace, justice and freedom for all and where a higher standard of civilisation has evolved, and is still evolving, than anywhere else. But this is not only concerning our own land. Today we are faced with the greatest organised challenge to Christianity and civilisation that the world has ever seen, and I count myself lucky and honoured to be the right age and fully trained to throw my full weight into the scale. For this I have to thank you, yet there is more work for you to do, the Home Front will still have to stand united for years after the war is won. For all that can be said against it, I still maintain that this war is a good thing; every individual is having the chance to give and dare all for his principle like the martyrs of old. However long time may be, one thing can never be altered. I shall have lived and died an Englishman, nothing else matters one jot, nor can anything ever change it.

You must not grieve for me, for if you really believe in Religion and all that it entails, that would be hypocrisy. I have no fear of death, only a queer elation. I would have it no other way. The Universe is so vast and so ageless that the life of one man can only be justified by the measure of his sacrifice. We are sent to this world to acquire a personality and a character to take with us that can never be taken from us, those who just eat and sleep, prosper and procreate are no better than animals if all their lives they are at peace.

I firmly and absolutely believe that evil things are sent into the world to try us; they are sent deliberately by our Creator to test our mettle, because He knows what is good for us; the Bible is full of cases where the easy way out has been discarded for moral principles.

I count myself fortunate in that I have seen the whole country and known men of every calling. But with the final test of war I consider my character fully developed. Thus at my early age, my earthly mission is already fulfilled and I am prepared to die with just one regret and one only – that I could not devote myself to making your declining years more happy by being with you; but you will live in peace and freedom and I shall have directly contributed to that so here again my life will not have been in vain.

Your ever loving son.

Sir John Cordingley was aged seventy-one when he retired at the end of May 1962. It is no disrespect to the President, the Chairman, members of the Council and Committees or to the staff at Portland Place to write that not only had Sir John served the Fund for fifteen years as Controller after eleven years' membership of Committees and the Council, but that to many people within and without the Fund he was the 'Father of the Royal Air Force Benevolent Fund' and was so described by his successor at the Council meeting in 1968.

He drove, cajoled and charmed the Royal Air Force Benevolent Fund into becoming the universally respected institution that it is, and although he affected a gruff disciplinary manner he drove himself so hard that he received the ungrudging support of those he kept under pressure. Cordingley's car driver, Sidney Kemp, who knew as much about the Controller's working hours as any man, reflected in a British Broadcasting Corporation overseas broadcast:

The work that man used to do was amazing. I used to take him a bag home every evening. At about 6.30 p.m. to 7.00 p.m. he left the office. He'd go home, have his dinner and then he'd work till 10.00 or 11.00 at night; and then on the weekend or Friday evenings, he used to take about three despatch cases and he'd sit all day Saturday and Sunday working and then I'd bring them back on Monday morning. That man used to do some wonderful work for the Royal Air Force Benevolent Fund. It was simply amazing.

Kemp's humble opinion was held in higher quarters. When Sir John retired for the second time the Queen appointed him a Knight Commander of the Victorian Order. It was exceptional for an officer, knighted in his service career, to have his retirement crowned with a KCVO.

At the last Council attended by Sir John as Controller on 22 May 1962, Princess Marina devoted the greater part of her address to expressing her own thanks – and those of the Council – to him in the following words:

> There is not one of us sitting round this table who is not aware of his immense services to the Fund ever since he became Controller in 1947. Throughout all these years he has been largely responsible for the magnificent reputation that the Fund undoubtedly has throughout this country, and not only in this country but in the Commonwealth and in many foreign countries as well. It has been due to his wisdom and skilful administration that the Fund has been in a position, during the period of his office, to expend nearly £9 million in relieving distress and suffering. We are going to miss him, and his great wealth of experience, very much; but perhaps I may say that we are going to miss him even more in the capacity of a friend.

At the same meeting the Controller paid the following tribute to the staff:

> The volume of thanks which could be offered by me on an occasion such as this is tremendous, but time restricts, and I therefore would seek your indulgence to emphasise my thanks and appreciation to all members of the staff. I have had the most loyal support from all members of the staff; a keen, loyal, hard-working and, I do not think it is an exaggeration to say, a team dedicated to their work. The Fund receives thanks and praise for its efficiency, and for the good it does, and this is so very often almost solely due to the magnificent manner in which the staff perform their duties. I cannot take leave of you without emphasising as strongly as possible how much of our success is due to the manner in which the staff carries out your policy.

After retiring Cordingley resumed membership of the Council and was elected a vice-president in 1975. He died on 5 January 1977 at the age of eighty-six. A crowded Memorial Service, at which Air Marshal Sir William Coles gave the address, was held in St Clement Danes Church on 22 February 1977.

Air Marshal Sir John Whitley succeeded Cordingley on 1 June 1962. It was no easy matter to follow a Controller who had so wholly and personally identified himself with the office and with the Fund. Where lesser men might have been tempted to put the helm hard over and set a new course, Whitley deliberately kept her steady as she went and sailed the Fund sedately towards its fiftieth birthday.

Air Marshal Sir John Whitley, Controller 1962–68.

Inheritor of proven organisation and having many years of personal contact with the service, Whitley set out to – and was more free to – renew the knowledge of the Fund throughout the service, a task for which he was ideally suited as the recently retired Inspector General of the Royal Air Force and having been Air Member for Personnel on the Air Council. Moreover, something of Whitley's flying career was known in the service. It brought comfort and confidence that the new feet under the Controller's table in the Council Room at Portland Place had climbed into operational bomber aircraft, had dangled over enemy-occupied France, their owner suspended dangerously by only half a parachute harness.

Early in the war, Whitley, who flew habitually with a civilian suit under his uniform and carrying a self-assembled escape outfit, had evaded capture and returned to Britain in a story-book manner, which is part of the escape lore of the service. Speaking from this background, it went home when Whitley told his Royal Air Force audiences: 'I think you can look on me as someone who has spent a great deal of his life in the service, who has gone into the Benevolent Fund, had a good old nosey around, and can report to the service on what he has found.'

He spoke simply, compellingly, telling officers and airmen wherever he went just how the Fund works. So effective was Whitley's approach that, within the very small margin left to him by his predecessor, he further improved the voluntary subscriptions coverage from eighty-four

per cent of service people to ninety-two per cent. By the time of his retire- 92%
ment in the summer of 1968, Sir John Whitley jokingly claimed that he   RAF
had also reduced the number of 'howlers' in officers' promotion examination papers – such answers to the question 'What does the Fund do?'
as 'Builds swimming pools', 'Helps dependants of RAF wives, who die
fighting', 'Provides widows for RAF personnel.'

This is how Sir John Whitley told the story about the Fund:

> The staff who deal with the applications for help are almost entirely people
> who have served in the Royal Air Force. They have to prepare their cases
> and put them before a Grants Committee for a decision. The members of
> the Grants Committees are mostly people who have been connected with
> the Royal Air Force. The Committees sit once a week and have the cases
> presented to them by the relief secretaries and they judge the cases purely
> on their merits.
>
> If the staff want further information about a case, well, if it's a serving
> case they go back to the Station Commander or his representative. But, the
> majority of cases, I find, apply to people who have retired and to widows
> and dependants of those who have died. Then they get in touch with one
> of the various organisations up and down the country, like the Royal Air
> Forces Association, the Soldiers', Sailors' and Airmen's Families
> Association, the Officers' Association, Red Cross, Royal British Legion,
> Forces Help Society, and so on.
>
> We have not got our own investigatory service and we avoided setting
> one up deliberately, because if we did, it would involve us in more admin-
> istrative overheads. These organisations already have their welfare officers
> and, after all, they collect money on behalf of the three services. We look
> upon investigations by these organisations as their contribution to the
> Royal Air Force. We don't pay them for their services. Of course, a further
> advantage of doing it this way is that it gives us tremendous coverage
> throughout the country. For instance, the Soldiers', Sailors' and Airmen's
> Families Association has something like 12,000 welfare officers, almost one
> for every village, so if they hear of someone who served in the Royal Air
> Force who is in distress, they let us know, because in the main, they do not
> disburse money themselves. If financial help is required, they come to the
> Benevolent Fund, to 67 Portland Place.

Air Marshal Sir John Whitley retired on 19 August 1968. During his
six years as Controller, the Fund made over 73,000 awards and the
amount spent on the relief of distress totalled nearly £4.5 million – a
record expenditure for any six years since the Fund's inception. Income
(including legacies) during the same period totalled £5,663,954, which
was almost £600,000 greater than total expenditure, including administration expenses. An excellent addition to capital in these difficult days.
During Sir John's Controllership the Insurance Advisory Service had
been most successfully developed, and the Royal Air Force Dependants

Fund inaugurated in 1967, in co-operation with the Air Force Board, and accommodated at 67 Portland Place.

No mention of the Fund's work in this period would be complete without a tribute to the devoted services of Squadron Leader Jock Beaton, Personal Assistant to Air Vice-Marshal Sir John Cordingley and to Air Marshal Sir John Whitley during their Controllerships. Squadron Leader Beaton, who had worked with Sir John Cordingley at the Royal Air Force Record Office in pre-war days, put in over twenty years' magnificent work at Portland Place, preceded by twenty-five years in the Royal Air Force and about nine years in the Army. He acquired a positively encyclopaedic knowledge of the Fund's history and activities, which he freely dispensed to younger colleagues. To the entire staff, as well as to his chiefs, he was a guide and philosopher but, above all, friend. When he retired in 1968 he was seventy-two.

CHAPTER 11

HEAD OFFICE

*'There are no words to thank you for so much. Perhaps the best way I can
put it is that although my husband is dead, I cannot regret that he chose to
fly with the Royal Air Force.'*

An aircrew NCO's widow, 1965

F
ew service or ex-service people, or their dependants, visit
67 Portland Place, but the front door is always open during business
hours by appointment, and any eligible person will receive sympathetic attention. Until Mr Walter J. Chandler retired in January 1977, he
had been the Interviewing Secretary for many years and an assistant
secretary in the Welfare Branch. He was Personal Assistant to the first
Controller and during his thirty-two years with the Fund he served under
all five Controllers. He is a member of the Goldfish Club, having been
shot down over the North Sea during the Second World War. The Head
Office staff do a certain amount of personal investigation themselves of
nearby cases. Written and telephoned inquiries which are subsequently
investigated are more frequent. But, while the cheques are written at
Portland Place, investigation and the relief of distress in the field have
been carried out locally through such organisations as the Royal Air
Forces Association, the Soldiers', Sailors' and Airmen's Families
Association, the Officers' Association, the British Red Cross Society, the
Department of Social Security, the Fund's own Branches, County
Representatives, Helpers and Education Advisers, to all of whom the
Fund is indebted.

A modest and separate benevolent fund belonging to the Royal
Observer Corps is also administered here. The object of the Royal Observer Corps Benevolent Fund is to provide relief to members and
ex-members of the Royal Observer Corps and their dependants in neces-
sitous cases arising after the end of the war. Many 'Observers' have not
served in the Royal Air Force and thus are ineligible for help from the
Royal Air Force Benevolent Fund.

Primarily, Portland Place provides a meeting place for Council and
committees and is the workshop where cases are prepared for submission
to the Grants Committees.

An impression should not be gained, however, that where acute distress exists an applicant must await the decision of a weekly committee. The welfare secretaries, now assistant directors, are authorised to make immediate grants within a limited amount and can seek the Controller's authority to grant or to loan more substantial sums at any time. The splitting of relief cases under three separate headings – main, including house purchase; education and dependants; serving and ex-Royal Air Force – provides the benefits of specialisation and also helps to hasten their arrival in committee. During the peak period after the Second World War seven Welfare sections evolved: Main, Education, Dependants, Disablement, Serving, Ex-Royal Air Force and House Purchase.

Generally, unless further investigation is required, the relief staff expect to submit an application to a Grants Committee within a week of receiving it.

The other departments at Portland Place in this period were similarly organised with directors for Administration, Finance and Appeals, and a senior executive responsible for the Insurance Advisory Service. The 'admin secretary' at the time of the fiftieth and sixtieth anniversaries was Mr Paul Cutting (Administration), a wartime Squadron Leader who flew with Bomber Command and joined the Fund on release leave in January 1946. He had been Secretary to the Council and to the Finance and General Purposes Committee for many years and took on the task of editing this book. Both he and his assistant, Squadron Leader F. Hawley spent several years on relief work, as did Flight Lieutenant J. A. B. Cairns (Finance), responsible in war for No. 54 Group postings. Cairns came to the Fund on 1 January 1946, the very day of his release from the Royal Air Force, and he was assisted by Mr E. G. Abbott, who had been responsible for keeping the accounts since joining the Fund at Hove in 1945. Group Captain T. J. Arbuthnot (Appeals) joined the staff in 1963, following Group Captains S. J. Bailey and G. P. Woodhouse. Group Captain S. L. Swain (Insurance) succeeded Air Commodore C. V. Mears.

The executive staff is headed by the Controller, who by custom and design, since Air Vice-Marshal Sir Hazelton Nicholl's appointment in 1944, is a retired senior officer. So the desks at Portland Place were customarily 'driven' by experienced aircrew.

Although realistic salaries and wages are paid and there is a staff pension scheme, general administrative costs are pared at Portland Place, where the emphasis is always on economy. Although the council room which for many years doubled as the Controller's office was appropriately furnished at an exceedingly low price, the remaining offices were furnished with second-hand items purchased after the war. The anecdote about the air commodore who, arriving on his first day, was handed a hammer and a bag of nails to repair a dilapidated desk makes a cheerful canteen topic to impress visitors!

But when Fund money is spent on furniture, it is in the Grants Committee that such expenditure takes place, substantial assistance being not infrequent in the furnishing of new homes for young widows and disabled applicants with young children.

Apart from the Main Grants Committee and the Education Committee, to which cases requiring substantial financial assistance are referred, the committees are specialists, considering serving, ex-serving (including disabled), and dependants cases. When a committee sits, the secretary, who is generally a retired Royal Air Force officer, submits the week's list of applications. The cases are presented with a guide to eligibility, detailing the family and dependants involved; the financial position; and, finally, details of the request for assistance together with the remarks and recommendations of the commanding officer or the local representative. Facts for and against an application are given so that the committee can reach a decision within the Council's policy.

The Fund, being a Service fund, must take into account not only the human side but also the service given. Consistent with this policy, it was decided that national servicemen who entered the Royal Air Force under the peacetime acts between 1 January 1949 and 18 November 1960 were eligible to be considered for assistance from the Fund during their actual period of National Service and for an equivalent period thereafter. Exceptions to this rule were made in cases of death and disability or sickness attributable to or arising from actual service in the Royal Air Force. There were no restrictions on the period of eligibility for National Service officers and airmen who ultimately undertook regular service. Had the Fund accepted liability for all Royal Air Force national servicemen it would have faced a potential demand from a further 500,000 men and their families. All requests from national servicemen were considered by the Main Grants Committee. Policy was eventually changed, as will be related, in the 1990s to give National Service people full eligibility.

Over the years committees become familiar with some cases which cover long periods, some originating in the First World War, as in the following examples from the 1960s.

A Royal Flying Corps observer was shot down during the First World War and was taken prisoner. After the war, when flying with his brother, they crashed and he was very badly injured trying to rescue his brother, who was burned to death. He spent eighteen months in hospital before he resumed flying, and he was so grateful to the woman who nursed him through his convalescence that he expended practically all his resources in purchasing a home for her. On another occasion he was being driven in a car over a level crossing when a train hit the car. In 1938 he was again badly injured in another aircraft crash whilst serving abroad and was subsequently invalided with a 100 per cent disability pension. Later on the Fund heard of his difficulties and the Committee approved assistance with house purchase at a time when his wife was suffering from bad health. Two years later the officer had a stroke which rendered him paralysed, blind and speechless. The Fund assisted with maintenance and the cost of nursing attendance until he could be admitted to a home, where he remained until he died. His widow occupied the house purchased with the help of the Fund.

Following a long illness, a Royal Flying Corps air mechanic of two years' service had insufficient money to clothe himself for the winter, so the Committee assisted. He wrote, 'I am going to buy an overcoat and winter boots and socks. A nice thought that this winter I shall be warm and have dry feet.'

An ex-warrant officer, aged seventy-three, who served in two wars, was ashamed to go out of doors. His clothes were too shabby. He had not had a holiday for many years and his clothes were too bad for him to be accepted by a home. He was too proud to ask for help but his case had been reported to the Fund. His income was £4 a week. He received an immediate grant for clothing.

A former Royal Flying Corps pilot, decorated for gallantry and aged seventy-two, was as badly off as the warrant officer, although his wardrobe was respectable. Until recently, post-war 'deals' had prospered but now he was down on his luck. He had a large bank overdraft secured by his house. He had local debts. Unable to draw from the bank, he and his wife had a total income quite inadequate for their basic needs. The Committee granted immediate assistance and accepted that 'he would probably be with them until he died'.

CHAPTER 12

GRANTS PROCEDURE

'It is really a tremendous inspiration . . . the way the Fund comes to the
rescue of the men, particularly amongst the aircrew who marry very young
and have no resources and sometimes leave a widow and young children
suddenly faced with a new life.'

Air Chief Marshal Sir Harry Broadhurst, 1955

A major disaster such as that of the Hastings aircraft crash in 1965, when thirty Royal Air Force servicemen died, will make the headlines and the Royal Air Force Benevolent Fund does not need to await official confirmation before it acts.

It is, however, routine for the Fund to learn officially of every Royal Air Force officer, airman and airwoman who is killed or missing or who dies while serving; and of the deaths of retired officers and airmen pensioners. Such is the Fund's liaison with the Air Force Department of the Ministry of Defence that within twenty-four hours of notification Welfare dispatches a letter to the next of kin, expressing the sympathy of the Fund and asking whether the Fund can help.

From experience, though, the Fund knows that even today some widows and dependants are reluctant to come forward or lack knowledge of how the Fund can help them. There is also the possibility that the Fund's readiness to help will not necessarily register with a bereaved person who is suffering from shock. Whenever practicable, therefore, the next of kin is visited by the station commander or his representative where the next of kin is living in married quarters or locally, or by one of the Fund's Honorary County Representatives or Helpers where the bereaved is living far away.

The Helper sends in a general report about the situation and the Fund can then decide what is the next step to take. If, after some six months, the next of kin has not applied for any help the Fund sends another letter saying, virtually, look, are you still all right? Do remember that if you want help now or in the future the Fund is here to help you.

Fortunately, peacetime disasters on the scale of the Hastings accident are rare but the call this single accident made upon the Fund's resources provides an example of the enormous liability that is never far from the Fund's front door.

When the Hastings crashed on 6 July 1965, forty-one servicemen were killed, of whom thirty were members of the Royal Air Force. There were no survivors. The object of the fifteen-mile flight from Abingdon to Benson in Oxfordshire had been to drop parachutists over an exercise area. Shortly after take-off the pilot reported that there were difficulties and he was returning to Abingdon. Within seconds of that message the aircraft crashed into a field of ripe barley near the village of Dorchester. The thirty Royal Air Force dead comprised six members of the crew, eight instructors, three air quartermasters and thirteen volunteers learning to jump. There were five single and five married officers and five single and fifteen married airmen. In less than a year assistance in twenty-two cases arising from this disaster had cost the Fund more than £40,000. In 1969 it had reached £60,000.

The commitment did not end there. In some cases education was a recurring expense for many years. Since the introduction of education allowances for the services, the practice of educating children at boarding schools has extended greatly, but if a father dies the allowances cease and the Fund, subject to satisfactory investigations, steps in to complete the children's education.

During the decade 1952–61, when the bulk of the children whose Royal Air Force fathers had been killed or disabled in the Second World War reached school age, the Fund made over 20,000 educational awards and spent on this largest item during that period almost £2 million. These figures underline the great and unique achievement of the Fund in the field of education. In 1962 assistance relating to house purchase drew level and from 1963 onwards edged ahead as the most expensive single item in the Fund's budget on relief of distress.

House purchase assistance usually takes the form of a mortgage loan but it is exceedingly long-term because no loan repayment or house surrender is likely in such cases unless a widow's circumstances alter materially, or she dies. Even then the accommodation may have to remain available for any young children who survive her, provided they can be cared for, say, by a relation.

Indefinite 100 per cent house purchase loans in the 1960s were not made indiscriminately. They were normally available only to widows and those seriously disabled, with young children, where death or disability was attributable to service and where rented accommodation proved to be impossible to obtain or beyond the applicant's means. For many years such cases were presented to the Grants Committee by Mrs Ethel Page and later by Mrs Hazel Chapman.

Naturally, numerous considerations qualify the Grants Committee's awards throughout the range of relief and some of these are well demonstrated among the following examples arising out of the Hastings disaster.

Mrs A was living in married quarters when she was widowed and her eight-year-old son was attending a local school. As very often occurs, an officer with whom her husband, Corporal A, had served, offered to assist

Mrs A with formalities – assistance which Mrs A gladly accepted because she was a German national by birth with insufficient English. The officer, a flight lieutenant, and the husband had served together in the Jungle Rescue Team of the Far East Air Force and he set out to obtain every possible form of relief for the widow. Thus, when Mrs A received the Fund's routine letter of condolence the flight lieutenant approached the Fund on Mrs A's behalf. He explained that the four worries on Mrs A's mind were a bank overdraft which would swallow up most of her husband's life policy, the future education of her eight-year-old son, house purchase, and a job.

He knew of the existence of Vanbrugh Castle School and it seemed to him the ideal school for her son. Mrs A was not at first persuaded about Vanbrugh, although the headmaster, after interviewing mother and child, noted 'the boy is above average and acceptable. Excellent for him to come. But mother very weepy and reluctant to part with only child.' However, John Corner had a well-tried remedy for weepy mothers and he applied it to Mrs A, putting her in touch with a previously weepy and by this time appreciative mother who had experienced similar misgivings before allowing her son to board at Vanbrugh.

There can be no more suitable person to speak or write for the virtues of this school than a mother who has been bombarded with Vanbrugh anecdotes in the school holidays . . . 'there's rock-climbing . . . you ought to hear the school band and hear Paddy Purcell in action. He's director of the London Military Band too.' Mr Purcell retired from Vanbrugh Castle in 1968 and died a few years later.

Then there were the visits to Royal Air Force stations at home and abroad, the Christmas party with individual presents, a tradition started in 1948 by Mrs Ackerman, wife of Brigadier-General John B. Ackerman, the then Air Attaché at the United States Embassy, and for many years a much-appreciated annual event. Cricket, football, athletics, swimming, the choir at the Royal Naval College, Greenwich . . .

To all of which, and more besides, John Corner, then headmaster, would not be human if he had not added with justifiable pride, in the brochure giving facets of life at the Royal Air Force Benevolent Fund's boarding school:

> The boys are taught in small classes and take the Common Entrance Examination at the age of thirteen when they usually transfer under the guidance of the Fund to other boarding schools. Experience has shown that these boys are well up to the standards demanded by other boarding schools, both as regards their scholarship and their general attitude and character.

But it is the appreciative mother who perhaps finally convinces a new and undecided widow, writing:

I know as the time approaches for my son to leave Vanbrugh he will have
a heavy heart. I feel sadness that school years could pass so quickly. I see
him so clearly on his first visit to the school wondering what was in store
for him, his first holiday at home, and his eagerness to return to Vanbrugh;
the time the headmaster assured me that he would enjoy rock-climbing,
how right he was. Above all, he has learnt respect, loyalty and to share the
joys and disappointments that a boarding school holds. How lucky to reap
a harvest from a very deep sadness. My children have much to be thankful
for, and so have I.

Perhaps it is needless to add that Mrs A's son was educated at Vanbrugh!

But to return to Mrs A's story. After her husband's affairs had been
settled she possessed only a small sum, comprising her husband's
gratuity, a gift from a local disaster fund and what was left of her
husband's insurance policy after repayment of the bank overdraft. She
was receiving a war widow's pension and was still living in married
quarters at the dispensation of the station commander, who had also
engaged her as a temporary part-time batwoman, raising her income to
a moderate figure. Obviously, neither Mrs A nor any Vanbrugh mother
was in a position to pay full Vanbrugh fees at the time of £441 a year
(£207 tuition plus £234 boarding), but no boy accepted for Vanbrugh
was prevented from attending because his mother could not afford the
fees.

In Mrs A's case the Ministry rejected the application but her Local
Education Authority agreed to contribute almost all of the fees, leaving
the widow to find a small amount annually, either from her own resources
or from the Fund. In this case, Mrs A paid her share of the fees.

With the boy's education arranged, the flight lieutenant turned his
attention towards Mrs A's accommodation problem, because she could
not remain indefinitely in service quarters. The Fund advised the widow
to seek a flatlet in the London area through the Douglas Haig Memorial
Homes, but Mrs A had set her heart on a 'front door of her own'. Initially
the Fund attempted to deflect her from this dream, suggesting that it
might be unwise of Mrs A to take on the expense of her own house when,
apart from the school holidays, she would be living alone. Nevertheless,
the Grants Committee later consented to consider an application for a
house purchase loan sympathetically if Mrs A was prepared to live in
a small and modestly priced property.

The Fund wrote:

In view of the limited capital resources the assistance would take the form
of an interest-free loan to cover the full purchase price of the property,
subject to survey and valuation, and the survey fee and all legal charges
incurred would be added to the loan, which would have to be secured by
a first mortgage on the property.

Any assistance sanctioned for furniture would be an extension of this loan and Mrs A would not be required to make any repayments to the Fund while she occupied the property herself and there is no material change in her circumstances, and she does not remarry.

Armed with this splendid news, Mrs A went house-hunting. She was offered a semi-detached by her local council, but preferred a private property at about the same price with a more pleasant outlook. The Fund loaned the money to buy it, adding assistance for furniture.

'This news', the flight lieutenant informed the Fund, 'has been a terrific fillip to her morale and she is a different person.'

Finally, the Fund assisted Mrs A to improve her English sufficiently to obtain work. Her son? 'Good in every way,' reported his headmaster. 'He is successful, well liked and loyal and can hardly fail to do well.'

Sergeant B who died alongside Corporal A in the accident was an air signaller with nine years' service. He left a widow, two sons aged eleven and four and two daughters aged eight and five.

Mrs B's first visitor was her husband's flight commander and he wrote to the Fund on the widow's behalf. He said Mrs B had met her husband when they attended school together. She had been a very service-minded wife and held no bitterness towards the service at the loss of her husband. She held a small insurance policy on her husband's life but this sum would not be released for some while because of inquest formalities. Apart from this money, Mrs B would only have her pension to support herself and her four children. 'Her most immediate concern,' the flight commander wrote, 'is that of housing her family when the time comes to vacate married quarters. She is most concerned that when she has to move from married quarters she is able to settle in one place permanently and will not be involved in a series of temporary moves.'

The flight commander's visit was followed up by the Fund's nearest Helper, who explained to Mrs B how the Fund could assist and in particular that the two boys were eligible for Vanbrugh. The elder boy entered Vanbrugh a few weeks after his father's death. In Mrs B's case a yearly grant of his fees was contributed by the Ministry of Social Security. But, unlike Mrs A, she did not fare so well with the Local Education Authority, where her application for assistance was refused.

As with Mrs A, Mrs B was asked by the Fund to approach her Local Education Authority Committee and the Ministry for assistance with the Vanbrugh fees. At the same time, the Fund assured the widow that, whatever the outcome of her application, her son would be educated at Vanbrugh and that she would only be required to contribute as much as she could reasonably afford. In fact, this generally meant in practice the child's war pension or state pension allowance, though in Mrs B's case the balance of the fees were waived by the Fund as her entire income consisted of a weekly pension.

With her elder son at Vanbrugh and her second son 'down for

Vanbrugh', Mrs B moved into a small house, bought and furnished by the Fund. 'Please note any change of address,' she wrote cheerfully, and continued:

> I would like to try to tell you how grateful I am for all that has been done for us. I could never have given my children such a lovely home without your help. Thank you also for the financial assistance granted to me towards the cost of furniture.
>
> My eldest boy is very happy at Vanbrugh Castle School. He is a strong-willed boy who needs a lot of discipline and I feel that this can only be carried out by a man. My husband and I had always wanted him to attend a boarding school.
>
> I feel that if any other woman in similar circumstances could be re-assured that she would receive real help the way I have, it would save her a lot of distress and worry at a time when she is full of sorrow. I also feel that if the general public knew more about the marvellous help that the Fund has given to so many families, more people would donate more freely to the Fund.

Each widow in these cases, it will have been noted, stood to benefit from small insurance policies on her husband's life. In an increasing number of instances the deceased's life insurance cover is sufficient to complete the purchase of a house. The Fund does not desire to penalise the provident but distress must always be the ruling factor.

There was the case, for instance, of a flight lieutenant who had been buying a house on a mortgage covered by insurance policies. The widow was extremely reluctant to seek help but the Fund discovered that, although she owned the house, it was sparsely furnished. So they assisted with the purchase of essential furniture, the legal expenses in connection with the settlement of her late husband's estate, and the education of her eldest son, whose ambition was to be a pilot.

In another of the Hastings cases, a flight sergeant left a widow with four sons aged fourteen, twelve, nine and eight. In order to settle the family quickly in a home of their own, the Fund loaned money for house purchase, expecting the widow's capital not to exceed a moderate sum. When it was learned later that the flight sergeant had taken out four in-surance policies, the widow promptly agreed to contribute towards the purchase of the house.

Throughout the 1960s there was an increasing interest among all ranks of the Royal Air Force in life assurance. Even so, of the ten officers and twenty airmen who died in the Hastings accident only five officers and fourteen airmen had taken out policies on their lives, thus helping to reduce the burden on the Fund. In the loss of three Shackleton aircraft of Coastal Command in 1967 not one member of the crews of ten men each was insured.

For every serviceman, such as the Hastings flight sergeant with adequate life assurance, there were many other officers and men who were not insured in this respect.

Until the introduction in 1962 of the Fund's Insurance Advisory Service, then under Air Commodore C. V. Mears, knowledge of life insurance within the Royal Air Force, notwithstanding Air Ministry publicity and in certain cases assistance with premiums, was in practice largely confined to talks from itinerant salesmen or the activities of the hut corporal, who happened to be making something on the side as a sub-agent.

The Advisory Service at this time helped service people select the policy best suited to their individual needs. Glad to assist with the taking out of policies, Group Captain S. L. Swain and his successors acted as intermediaries between service people and the insurance market. Every case was examined minutely and expert advice was sought from Lloyds Bank Insurance Services Ltd. When the Fund recommended an insurance policy the decision represented the joint advice of the Fund and the insurance department of the bank concerned.

This service was free of charge and of particular value to those wishing to buy their own home and requiring advice on assurance policies in connection with house purchase. The Fund derived no commission from the business transacted but the bank made an annual donation.

The Insurance Advisory Service did not preclude individuals from making their own arrangements, but it did offer them the opportunity of a very sharp scrutiny of any policies on offer and advice on their suitability or otherwise. Moreover, special arrangements were made with insurance companies to meet particular service needs. In numerous instances the Advisory Service has been able to counter an airfield salesman's contract with considerable improvement.

One of the more frequent calls for the relief of distress is caused by the financial vacuum in which many widows find themselves within hours of the death of their husbands. There is the need for sufficient cash to live on and there are often continuing hire purchase commitments, household expenses and the extra cost of the funeral. There may also be debts which the husband had intended to pay shortly.

Potentially, the widow may possess ample funds to meet all commitments and to leave a fair balance after settlement, but her husband's bank account has been frozen at death and his life policy, if there is one, cannot be realised until the completion of formalities, which may include an inquest.

In 1967 a new and separate organisation, the Royal Air Force Dependants Fund, was established at 67 Portland Place on the recommendation of the Air Force Board to ease this particular burden. The Trustees of the Dependants Fund, in the main, are serving officers with the Air Member for Personnel as President and the Controller of the

Benevolent Fund as Chairman of the Executive Committee. The Secretary, on inception, was Wing Commander Innes Westmacott, another Battle of Britain pilot. Started with a donation of £50,000 from the Royal Air Force Central Fund, the Dependants Fund is self-supporting. At its inception, members of the Royal Air Force and the Princess Mary's Royal Air Force Nursing Service were encouraged to subscribe sixpence a week from their pay at source.

When a subscriber dies the Dependants Fund sends a grant – in the late 1960s it was £500 and by the late eighties had risen to more than £1200 – to the nominated dependant within forty-eight hours of death being reported. Eligibility remains so long as a subscriber remains in the service and maintains the subscription.

The operation of the Dependants Fund in no way affects the normal activities or concern of the Royal Air Force Benevolent Fund, whose prompt help is available both to serving and past members of the Royal Air Force and their families, and can be of a much longer-term and more permanent nature.

CHAPTER 13

THE 1970S

'There is no doubt that so long as the Royal Air Force exists and trains, as well as fights in the air, there will be a need for the Royal Air Force Benevolent Fund, which in memory of those who died or were disabled whilst serving, must not lower its standard of relief to their dependants.'

Air Vice-Marshal Sir John Cordingley, 1962

S adly, the setting of the seal on the establishment and accommodation of the RAF Dependants Fund was one of the last actions of Lord Knollys before his death at the age of seventy-one in 1966. Inheriting the responsibilities of great charitable wealth which had been collected in war by his predecessors, Wakefield and Riverdale, Knollys had dedicated himself to the more difficult task of persuading the public that a Benevolent Fund for the Royal Air Force was every bit as necessary in a long and, it is to be hoped, permanent peace.

Greatly concerned by the mounting expenditure on relief, Lord Knollys had taken a strong interest in the Insurance Advisory Service established in 1962 and the new Royal Air Force Dependants Fund. His enthusiasm for the encouragement of self-help was as evident as the enthusiasm with which he had broadened the Fund's investment portfolio at the outset of office. But, of all Lord Knollys's service to the Royal Air Force Benevolent Fund, perhaps the most important was the sang-froid with which he accepted the Fund's time-honoured principle that over the years capital would be used if income was insufficient to enable the Fund to meet its objects; and this included the traditional but expensive principle of contributing heavily to kindred organisations providing facilities for the benefit of Royal Air Force personnel and their dependants. In his last year, for example, £10,000 was given to the recently opened Royal Air Forces Association Home at Sussexdown to endow one bed in perpetuity for a chronically sick or elderly Royal Air Force patient. As it happened the first beneficiary was an elderly ex-member of the Women's Auxiliary Air Force who, after serving as a corporal cook in the war, had fed the Vanbrugh boys for fifteen years.

That there is no question of budgeting by the Grants Committees, that awards are made in all cases on their merits, that outside organisations continue to be generously supported – this big-hearted, open-handed

approach was Knollys's prime legacy to the Fund. But it is in the hearts of men and not in accountants' ledgers that actions and the names attached to them live on. So long as former Vanbrugh boys make their way in the world and new generations of children attend Duke of Kent School, Lord Knollys's leadership of the Royal Air Force Benevolent Fund will be recalled by those who passed through the Knollys Wing, and especially each year by the six or seven boys who benefit from the Knollys Holiday Fund, created by donations received in his memory.

On 3 May 1967 Mr Harald Peake, Chairman of Lloyds Bank, and a Director of Rolls-Royce among other appointments, was appointed Chairman of the Royal Air Force Benevolent Fund in succession to Lord Knollys.

In accordance with custom, the Fund had turned to the City and to business for a leader. Nevertheless, as with Lord Knollys, Mr Peake had been in the armed forces. In 1918 he served for a year in the Coldstream Guards, at first in the ranks and later as an officer. Three years before the outbreak of the Second World War he raised and commanded No. 609 (West Riding) Squadron of the Royal Auxiliary Air Force.

In November 1938 Mr Peake was appointed Director of the Auxiliary Air Force at the Air Ministry with the rank of Air Commodore. Following the outbreak of war he occupied the posts of Assistant to the Air Member for Personnel, Director of Public Relations, and Director of Air Force Welfare, before being transferred to the Foreign Office for special duties from November 1943 to 1945. He married Air Commodore Dame Felicity Hanbury, a former Director of the Women's Royal Air Force. Altogether a formidable and highly practical background from which to take the chair at 67 Portland Place, and, incidentally, to join Dame Felicity, already a member of the Council since 1956, and now, as her husband arrived, a vice-president and member of the Finance and General Purposes Committee.

To the uninformed, the chairmanship of a service charity twenty-two years after the 1939–45 war might seem a sinecure but Harald Peake's election by the Council coincided with the publication of the 1966 Annual Report, which revealed a record relief expenditure of £890,272 that year.

Throughout the 1960s relief spending rose progressively, climbing from £527,979 in 1960 to £803,885 in 1967 and in 1969, the fiftieth anniversary year, an expenditure of £905,199 for 9552 awards was more than ever before.

Now, why should this be? As the Fund saw in 1969, some of the financial burden might have been lifted as the life insurance advice and the Royal Air Force Dependants Fund gained impetus. But, outside this hope, experience suggested that the Fund could expect little or no lightening of the load.

House purchase loans which then accounted for forty-three per cent of the Fund's annual relief expenditure were, of course, technically recoverable – one day. The value of today's money in 2019 is also uncertain, if comparison between the values of 1919 and, say, 1979 is anything to go by. Much depends on international stability and world peace, a cause in which even a much reduced Royal Air Force is still not without influence.

Meanwhile, it was particularly reassuring that in the 1970s it was necessary to write off or convert to grant less than one per cent of loans sanctioned.

Although each house, for which such substantial purchase loans were made in the 1960s, was put in the widow's name, the Fund took a first mortgage on the house so that if the widow remarries or dies the house cannot be sold without the Fund recovering its money. It was said in criticism of house purchase loans that they were unnecessarily generous and that the Fund ought not to spend so much a year on making them. But the Royal Air Force Benevolent Fund is constituted to relieve distress and if the provision of a home for a widow and her children is necessary to meet this object then a house, and one that is within reason of the widow's choice, will be bought, subject to professional survey. It is the Fund's experience that houses and flats for letting to families with young children at reasonable or even unreasonable rents are almost non-existent.

Looking to the future the Fund correctly anticipated greatly increased demands upon its resources in the 1980s and onwards from aged widows and from officers and airmen whose earning power and whose savings had expired.

Some elderly widows from the First World War must have looked with wonderment at the lot of Royal Air Force widows as they reflected upon the long and hard road they themselves had travelled since 1919.

Indeed, the world had moved on at twice the pace since Princess Marina accepted the Presidency in the moment of her own service widowhood in the Second World War. Sadly, the Princess did not live to lead the commemoration of the fiftieth anniversary. Princess Marina died in August 1968, only sixteen weeks after receiving in Council the congratulations of the Fund on the occasion of the Silver Jubilee of her Presidency. In twenty-five years Princess Marina had not missed a Council meeting. It was an annual duty which the Princess characteristically enriched with her deep and understanding sense of humanity, while at the same time being always ready to relieve a necessarily businesslike occasion with a ready sense of humour, attributes which are clearly reflected among Princess Marina's remarks to the Council in May 1968.

Replying to the Chairman's congratulations on her Silver Jubilee, Princess Marina said:

> You say, Mr Peake, that you can hardly believe I have been President for so many years. Nor can I! I assure you that I too find it very difficult to believe – and that it makes me feel like a sort of Methuselah! All the same I think I must remind you that Lord Portal and Mr de Rougemont, who

both joined the Council immediately after the war, are almost as pre-
historic as I am!

And here I must mention the remarkable good fortune that the Fund has
enjoyed in the wonderfully long and loyal service given to it by successive
Chairmen and Controllers, and members of Council as well. In the whole
of my time here, we have had only three Chairmen: Lord Riverdale, Lord
Knollys, and now Mr Harald Peake; during the same period, there have
been only three Controllers, two of whom are with us today. I am so
pleased to see Sir John Cordingley once again, but it is about Sir John
Whitley that I should now like to say a few words.

Like every member of the Council, I have been extremely sorry to learn
that Sir John will be resigning his appointment which he has held for the
past six years. You have only to look at the details of the Fund's finances
and other developments which are shown in the Report before you, to
appreciate the progress the Fund has made during Sir John's term of office.

His enthusiasm, tact, courtesy and great abilities have been of
outstanding service to the Fund, and on behalf of the entire Council I want
to express our thanks and congratulations to him, and to wish him and
Lady Whitley every happiness in retirement.

I want also to mention the retirement of Sir George Erskine who has
been the Fund's Investment Consultant for the past eleven years. His
immense contributions to the Fund throughout that time are known to all
of you, and I can only say – in thanking him for his great services – how
delighted we are that he, like Sir John Whitley, has agreed to remain a
Member of the Council.

It remains for me to thank you all, once again, for the great kindness –
and honour – that you have done me today and to express my best wishes
to you and to everyone who works for the Fund during the coming year.

To mark the occasion of Princess Marina's silver Jubilee as President
on 11 March 1968, those who had been members of the Council at any
time in the twenty-five years personally subscribed to a gift of garden
furniture chosen by the Princess.

In a letter to the Chairman, Princess Marina expressed her great
pleasure at this gift and suggested that next year's Council Meeting might
take place at her home at Kensington Palace to enable the Council to see
'my lovely present displayed in my garden'. It was not to be.

With the President's death, Mr Harald Peake's first full year in the
chair, Sir John Whitley's decision to follow Sir John Cordingley into
retirement, and Sir George Erskine's retirement as Honorary Investment
Consultant, 1968 was a year of great change among the Royal Air Force
Benevolent Fund's officers.

However, there was no gap in the executive control of the Fund's day-
to-day business. In accordance with long established policy the post of
Controller was offered to a retiring senior Royal Air Force Officer and
Air Marshal Sir John Whitley handed over to Air Marshal Sir William

Coles in August 1968. Sir William Coles, a former Director General of Personal Services, came to the Fund almost directly from his former headquarters as Commander-in-Chief of Royal Air Force Technical Training Command and entered 67 Portland Place with what can be described, perhaps, as a very useful 'entrance fee'. As a result of Sir William's great personal enthusiasm his Command, in his last year of service, raised the record sum of £17,216 for the Fund.

Sir William had not been long in office when, to the Council's delight, The Duke of Kent, whose father had been killed flying on active service in August 1942 while Chairman of the Fund, agreed in the fiftieth anniversary year to accept the Presidency in succession to his mother.

CHAPTER 14

BILL COLES AND
DUKE OF KENT SCHOOL

While Cordingley had been a paragon of all the virtues which had
been required to consolidate the Fund and its organisation after
the Second World War, and Whitley, his successor, had kept it
very much on course, Coles, who now took the controls, was the inno-
vator and opportunist the Fund needed to work with the Chairman and
Council towards the creation of investments and facilities more suitable
to the demands of the 1970s.

Each step in Coles's career had helped to prepare him for his task,
accumulating the mixture of opportunism, dash, social concern, compassion and understanding of human nature which was to stamp itself on
his seven-year tenure as Controller.

At first he was a youthful Metropolitan Policy bobby, who learnt about

Air Marshal Sir William Coles, Controller 1968–75.

life on the beat, and who encountered the Royal Air Force while playing
rugby so impressively for his native Oxfordshire that his opponents,
coveting such a useful player, suggested he ought to apply for a commission as a pilot.

But there was the problem that in 1938, after four years in the police
and at the age of twenty-five, Bill Coles had no exams to his name. He had
failed to qualify for entrance to the Police College which Trenchard
had founded at Hendon and acceptance as an officer in the RAF seemed
an impossible dream.

Fortunately, however, the pilots whom Coles had met on the rugby
field were determined to recruit him for the Service's XV and an enterprising flying officer invited him to the airfield at Hendon for an unofficial
flying aptitude test. After the joy-ride the policeman was declared a
natural pilot and, on the strength of this, submitted an application for
a short-service commission and was accepted as an Acting Pilot Officer
in October 1938. The DSO, DFC and bar, and AFC decorations,
together with the United States DFC, which were to come his way were
in time to justify the confidence of Coles's rugby friends. In all appointments of command Sir William was decorated. Much later they were
astonished to find that they had also discovered the leader of the nation's
first post-war Olympics bobsleigh team, which was provided by the RAF
in 1948.

As Coles arrived at the Fund there could have been no more appropriate moment for planning for the future, because Peake's first year in the
chair had convinced him of the need for gusts of change – a conviction
which was strengthened, as it happened, by preparations for the
commemoration in October 1969 of the Fund's fiftieth anniversary.

In its way the observance of the Fund's half-century served to under-
score the need to move forward. As Peake laid a wreath at Trenchard's
statue on Victoria Embankment on 23 October, the very day of the first
meeting in 1919 of the Executive Committee of the Royal Air Force
Memorial Fund, he and Coles knew that in some respect the Fund's attitudes and actions were almost as outmoded as conditions prevailing after
the First World War. Even the Queen's attendance at a Royal Gala
performance of the film *The Battle of Britain* served as a reminder that
much of the Fund's financial strength was based upon the rewards of
Trenchard's appeal in 1940 and on legacies and donations inspired by
memories of the exploits of the Few.

Within four months of attending the gala showing of the film, Lord
Dowding, Leader of the Few, was dead, a loss which further alerted those
responsible for the Fund's future that before very long the Battle of Britain
might become as much a part of history as Nelson's victory at Trafalgar
– a battle which could no longer be said to provide an income for seagoing
charities. Certainly, the fiftieth anniversary commemoration of the battle
in 1990 seemed likely to be the last opportunity for a major appeal.

During Coles's service career in the twenty years which had elapsed between 1948 and his arrival at Portland Place, social conditions in civilian life had altered radically. The new Controller, in consultation with Peake, decided that the Fund should realign its finance, welfare, educational and appeal policies with the needs of the new society which an absence of war, the introduction of socialism and the Macmillan never-had-it-so-good years had combined to create.

Among the advantages to the Royal Air Force Benevolent Fund of Coles's recent appointments as Director General of Personal Services at the Ministry of Defence and Air Officer Commanding-in-Chief, Technical Training Command, and his proven career as a leader, was his knowledge of a fundamental change of attitude towards education at the Ministry of Defence. Broadly, the educational allowance had been extended to include all personnel serving at home as well as overseas. Taken together with educational problems arising from overseas service and postings, this suggested that the Royal Air Force would welcome a boarding school to assure continuity of education for children of families on the move.

Well, there was Vanbrugh Castle at Blackheath, the Alexander Duckham Memorial School, but it could accommodate only sixty boys and at this maximum had become uneconomic. Investigation by an architect of the possibility of expansion revealed that the idea was not tenable. Of its many disadvantages, one was particularly plain to Coles. As a former member of the Blackheath XV, among his rugby caps, Coles was well aware that Vanbrugh Castle School had no playing fields and was obliged to borrow them from the Blackheath Rugby and Cricket Club. Nor were there any recreational facilities, swimming-pool, or even a house for the headmaster – although until John Corner, a bachelor, retired in the autumn of 1973 and was succeeded by Mr W. P. Jones, a married man, this was not a major consideration.

Bill Jones was selected out of sixty applicants for the post and had served as a wartime flying instructor at the Central Flying School, Upavon, and later in India. He was as right for Vanbrugh and the transfer that lay ahead as had been Corner for the school in the years since its reopening after the Second World War, a headmastership which was recognised with an OBE shortly after his retirement.

After six years as headmaster of St Michael's School at RAF Nicosia in Cyprus, preceded by fifteen years as head of the junior school at Kimbolton in Huntingdonshire, Jones understood the RAF's educational problems, particularly that of parents serving overseas. He was, there-fore, wholeheartedly in favour of change in accordance with Coles's vision of the future for Vanbrugh.

'Vanbrugh,' Coles said, 'ought to look more like a preparatory school and less like a fortress.' And in early 1971, as the school celebrated its Golden Jubilee, the Alexander Duckham Memorial School Committee, chaired by Air Chief Marshal Sir Walter Merton, took a step in this direc-tion. After consulting the Fund's solicitors and the Duckham family it decided to offer admission from September 1972 to the sons of deceased and severely disabled officers in addition to those of NCOs and airmen. It was the first break in a long tradition and the beginning of a series of events which was to result, seven years afterwards, in the Fund's Diamond Jubilee year, in the already well-established Duke of Kent School having an ever-broadening field of admission, including the boarding of girls.

But now, as the School Committee recognised, the service educational allowance would result in an ever-increasing demand for places and, in any event, the economic advantages of a larger school must take precedence over a very human reluctance to accept change. There were also the considerations that cramped conditions and a necessarily restricted range of educational facilities and extra-curricular and sporting facilities were inhibiting opportunities for Vanbrugh pupils to compete for scholarships and bursaries available to the Fund at many public schools.

Eventually, resolution of the conflict over the removal from Blackheath proved easier than the search for an alternative property, the burden of which fell on Bill Coles with the professional help of Martyn 'Sandy' Sanders of Debenham, Tewson and Chinnocks, Chartered Surveyors, and the practical help of Paul Cutting, Secretary (Administration), who had dealt with the Fund's property investments since 1951. Briefed, as Coles recalled, 'to search the south of England for a place that looked more like a prep school with its own playing fields and capable of boarding between 120 and 140 pupils', they had spent two abortive years viewing fourteen unsuitable properties.

Then, in late 1973, when hopes were at their lowest ebb after investigating yet another unsuitable property near Ewhurst in Surrey, Coles, Paul Cutting, Bill Jones, Vanbrugh's headmaster, and Sandy stopped off at a village pub to refresh and console themselves.

It so happened that on the way to the rejected estate they had noticed an imposing Victorian building in extensive grounds which housed a school called Woolpit. As the party lifted its glasses Coles, the opportunist, observed: 'If only we could find a place like that, somewhere we could build on to if necessary. Let's ring up and ask if we can just come and have a look.' Within half an hour they were being shown round by the headmaster. Just as they were leaving Coles asked point-blank: 'I suppose you wouldn't want to sell this place?'

At last Coles's luck had turned. He had put his blunt question at the very moment when Woolpit faced problems. After twenty-eight years in the ownership of The St Thomas's Church Schools Company, it lacked the financial resources to pay for the expansion which would enable it to almost double the total of its eighty-five boarders and twenty-five day boys to an economic number. Mr John Hall, the headmaster, advised Coles that an approach to the Board of Governors might be welcomed, especially as Mr Trevor Jones, then Deputy Chairman, had served in the RAF.

Thereafter, events moved swiftly and shortly after the visit Coles received a letter from the headmaster offering amalgamation. On 10 January 1974 the Controller returned to Woolpit for a further recon-naissance and a week later Peake, Coles, Trevor Jones, together with Alan McLintock and other colleagues of the school board, put their heads together to examine the prospects for a merger.

From the start the Woolpit governors could not have been more helpful and co-operative. They had the will and the room to expand the school to an economic size but were without the wherewithal; whereas the Fund, facing an almost identical expansion problem so far as numbers were concerned, could find the money but was unable to enlarge Vanbrugh in the claustrophobic urban environment of Blackheath, in south-east London.

Before the end of February John Hall and Bill Jones, the headmasters of Woolpit and Vanbrugh, had exchanged visits and each side had accepted in principle that the Fund should take Woolpit over in return for discharging its liabilities. On 4 April 1974, Peake headed a joint meeting of the Fund's Finance and General Purposes and Alexander Duckham School Committees at Woolpit and members were over-whelmingly in favour of going ahead.

However, such a large undertaking could not be entered into without the observation and completion of certain formalities. Thus, Peake, after obtaining the Council's approval of the merger in principle on 8 May 1974, informed the President and Council Members by letter that, subject to the approval of the Charity Commissioners, the Woolpit governors would convey the school, playing fields and about fifteen acres of free-hold land to the Fund as a gift. In return the Fund would continue the fee-paying education of children already at the school or previously accepted for places.

Delightedly, the Chairman wrote that the Fund's surveyors estimated the value of the gift as at least £225,000 and that it had been arranged to buy a further ten acres, with buildings, known as Woolpit End – hitherto leased to the school – for £25,000. An additional fourteen-and-a-half acres of woodland had been offered to the Fund and this land would be purchased for £7250.

He explained that work on the Woolpit buildings would probably cost £35,000, while a new block of classrooms and dormitories had been esti-mated at £150,000.

Formal negotiations were opened and, after their completion during the year, the Fund, thanks to the generosity of the Woolpit governors, took possession of the fine Victorian mansion and the freehold of some forty acres in the Surrey countryside. Peake wrote to tell his colleagues on the Council that the Fund planned to transfer its Vanbrugh pupils for the start of the September term in 1975. However, the amalgamation depended at least upon the completion of the new dormitory/classroom block to provide the additional accommodation required. Subsequently, as plans were prepared, it was decided, on Peake's insistence, to provide a general-purpose gymnasium/assembly hall and six houses or flats for the staff. Air Commodore Peter Vicary, the Fund Branch Secretary, Education, was given the task of overseeing and co-ordinating the whole development project.

Then came delay because of alarm in the Waverley Planning Authority about the immensity of the development proposed for Woolpit. Quite reasonably, it explained that Woolpit lay within the Metropolitan Green

Vanbrugh Castle, the Fund's first school.

Belt and enjoyed the particular advantage of being situated in the Surrey hills in an area of outstanding natural beauty. Conferring with Peake and Coles at Woolpit, Sir Michael Creswell, Chairman of the Authority's Planning Committee and a member of Surrey County Council, explained sympathetically that the area was about to become part of a national park.

These and other detailed difficulties overcome, the contract for the whole development was finally let and the construction of the dormitory/classroom block and the modification of the main house, particularly of its kitchens, went ahead as rapidly as possible.

Meanwhile, with the encouraging approval of Professor A. N. Duckham and his sister Mary, Lady of Cults, the freehold of the Vanbrugh Castle School buildings was sold to the Blackheath Preservation Trust Limited in March 1977 for £177,500, which the Duckham family most generously agreed should be devoted to Duke of Kent School.

The Variety Club of Great Britain decided to finance four scholarships for Foundationers at the school for six years. They also presented a school bus, bringing the Club's ultimate contribution to the school to £35,000.

Since the playing fields were to become a central feature of the school a most generous and helpful offer was received from the MacRobert Trusts, through its Administrator, Air Vice-Marshal Frank Dodd, to provide a grant of £20,000 (subsequently increased to £22,000) to

The Duke of Kent School in the Surrey hills succeeded the Fund's original school at Vanbrugh Castle, Blackheath, in 1976.

This splendid library at Duke of Kent School was provided by the generosity of RAF personnel serving at Bruggen in West Germany.

increase the playing field area, which would thereafter be known as the MacRobert Playing Fields.

The source of the MacRobert fortune was Sir Alexander MacRobert, an industrious Scot of humble origins who had worked hard at night school in Aberdeen before sailing for India in 1884. He was vastly successful, managing Cawnpore Woollen Mills and becoming Chairman of the British India Corporation and receiving a baronetcy. When he died in 1922 he left a fortune.

MacRobert's first wife, Georgina, had died in 1905 and he married Rachel Workman, an American who inherited a considerable estate. He had three sons by his second wife and this is where the link with aviation and the RAF begins. Alasdair, who inherited the baronetcy, was Chairman of the British India Corporation when he was killed while piloting his own aeroplane near Luton. Succeeding his brother, Sir Roderick MacRobert joined the RAF before the outbreak of the Second World War with a short-service commission. Among his appointments before being killed in May 1941, in a Hurricane attack on Mosul airfield, was that of ADC in Palestine to Air Vice-Marshal Arthur Harris, who was later to become Marshal of the Royal Air Force Sir Arthur Harris, or, more popularly, Bomber Harris. Within weeks the third MacRobert brother, Sir Iain, had also died when his Coastal Command Blenheim failed to return from a North Sea air search for the crew of a missing bomber.

Shortly after the loss of her third son, Lady MacRobert bought a Stirling bomber and four Hurricane fighter aircraft for the RAF. The bomber went to war with the name 'MacRobert's Reply' painted on its nose and three of the Hurricanes were named after Alasdair, Roderick and Iain, while the fourth was simply called 'The Lady'. All four Hurricanes fought in the desert war with No. 94 Squadron, in which Iain MacRobert was serving on the day he died in the Middle East. Lady MacRobert took a strong personal interest in all her benefactions to the RAF and the MacRobert Trusts have carried on her good work since her death in 1954.

After such a generous gift from the MacRobert Trusts the Fund went ahead to make a showpiece of Duke of Kent School's playing fields. The headmaster was authorised to buy a powered roller and to arrange for the drainage of the cricket and rugby fields.

Another generous gift was received from the Hayward foundation. Sandy, the Fund's surveyor, knew Sir Charles Hayward and mentioned the Duke of Kent School development to him. When Coles wrote to the Hayward Foundation, giving them details of the impending expansion of this RAF school and sending a copy of *The Debt We Owe*, a cheque for £10,000 was received by return.

During 1975–76 John Hall and the Woolpit School continued to function amid the contractor's rubble and the combined school started work on the first term of the 1976–77 academic year. A Board of Governors appropriately chaired by Sir Walter Merton was appointed to include the former Chairman of the Woolpit School Governors, Mr Trevor W. Jones, and two other Woolpit Governors together with Mrs Ruth Croome, Mr Alexander Duckham's youngest daughter; the wife of the Commandant, RAF Staff College (Lady Williamson, succeeded by Mrs Peggy Curtiss); Mr Tim White; the Director of Training (Education); and Air Commodore Peter Vicary. All the Fund Governors are former members of the Vanbrugh Castle Management Committee.

Within the first year of operation the new school, with the permission of the Queen and the agreement of the Fund President, was renamed Duke of Kent School and was honoured by an informal visit by the Duke on 3 March 1977. It was also decided to open the school to the children of all serving personnel as full fee payers to fill available vacancies, priority having been given to children who had lost their fathers in the service.

It was further decided to make twenty places available to girls, thus making Duke of Kent School one of the first co-educational boarding preparatory schools in the country.

CHAPTER 15

PRINCESS MARINA HOUSE

Throughout the period of the negotiations which were to result in the removal from Vanbrugh to Woolpit, the Controller and his staff, enthusiastically encouraged by Peake, were also heavily engaged in preparing the way for Princess Marina House, an equally ambitious and expensive development, which was not to reach full fruition as a residential and convalescent complex at Rustington on the Sussex coast until the Diamond Jubilee year. But this is to look ahead from the Golden Jubilee, when an outstandingly generous action was to provide the Fund with a landmark at the close of its first fifty years.

The origins of Princess Marina House – whose existence owes everything to the moment on 30 September 1969 when Mrs H. Newton Driver

Princess Marina House, the Fund's convalescent and residential home at Rustington in West Sussex.

handed a cheque for £100,000 to Lord Ward, a former Air Minister and the Fund's Honorary Treasurer, to endow the Newton Driver Memorial Fund in memory of her husband – are to be found in the Second World War when Mrs Newton Driver ran an officers' club in the West End of London.

As Mrs Newton Driver explained at Portland Place when she presented the cheque,

> During the Second World War we had a very strenuous time at the English-speaking Officers' Club in Park Lane. None of my staff would live in because of the bombing. I was alone there with just one young girl who said she would like to die with me.
>
> Night after night I just went to bed with slacks and jumper on. The telephone would often ring and it would be the Railway Transport Officer asking for accommodation for servicemen who had nowhere to go. They would never take no for an answer. Very often I had to put a mattress on the floor and to make up those and our chesterfields into beds. When they arrived out of the blackout I would always ask 'Are you hungry? Have you had a meal?' and invariably they would reply, 'We are famished'. So we would all go to the kitchen and they would sit on the kitchen table, on the dresser, sinks, everywhere, and have cocoa and sandwiches. Throughout the war that went on.
>
> The one big topic of conversation was: what were they going to do after the war – these brave, eager boys, especially the Royal Air Force? They had marvellous plans. Then a few weeks later I would hear that they had crashed. It did something to me and I always said that if I could help the Royal Air Force in any way I would do so.
>
> Therefore, now that I am semi-retiring, I would like to give the proceeds of my work from all these years to the Royal Air Force Benevolent Fund and it will be a most wonderful thought to me that when I have passed on I shall be still helping the Royal Air Force.

Twenty-one years earlier in 1948, three years after the end of the Second World War, recognising that her London club had served its purpose and that the post-war period of resettlement and rehabilitation had created new needs, Mrs Newton Driver transferred the club to a beachside property at Rustington, where it was opened by Prince Philip.

In those days, conforming with its wartime status as an officers' club, it received British Commonwealth and United States Army, Navy and Air Force officers and ex-officers, including those of the women's and nursing services, and their relatives and friends.

Thus, as the Royal Air Force Benevolent Fund took over The Newton Driver Services Club it seemed appropriate to continue the tradition of convalescence and very soon up to sixty men and women were guests at any one time. There was the difference, however, that rank was irrelevant as a qualification and admission was at first restricted to elderly or partially disabled serving or ex-members of the RAF and WRAF, Princess Mary's Royal Air Force Nursing Service, and their adult dependants. Within a year, though, this exclusivity was reconsidered and admission of Army and Navy personnel was approved, when vacancies existed, as being in accordance with the spirit of Mrs Newton Driver's wishes.

In permitting the Fund to acquire her club under the endowment arrangement of 1969 Mrs Newton Driver received deep personal satisfaction and was further heartened by its immediate success under the Fund's management. After her death on 19 June 1970, from injuries received in a motoring accident, the Fund learnt that Mrs Newton Driver, who was well into her eighties, had bequeathed her adjacent land and property of considerable value and potential use to the Fund.

Shortly after its acquisition of the club the Fund's first guests were enjoying the restful and comfortable centre for which its management committee, chaired by Air Chief Marshal Sir Wallace 'Digger' Kyle, with Wing Commander Ted Holloway as the first Secretary, and its manager, Group Captain G. F. Corden, now held responsibility.

Very soon the eligibility of all ranks for accommodation was emphasised by the presence of Air Marshal Sir Richard Atcherley, a former Council member of the Fund, who spent most of the last few weeks of his life there. The Air Marshal subsequently was taken ill *en route* to Cape Canaveral, where he had been invited to watch the launching of a moon mission and was rushed to Aldershot Hospital where he died.

Among the earliest guests at Princess Marina House were some who had stayed there when it was the Newton Driver Services Club and naturally one of the first questions they asked was why it had been renamed

Special events create links between the Fund's establishments as when Duke of Kent School pupils sang carols with Princess Marina House residents at Christmas in 1982.

Princess Marina House. The explanation was that, since Princess Marina's death in August 1968, the Fund had sought a suitable memorial to its long-serving President and had been delighted when the Duke of Kent approved the use of his mother's name for the centre at Rustington. Nor was the wartime effort and peacetime generosity of Mrs Newton Driver to be overlooked, because Banner Cross, one of the adjoining houses she bequeathed to the Fund, was renamed Newton Driver House and has been converted into a nurses' residence.

From the outset Princess Marina House was not self-supporting, those with RAF connections being charged about £16 a week or according to their means, while Army and Navy guests had to pay a full economic rate.

In 1971, its second full year, Princess Marina House accommodated 279 RAF guests for a total of 593 weeks and fifteen former members of the Army or Navy for twenty-four weeks at a cost, after contributions, of £30,149. Days out by the sea were organised by other service charities, including the Not Forgotten Association, one of the Fund's oldest associates, which maintains an ambulance coach and provides outings, entertainments and personal gifts for disabled and wounded service or ex-service people.

It was at this stage that the Fund, taking note that of the fifty places at the centre nineteen were occupied by long-term residents, began to consider the problem of caring for those who needed periods of nursing. Until now it had relied considerably on the Royal Air Forces Association's acceptance of some such cases at its nearby Sussexdown home, but, as the demand for such treatment grew, it became clear that Sussexdown, for all RAFA's good will, could not be expected to meet all the Fund's needs indefinitely.

While this all-important matter of expansion was being considered, certain problems arising out of Mrs Newton Driver's will were resolved and Coles was relieved to hear from her executors that the Fund could take possession of Banner Cross and St Bega, another adjacent house, thus facilitating a first enlargement of Princess Marina House. Consequently, in 1972 as many as 331 RAF guests and nineteen long-term residents benefited from the peaceful seaside surroundings, as did also ten Army or Navy guests, at a total cost of £52,127, reduced to £35,629 from income. Thereafter the occupation rate rose progressively, a record being set in 1973, with 383 RAF guests spending a total of 772 weeks, twenty long-termers in residence and eight ex-Army visitors. The cost was £65,350, offset by an income of £47,030.

Satisfactory though this occupation rate was, particularly in view of the closure of the main building for rewiring in December, the management committee felt that Princess Marina House was not being used sufficiently for convalescence by RAF servicemen and women or their wives and husbands. Ex-service people were every bit as welcome, but the Fund wished to encourage younger men and women from RAF stations to make use of the centre. Certainly, there could be no finer place to relax and regain strength after an illness or operation than at the RAF's very own seaside resort, which now comprised five buildings, including a club-house, a putting green and tennis courts with changing-rooms and showers. But good reports spread throughout the service and as a result the Committee decided to enlarge the lounge, dining room and sun lounge.

Throughout the gradual development at Rustington the Duke of Kent, while following every aspect of the Fund's advances since succeeding his mother as President, understandably had retained an especial interest in Princess Marina House. Knowing that expansion was planned for the new year he dropped in by helicopter on 29 May 1974, to see what the Committee had planned to further improve the centre and to find out for himself why it had proved so popular and established such an excellent reputation for convalescence.

It seemed to the President, as he remarked to the Management Committee during his visit, 'marvellous value', a plaudit which, expressed in figures for that year, reflected net expenditure of £61,852 for 418 RAF guests, twenty long-term residents and seven guests from the other services.

Thus, in the following summer of 1975, as Coles cleared the Controller's desk in the Council chamber at Portland Place he knew that to the groundwork for the removal from Vanbrugh to Woolpit he could add the achievement of helping to transform Mrs Newton Driver's club into a convalescent centre comparable with the best elsewhere in Britain.

The Duke of Kent had observed that there seemed little scope for improvement, but Peake, Air Marshal Sir Denis Crowley-Milling, Coles's successor, Air Marshal Sir Harry Burton, who had succeeded Kyle as Chairman of the Princess Marina House Committee, Wing Commander Allan Scott, who was now the Secretary having recently retired from the Royal Air Force where his last appointment had been Air Attaché in Madrid, and Wing Commander A. F. Carvosso, the centre's new manager, were already looking further ahead.

CHAPTER 16

THE ROYAL AIR FORCE BENEVOLENT FUND HOUSING TRUST LTD AND WELFARE WORK

Ranking high among the radical changes of course during Coles's controllership was the Fund's policy on housing widows and their families. In the early 1970s the property boom obliged the Fund to spend ever-increasing sums on homes. Characteristically, it was the Scottish Branch which set the alarm bells ringing at Portland Place.

Attending an Annual Meeting of the branch in Edinburgh, Coles was warned by Sir Ian Johnson-Gilbert that the Scots felt the Fund was being too prodigal in the manner in which it provided houses for widows.

It was true that although the houses were put in the names of their widow owners, in the event of remarriage a widow was expected to return to the Fund as much money as it had provided at the time of her bereavement. But the Scots regarded this as a bonus for the new husband who in all probability had not served in the RAF. It was wrong that such men with no call on the Fund should benefit from it, however indirectly.

Coles returned from Scotland with the clear message that a means should be devised through which the Fund could retain an interest in all such homes and thus gain from any rising values. The outcome was the introduction of the Royal Air Force Benevolent Fund Housing Trust Limited.

At the time of the incorporation of the Housing Trust in 1972 it was still the Fund's general policy to resort to house purchase where a widow or a severely disabled ex-member of the RAF with young children had been unable to find a suitable home to rent. Applications from fit ex-service people with dependant children and, exceptionally, from serving personnel, were also considered when rented accommodation was out of the question.

However, over the years, the reduction of suitable rented property on the market and ever-rising rents were to turn the Fund almost exclusively towards a policy of house purchase and also towards broader qualifications. Consequently, applications from ex-members of the RAF with dependent children were no longer exceptional. Further, serving members, with long or pensionable service, were to be eligible for interest-free loans as they prepared to leave the RAF, to help them put down a deposit on a house, such loans being subject to repayment from gratuities or terminal benefits.

In its operation of the Housing Trust the Fund observes two ground rules. Where it has to contribute more than half of the purchase price it buys and owns the property under the Trust so that after its sale the Fund benefits from any appreciation and can use the money to help another family. On the other hand, if an applicant can provide more than half the purchase price then the Fund will ease the burden of buying the property by awarding an interest-free mortgage loan.

Yet, as in all its welfare activities, the Royal Air Force Benevolent Fund is always ready to take a view of particular circumstances and the Housing Trust enjoys considerable elasticity. For instance a young corporal, who was happily married with two children, had completed a twelve-year engagement in 1973 and had bought a house with some assistance from the Fund, intending to start a business as a photographer from home. But before they could move into the house the couple were involved in a serious motor accident and each received severe facial, hand and body burns. The injuries were so bad that the husband was unlikely to be able to go ahead with his plan to launch himself as a photographer. In these distressing circumstances the Housing Trust bought a house for the family outright and put in a washing machine, washing-up machine and special door handles to enable the corporal and his wife to live as normal life as possible with the children.

The corporal wrote:

> I am finding it hard to put onto paper the words I use daily to describe your organisation to social workers, friends and family. Apart from the considerable financial help, which not only allowed us to survive, but put both our minds at ease, there have been the social visits to the hospital and our home which have been invaluable for the encouragement they have given us. I'll never be able to repay your personal help and your organisation will always have our gratitude.

Lest spending on the scale required for such large developments as the Duke of Kent School and Princess Marina House and the purchase of houses – 145 families costing £318,193 in 1969 – should seem to distort the picture of the Fund's welfare activities, the Grants Committees, the Controller and staff were as much exercised by day-to-day calls for assistance as had been their predecessors during the first fifty years. There was the difference, however that in spite of inflation the Fund's income and capital additions from investments, the pay deduction scheme, other RAF self-help schemes, and legacies and donations enabled the Grants

Committees to make individual awards without drawing on the Fund's capital, which they were always prepared to do if necessary.

Examples selected at random from beneath the heading 'Kinds of Assistance' in the annual report for 1969, the Golden Jubilee year, reflect the variety of the Fund's welfare actions. For instance, help with prams in two cases, £56. Tools and working equipment were bought for sixteen people at a cost of £702. Travel and removals ran to £10,742 for 292 families. Clothing, bedding and footwear are itemised at 1033 awards totalling £17,253; debts due to sickness and other reasons, 2048 awards amounting to £100,318; and all aspects of the Fund's educational help cost £123,792 for 808 cases.

Thus, while hundreds of thousands of pounds were spent or appropriated for the two major developments, thousands of comparatively small individual awards were made after investigation in the field and discussion in committee, contributing to a grand total in Golden Jubilee year of £905,199 for 9552 awards.

In Diamond Jubilee year, when welfare expenditure was running at a rate of £2 million a year, it may be asked how much could be achieved for less than £1 million. The answer, as in previous years, was to be found not so much in statistics as in the human stories presented to the Grants Committees. If the following examples from 1969 can only give a general impression of the Fund's welfare assistance in that year, they bring out two emerging factors. These are the complicated nature of many cases and, in consequence, a growing demand on the knowledge and expertise of the staff at Portland Place, in the branch offices, and among the Fund's regular helpers and associated members of such bodies as the Royal Air Forces Association. Paying funeral or pram expenses where necessary was a stroke-of-the-pen decision, but, as the following examples illustrate, many cases called for tact, discretion, patience and understanding. In other words, more than mere money.

An aircraftman second class, young and single, had served five years before being discharged because he was schizoid, a condition which prevented him from retaining a job. Nevertheless, he was a brilliant mathematician and keen to take a two-year electronics course. The Fund helped him complete the course. He passed five examinations, three with distinction. Then he suffered another breakdown in health, but recovered sufficiently to take the City and Guilds Certificate with a view to settling into a job for which he had qualified.

Many years after a young pilot officer had been killed in a bomber brought down over Germany, his elderly and partially-blind mother, unable to find suitable accommodation, was much distressed because she had been obliged to put her faithful dog into kennels. It was urgent, her doctor said, that she should have a home with a ground floor. The Fund assisted with the purchase of a maisonette and some extra money to put it in good repair. The elderly lady and her dog were reunited. The pilot officer's sister who lived with her mother wrote:

It is very difficult to word the gratitude I feel towards the Royal Air Force Benevolent Fund. I thank you for helping my mother and I, when no one else could or would: for giving us a new start when we both thought we had reached the end.

In the 1960s and the 1970s survivors or their dependants of the First World War were a dwindling responsibility, but in Golden Jubilee year the following letter from the widow of a private in the Royal Flying Corps typified their needs:

I feel I must write and say thank you for the grant you made me. You cannot know all this has meant to me. I am not a woman who gets into debt needlessly, but what I had to get was a real necessity. Now, thanks to you, I have settled my debts. You see I am seventy-four and I was afraid I might have died with the debt unpaid.

Among the criteria taken into account by the Grants Committees is the extent to which families were able, have made provisions for themselves. The Committees warm to the provident who despite their own best efforts are subjected to worry and distress in the moment of crisis.

During Coles' controllership the Insurance Advisory Service continued to go from strength to strength, considerably broadening its scope beyond impartial advice or a second opinion on life assurance matters to advising on all aspects of family protection, savings, house purchase, education, financial planning and commutation of retired pay. At the end of 1974, following the retirement in September of that year of Group Captain Swain, his successor as senior executive of the Insurance Advisory Service, Group Captain R. J. Gosnell, could report savings-type policies of more than £1,125,000 in sums assured with a further £970,000 of temporary life assurance comprising convertible-term assurance or family-income policies.

At this rate the Insurance Advisory Service had become the source of a considerable flow of business in collaboration with the insurance department of Lloyds Bank, Cox's and King's branch, the RAF agents, who, if required, help applicants to negotiate such policies as are recommended.

By the end of 1974 the RAF Dependants Fund had nearly 90,000 members, subscribing 10p a month, and the basic death grant was £800, subject to the Trustees' discretion.

Visiting RAF units, Coles found that the prudence of subscribing such a small sum voluntarily was brought home convincingly on the occasions when an accident resulted in the deaths of several men on the same station and their comrades heard of the immediate cash payments received by widows.

Indeed, such was the reputation of the Royal Air Force Dependants Fund that many subscribers wrote to the Trustees asking if they could increase their weekly subscription in order that their beneficiaries could receive a greater cash sum. This was investigated by the Managing Trustees, who included Coles as Controller. He, in conjunction with Sidney Swain, looked into this possibility but, as this would change the basis of making the Dependants Fund a separate charity, it was not possible.

Faced with the ever-increasing number of servicemen who wished to protect their families beyond the single cash grant made by the Dependants Fund, Sidney Swain, in conjunction with the Air Member for Personnel's department, did some more homework. As a result of this, on 1 July 1971 the Air Force Board, in conjunction with the Finance and General Purposes Committee of the Benevolent Fund, launched the Royal Air Force Dependants (Income) Trust, underwritten by the Provident Mutual Life Assurance Association, under the Secretaryship of Wing Commander F. W. Tame. This enabled members of the Dependants Fund, if they so wished, to subscribe more to make their beneficiaries eligible to receive a monthly income, or, alternatively, a lump-sum payment. This enabled the Trustees to follow up the single lump-sum payment from the Dependants Fund by a tax-free monthly income from the first day of the month following the death of the subscriber. Such an income is payable until the subscriber would have reached the age of fifty-five, or sixty in some instances. A bonus increase from the date of joining is added each year to the income and this bonus growth, currently six per cent compound, also continues to be added if it becomes payable. Alternatively, the beneficiary of the deceased subscriber can, at the Trustees' discretion, commute the income for a tax-free cash payment. At the end of each accounting year, on 30 June, any net income from the Trust is covenanted to the RAF Benevolent Fund.

Well, those are the bald terms, but what makes the effort so very worthwhile to the staff of the Insurance Advisory Service and the RAF Dependants Fund and Income Trust are the letters of appreciation which arrive in every post. Group Captain Swain made the point to the Finance and General Purposes Committee shortly before he retired, bringing to its notice a letter from a flying officer of the Air Movement Squadron in Hong Kong. Not only did this young officer express surprise at the existence of 'D Income', as the service short-hands the Trust, but the accounts staff in the colony were 'perplexed at the remarkable protection for such a small premium'. Stating that he intended to make use of its Mortgage Saving Scheme, the flying officer wrote to Swain:

> I feel considerably more at ease than before I received your advice. The letter was logical to a layman and all the enclosures were explicit and of value . . . My fear of being caught by a pushing salesman has been slightly relieved and my understanding of jargon has been improved. Many thanks for the care you have taken.

Early in his tenancy of the controllership Coles had become concerned at the rapidly increasing burden that the casework mountain was imposing on his staff. For this and other reasons he felt that a reappraisal and possible overhaul of some of the administrative and staff recruitment machinery at headquarters was required. There were those on the staff, among them his secretary Elizabeth Ticehurst, whom he promoted to private secretary after Squadron Leader Stansfield's retirement – she is now at Sir 'Jock' Kennedy's side as personal assistant – who were not receiving the responsibilities and rewards for which they were experienced and equipped. There was also the problem of replacing retiring or resigning staff with people of sufficient ability, because salaries at the Royal Air Force Benevolent Fund were no longer competitive in the open market.

Naturally, Coles was as concerned as had been any of his predecessors to conform with the Fund's long-standing policy of keeping administrative expenditure to a minimum. In 1969, the Golden Jubilee year in which £905,199 was spent on relief, this was £141,953 of which £103,563 covered salaries, wages and staff pensions. Yet he also feared for the Fund's future administrative efficiency if pay at Portland Place was not brought more into line with commercial standards and promotion prospects made more attractive.

Peake, with his banking and business background, wholeheartedly supported the Controller's opinion and the Finance and General Purposes Committee authorised a survey of the administration. This was undertaken in 1971 by the Management Services Department of Barton, Mayhew and Company, the Fund's auditors, and as a result certain customary business practices were introduced, including a modification to the establishment of typists to concentrate the work of shorthand and audio typists who had been working individually for the various departmental Secretaries. Possibly the most helpful change to emerge from this review was the removal to Portland Place of the all-important Appeals Branch from its outpost in two rooms on the top floor of the Oxford Circus branch of Barclays Bank, a move which enabled the Controller to have immediate personal contact with Group Captain Arbuthnot, the Appeals Secretary. Accommodation above the bank had been obtained with the help of Lord Portal, a Barclays director, and as Appeals moved out the Insurance Advisory Service, whose presence at headquarters was not so essential, moved in.

At the time of the survey the possibility of wholesale removal from Portland Place and out of central London, which had been considered and rejected in an earlier review, was reconsidered. As hitherto it was decided that such an upheaval would not be in the overall interest of the Fund's welfare objectives, particularly because of its extremely favourable lease of the building. Other arguments which helped to end the proposal were the headquarters' accessibility in the West End of London to the majority of members of the Grants and other Committees and the importance of the Fund's general and personal relationships with the Ministry of Defence, other government offices, associated charitable organisations and also with its professional advisers.

The latter consideration is excellently illustrated by the proposal for another fundamental departure which was considered during Coles's controllership. This was the possibility of applying for a Royal Charter. While the pros and cons were being investigated, the benefit of close consultative contact with Charles Russell and Co., the Fund's solicitors, was much appreciated. In the event, the Fund was advised not to make application because such a status would enable the Privy Council to insist upon certain restrictions on its powers of investment. The Fund was not prepared to surrender its investment freedom. It also rejected incorporation under the Companies Act and carried on its business under the High Court scheme which had served it admirably for more than thirty years.

CHAPTER 17

FINANCE AND FUND-RAISING: INTO THE 1970S

It was in this realm of investment and City of London expertise that Lord Portal's persuasion of Peake to accept the chairmanship was to prove exceptionally fruitful. Portal's death on 21 April 1971 was a sad and serious loss to the Fund. During the preceding quarter of a century he had served as Deputy Chairman to Riverdale, Knollys and Peake, in whose favour he had declined the opportunity to succeed to the chair. This was a characteristically selfless action considering that the chairmanship would have crowned a connection stretching back to 8 March 1939 when, as an Air Vice-Marshal and Air Member for Personnel, he was appointed to the Council, as indeed also on that day was a certain Group Captain Cordingley.

After the new Deed of Trust had freed the Fund from its low-yield investment fetters – effectively from 1 January 1949 – Portal, for all his other banking and business commitments, had not spared himself in assisting the Fund to mix its gilt-edged portfolio with a blend of equity and property investments.

In their four years as Chairman and Deputy Chairman, Peake and Portal, notwithstanding an expenditure on welfare of nearly £3.5 million, had seen the Fund's net assets increase from £6,027,086 in 1967 to £6,941,742 in 1971.

Throughout the inflation-scourged 1970s Peake's performance as Chairman of the Council and the Finance and General Purposes and Appeals Committees repeatedly reinforced Portal's inspired recruitment of Peake, who built a formidable financial team as Lord Ward of Witley, Air Minister from 1957 to 1960 and a vice-president of the Fund since 1958, accepted the office of Honorary Treasurer in 1969 following the resignation of Lord Thurso. In 1968 Lord Catto of Cairncatto joined his fellow Morgan Grenfell director, Sir George Erskine, on the Council, and succeeded him on the Finance and General Purposes Committee, becoming its Deputy Chairman in 1974.

At the time of the Golden Jubilee in 1969 the team's money management was already proving remarkably effective despite prevailing economic conditions. A decision taken in September 1968 to increase the equity investment target to £2.5 million at cost had been implemented. Advantage was also seized of the high interest rates available from local authorities and by the end of 1969 the Fund had placed about £250,000 in this sector. Although the London Stock Exchange index was down on the year the Fund had managed to mark the close of Golden Jubilee year with the market value of its stocks and shares exceeding book value by more than £1 million.

Financially the picture in 1970 was not so sanguine, with securities dropping to more-than-book value of some £650,000. Yet such were the Fund's liquid assets that there was no need to sell securities at depressed prices.

In 1971 Lord Ward was able to report a big improvement. Taking advantage of favourable opportunities and the City expertise provided by Peake and Catto, the Fund's stock market holdings at £7,603,567 exceeded book value by £2,322,711.

In 1972 Peake's prudence in getting the Fund out of fixed-interest stocks and into equities and convertibles – stocks and shares to the net value of about £300,000 were bought during the year – was manifest. For in this year equities and convertibles continued to appreciate eighty-five per cent above cost as against a fall to nine per cent below cost in the market value of the Fund's fixed-interest stocks. Between 1968, Peake's first full year as Chairman, and 1972, the proportion of equities and convertibles in the portfolio had risen from thirty-one per cent to fifty-two per cent – with a target of sixty per cent book value in view – and the annual rate of income from all investments had improved from seven per cent to eight per cent. It was a satisfactory end to an investment year at the start of which Peake had been honoured with a knighthood in the New Year Honours list – although the Council in congratulating him acknowledged that the honour also recognised Sir Harald's services to the Royal Air Force before and during the Second World War as well as to banking and the community.

Before passing forward from 1972, the retirement of Flight Lieutenant J. A. B. Cairns, the Finance Secretary, who had been responsible for so much of the day-to-day detail of the Fund's money business for twenty-six years, should be recorded. He handed over to Wing Commander E. J. Holloway, who had joined the Army shortly after the outbreak of War, transferred to the Royal Air Force in March 1941 for pilot training and seen operational service in Bomber Command and North Africa. In later service he commanded No. 58 Canberra Photographic Reconnaissance Squadron for three years and after Flying College, where he was on the same course as the then Controller, Denis Crowley-Milling, completed an Air Ministry tour in the Assistant Chief of the Air Staff's Intelligence Department. His last appointment was Senior Personnel Staff Officer of Coastal Command. He joined the Fund Welfare Branch in 1967, and was Secretary of Princess Marina House before taking over from Cairns.

Such is the contrariness of the City that a setback might have been expected in the following year. The *Financial Times* index fell by thirty-two per cent and the Fund was highly selective and restrictive in its stock market dealings. Cash available for new investment was placed for preference at high interest on short-term deposit. The Finance and General Purposes Committee noted gravely that the fall in market values had reduced the real value of all the Fund's investments to £6,892,251, a reduction of £1,740,300 on the previous year.

With continuing inflation and with a record annual outgoings of more than £1.6 million on the relief of distress, 1974 was another difficult year. Investment was all but at a standstill, the Fund being kept liquid while any surplus money was placed on short-term deposit with local authorities to take advantage of high interest rates.

Nevertheless, although the Fund, together with most investors, suffered from the effects of the home and overseas recession, Peake and his colleagues could fairly report that it had held its own in a year which had been the worst ever in the London stock markets. In contrast with a 46.8 per cent drop in the *Financial Times* index, the Fund's portfolio had declined by thirty-eight per cent, a net reduction of about £2.5 million in market values. Nevertheless, accumulated funds had risen from £8,355,974 to £9,037,342, but the annual report on the accounts warned that a testing time lay ahead.

Before moving into 1975, as a matter of record it merits note that amid all the problems of 1974 the Fund overhauled its form of accounts to give effect to the Statement of Standard Accounting Practices with regard to the treatment of reserves, laid down by the Accounting Standards Steering Committee. The effect was to necessitate the Fund taking all exceptional profits and losses, and income such as legacies, hitherto regarded as capital, into the income and expenditure account and then into the accumulated funds in the balance sheet. The opportunity was also taken to simplify the form of the income and expenditure account and the balance sheet by transferring much of the detail to separate notes.

In the event, in 1975 the Royal Air Force Benevolent Fund stood up rather better than the gloomy forecast of an expected 'testing time' and Peake confidently informed the Council that investment income had increased and that the portfolio's market value was substantially higher than in the previous year. In fact, this could be described reasonably as an understatement, because market values of stocks and shares had risen in the year from £3,841,746 to £6,704,552, a feat for which Peake in his annual Chairman's statement gave generous credit to Lord Catto, Deputy Chairman of the Finance and General Purposes Committee and Chairman of merchant bankers Morgan Grenfell, which company's advice had been so largely responsible for the improvement in a year of such perplexity for investors.

Stocks and shares were not alone among investments calling for careful monitoring in the years of Coles's controllership. In the Golden Jubilee year of 1969 the Fund's property portfolio remained at a book value of little more than £1 million. It was a time of much competition in the property market and even the Royal Air Force Benevolent Fund, expertly advised by its surveyors, Debenham, Tewson and Chinnocks, found it difficult to buy properties with good covenants and producing its expected average return of fifteen per cent. With boom conditions running into 1970, the Fund's holdings remained much the same and a target of £1.5 million was not achieved.

Then, gradually the picture changed and, while a continuing shortage of suitable buys prevailed in early 1971 – with the consequent investment of £100,000 in Charity Property Trusts – Debenham's efforts were more fruitful and Peake's Finance Committee raised its sights, setting £1.75 million as its property sector investment target. By the end of the year properties totalled £1,156,724 at book value.

This improvement, however, was short-lived and in 1973 no leasehold properties were bought because yields were less than could be obtained from gilts and other fixed interest stocks.

There was a similar standstill in 1974. No leasehold property was bought and book values, further reduced by amortisation, continued to fall and were £657,821 in 1975.

Among the challenges facing Coles as he succeeded Whitley in the summer of 1968 was the problem of creating income other than from capital investment. The Fund, as he knew, was currently finding about thirty per cent of the £900,000 it was spending on the relief of distress from its annual income. Coles had joined the Fund, as it will be recalled, from Technical Training Command after raising £17,216 within the Command and, therefore, he was already an acknowledged fund-raiser.

Early in his controllership Coles was concerned as to the extent to which the Fund's appeal to the public for money was linked to the past achievements of the Royal Air Force. It was a question which greatly exercised Peake, not only as Chairman of the Fund but particularly as Chairman of the Appeals Committee, and also, of course, Group Captain Arbuthnot, the Appeals Secretary. The difficulties were that the Service was contracting and that such routine operations as NATO reconnaissance flights, exercises in West Germany, even helicopter rescue flights and famine relief mercy missions did not stir hearts and minds and tended to be taken for granted.

The diminution of the Royal Air Force and its activities was reflected in the membership of the Council itself, its numbers dropping from thirty-five to thirty-two chiefly because of the amalgamation of Bomber, Fighter, Signals and Coastal Commands into Strike Command, demonstrating that even Air Officers Commanding-in-Chief are not exempted from the perils of redundancy.

Consequently, while the Fund, with the continuing advice of Peter Taylor, its public relations consultant, strove forcefully to publicise needs arising from the reducing commitments of the Royal Air Force, the Council conceded that large unsolicited donations and legacies must still depend on past exploits and people's memories of them.

Therefore, while it has been explained that after the Golden Jubilee

Numerous fund-raising occasions have been associated with the Battle of
Britain. Air Chief Marshal Sir David Lee, a long serving chairman of the
Grants Committee, was presented to the Queen at a gala performance of
the feature film *Battle of Britain* in 1969.

commemoration the Fund would have to look forward in the realm of
appeal, it remained inevitable that it still had to look back.

At the time, this policy paid the Fund handsomely, especially as 1969
was the year in which the feature film, *The Battle of Britain*, received a
Royal charity première on 20 October at London's Dominion Cinema.
It was a glittering occasion attended by the Queen, Prince Charles,
Princess Anne, the Duke and Duchess of Kent, the Duchess of
Gloucester, Prince Michael of Kent and Princess Alexandra. After the
performance the Chairman presented the Queen with a leatherbound
copy of the Golden Jubilee edition of *The Debt We Owe*, an edition which,
incidentally, has contributed over the years to the Fund's income. It is
impossible to attach a figure to the book's influence on donations and
legacies, but at least one sum of £10,000 can be attributed to it, in that
the donor's cheque arrived by return of post after receiving a copy. This
windfall was part of the year's total of £245,526 from legacies and capital
donations.

As well as providing the Appeals Department with such a splendid
opportunity to bring in money (in all the Fund and the Royal Air Forces
Association shared £12,520 from London and provincial premières),
that gala night, attended by so many aces and survivors of the Battle of
Britain, was the scene of numerous reunions and nostalgic conversations.

For the Chairman's wife, Dame Felicity Peake, the sequence in the film
where the airfield at Biggin Hill is bombed in daylight, and the actress

Susannah York playing an officer counts her WAAF dead, was particularly poignant. In August 1940 the then Section Officer Felicity Hanbury,
who was later to command the Women's Royal Air Force in the rank of
Air Commandant, had been that officer and the part had been written
round her experiences.

Other than its direct financial assistance to the Fund, the *Battle of Britain*
film contributed to Golden Jubilee year's total of £276,565 received from
all appeal sources, other than legacies and capital donations, at home and
abroad by stimulating a flow of free-will offerings, which included £7531
from church collections, £2675 raised by the Jersey branch of the Royal
Air Forces Association in Battle of Britain Week, and ten shillings from
an eleven-year-old boy who staged a model aircraft display.

The fiftieth anniversary year had provided an opportunity to remind
the public of the Fund's existence and work but the Royal Air Force and
related sources remained the Chief fount of the Fund's income. In that
year servicemen's and servicewomen's voluntary subscriptions through
the half-a-day's-pay-a-year scheme had reached £131,754 which,
together with £12,500 from the RAF Central Fund – the Royal Air Force
Benevolent Fund Second Development Trust also received £12,500
from this source – £6818 from retired personnel, £25,581 from RAF
units and numerous contributions from wives' clubs and other service
sources, provided £203,268 of the £276,565 total. That old stand-by the
Royal Tournament contributed £8219 and Battle of Britain Week collections, excluding the RAFA's Wings Appeal, enabled that organisation to
pay £17,636 into the Fund's exchequer. At £46,385 ordinary subscriptions and donations from the public were more than £16,000 up on the
previous year.

All in all a good year, but, like the Council, the Finance Committee
counted the cost of relief and members were not satisfied that it was good
enough. Ordinary income at £1,033,123 had fallen short of expenditure
by about £14,000.

The Appeals Committee was open to ideas, however modest, the
results of which might supplement such hardy annuals as the RAF
Anniversary Concert and the Souvenir Book. One such idea in this year
was the Used Stamp Scheme, through which service people and the
public were asked to collect stamps of all sorts and send them to the Fund
in packets of not less than 1000 stamps at a time. Arrangements were
made with the stamp trade to bulk-sell to collectors for the Fund's benefit.
Another enterprise was to stimulate the parks and gardens department
of country and seaside resorts to plant floral displays featuring the RAF
and the Fund. These flower beds offered the dual benefits of reminding
the public about the Fund and raising money. In 1969 a Folkestone floral
display brought in £720, despite the vandalising of a concrete collection
box.

In the following year Peake, reporting as Chairman of the Finance and
General Purposes Committee, noted with a hint of surprise that the deficit

between ordinary income and record welfare awards of £935,000 was again £14,000, despite a drop in support from the public; legacies and donations having fallen to about £200,000.

But the RAF had managed to prevent the gap widening and to enable the Council to record with gratitude that a total just short of £334,000 had provided thirty-five per cent of the amount paid to relieve distress. As Peake observed in his financial report, had it not been for the decision of servicemen and women to allow their annual subscriptions to remain at half-a-days-pay-a-year after the April 1970 introduction of new pay scales, the deficit would have risen to more than £60,000.

Such was the appreciation of the importance of the service subscriptions that Coles was at great pains during his visits to RAF units to emphasise that the Fund was looking for a 100 per cent of voluntary subscribers and to explain the desirability of entering into seven-year covenants, whereby for every £1 a year given the Fund could recover 63p from the Inland Revenue, thus receiving a total of £1.63. It was also publicised that, whereas covenant facilities had so far been restricted to officers, warrant officers and senior non-commissioned officers, they were available henceforth to corporals and airmen who paid standard-rate income tax. As in previous years every new penny counted and the Fund was indebted to the most modest of donors, not least among whom was the schoolboy – he was not a Vanbrugh pupil – who sent 75p at the suggestion of his headmaster after being caught running a book on the Grand National.

After the excitement of its Golden Jubilee the Fund had returned to a more workaday existence, yet 1970 was not without its brighter interludes, particularly a belated fiftieth anniversary reception, arranged at Lancaster House in London on 21 April by the Air Force Board of the Defence Council and which was attended by the Duke of Kent and the Rt Hon. Denis Healey, Minister of Defence. There was also the annual concert on 3 April, provided this year by the Birmingham Symphony Orchestra and, as ever, the Central Band of the Royal Air Force. The soloist was Jeffrey Siegel, the international pianist.

In October 1971 Group Captain Arbuthnot retired after running the Appeals Department for eight years, handing over to Air Commodore John McKelvey. Arbuthnot's last year was his best, the Fund receiving £410,913, which represented nearly forty-one per cent of the cash paid out to relieve distress. Service contributions of £337,748 had never been higher. If legacies and donations were a dismaying twenty-seven per cent lower at £151,691, Arbuthnot had still set his successor a stiff challenge. The concert at the Royal Festival Hall on 2 April, the last Arbuthnot was to organise, had, as Peake told the Council, produced 'a very happy result' for the Group Captain, all seats being sold within three days of the box office opening in early March. But then it was not every year that Princess Anne was guest of honour, that the Royal Philharmonic Orchestra was available to join the Central Band, and that Moura

Lympany was soloist. It was the sixteenth anniversary concert to celebrate the founding of the Royal Air Force on 1 April 1918, and it brought
the total concert revenue to £15,442.

Arbuthnot could also take pleasure in the fact that in his last year Prince
Philip offered to make an annual donation; and that a growing awareness
of the aims and achievements of the Fund, obtained through Peter
Taylor's regular news releases to RAF station publications, resulted in
two remarkable donations – £12,394.50 from Little Rissington and
£8736.27 from Akrotiri in Cyprus.

One of the Fund's strong points is that its permanent staff represent a
cross-section of service experience. While the Controllers, since
Cordingley's retirement, have been former pilots who achieved Air
Rank, others – among them Paul Cutting, for so long the Administration
Secretary, a war-time navigation officer of a Lancaster bomber squadron,
and Air Commodore Peter Vicary, whose last appointment was Air
Office Commanding, the RAF Record and Pay Office, Gloucester –
entered the ranks under the raw discipline of the pre-war service. Such
an officer was Air Commodore McKelvey, an engineer who had joined
as a fifteen-year-old aircraft apprentice in 1929 and retired in 1969 as Air
Officer, Wales, and Commandant of RAF St Athan.

Taking over from Arbuthnot in the autumn of 1971, McKelvey had
little time to influence the year's results, but Christmas provided him with
two modest opportunities to show his mettle. Finding that in 1970 the
bustling Air Marshal Ivor Broom, commanding No. 11 Group and to be
knighted in 1975 – a Baptist minister's son of whom, as a wartime
Mosquito pilot, it had been said he could drop a bomb on a postage stamp
– had raised £630 by the sale of Christmas cards, the Fund enlarged the
idea.

Although the production and sale of greetings cards had been ruled out
previously as unrewarding, experience proved that Broom and his wife
had organised a valuable pathfinding scheme. The Brooms were
delighted to hear from the Fund that of a range of eleven designs
218,890 cards were sold. In addition 26,050 issues of very special cards
had also been sold, and, while not quite so profitable, had produced
useful publicity for the Fund.

McKelvey's second opportunity was to organise the Annual Festival of
Nine Lessons and Carols at the Royal Air Force Church of St Clement
Danes, at which the Venerable L. J. Ashton, Chaplain-in-Chief, Royal
Air Force, received on behalf of the church a casket containing gold,
frankincense and myrrh from Group Captain E. G. P. Jeffery, the last
commander of the RAF's closed Muharraq base in the Persian Gulf. If
the collection of £137.26 that December Sunday contributed marginally
to the Appeals Department's total, the occasion was of much significance
to the future promotion of the Department's work.

From his seat in the congregation, McKelvey's attention was caught by
a wood carving above the altar, the 'Pelican in Piety', which appears on

Services of Commemoration are held at St Clement Danes, the
RAF Church in London's Strand, as on the occasion of the Fund's
sixtieth anniversary in 1979. The Pelican of Piety, the basis for the
Fund's crest, surmounts the altar.

the jacket of this book and which was to become the badge of the Royal
Air Force Benevolent Fund. At Christmas 1971, McKelvey knew that the
Fund, which had hitherto adopted the RAF badge, needed an emblem
of its own – and here above the altar of St Clement Danes stood the
answer.

One of Trenchard's many services to the Fund had been his swift
gaining of permission for it to use the RAF badge as its emblem. Thus
any potential benefactor receiving an appeal on notepaper bearing the
familiar circle broken by eagle's wings and inscribed with the motto 'Per
Ardua ad Astra' would recognise its authority. The motto had been
approved for the Royal Flying Corps under an Army Order of 1913, but
it was not until 1922 that Trenchard had obtained approval of the RAF
badge – by approaching King George V personally for an immediate
signature. Thereafter the paperwork had been minimal. The King had
signed that the design was registered with the Royal College of Arms.

The RAF badge had served the Royal Air Force Benevolent Fund for
half a century but, when Air Commodore McKelvey was appointed
Appeals Secretary and fund-raising attitudes became more aggressive,
even commercial and entrepreneurial, it seemed appropriate for the
Fund to match its RAF badge with a distinctive emblem of its own. It was
an aim which McKelvey thought would present few problems but which,
without a Trenchard to march into the monarch, took five years to
achieve.

The concept began to take off when Portal, attending his last Council
meeting before his death in April 1971, said that he thought the Fund

ought to have a tie, but that this would not be possible until it had a suitable badge.

Portal was spared the agonies of the five years in which the Fund, spearheaded by McKelvey, clashed in the most gentlemanly fashion with the Royal College of Arms until agreement was reached on a design for the badge. Indeed, it was not until January 1976 that McKelvey was able to inform the Controller: 'The receipt of a recommended design for a Fund badge from Garter marks the end of a battle with the College of Arms which started early in 1971. I was particularly pleased to see that the recommended design is almost identical to the original proposal.'

The design, the 'Pelican in Piety', was chosen because the Fund felt that the pelican, shown with its babies in the carving above the altar at St Clement Danes, symbolised the humanity which guides its decisions. At the outset, the suggestion had been approved by the Venerable L. J. Ashton, the then Chaplain-in-Chief of the RAF, who wrote: 'I cannot think there would be any ecclesiological or theological reasons why this emblem should not be used and indeed it would be a happy association between the Royal Air Force Benevolent Fund and the Church of St Clement Danes.'

The significance of the Fund's selection of and insistence upon the 'Pelican in Piety' can be found in an old belief that the pelican has the greatest love of all creatures for its young and pierces its breast to feed them with its own blood. It is on this basis that the pelican came to symbolise Christ's sacrifice on the Cross because of His love for all mankind, an interpretation which is supported by Psalm 102:6 – 'I am like a pelican of the wilderness', an accepted allusion to Christ.

In practice, the long beak of the white pelican includes a sac which retains the little fish with which it feeds its young. While feeding them it presses the sac against its neck, thus appearing to pierce its breast with its bill. The belief that the pelican drew blood from its breast was given credence in folklore by the reddish tint of its breast feathers and the red tip of its beak.

Although McKelvey's memorandum to the Controller had referred to 'the battle' with the Royal College of Arms, in fairness to Garter Principal King of Arms it should be explained that the College's procrastination involved no dispute over the use of the pelican. The chief difficulty was over the inclusion and style of the crown, for which Home Office permission was required. The Home Office was sympathetic in general but appeared to disapprove of the use of a crown badge on ties.

The Home Office viewed the Fund as a civilian organisation and, therefore, held reservations about the grant and use of the ensigned St Edward's crown in the interest of maintaining the value and significance of royal emblems.

The long delay was further compounded by the unfortunate circumstance that, before a painted design could be sent to the Queen for her approval, the Herald Painter was, as York Herald of Arms informed the

Fund, 'mugged on the underground railway on his way home from work'.

It will ever remain a matter of regret to McKelvey that he had no Trenchard to bypass the middlemen, gatecrash the Palace and get the design approved on the spot.

Gradually, as McKelvey settled in as Appeals Secretary, the more contemporary fund-raising image which had seemed so desirable once the Fund had passed its half century began to emerge. The Appeals Committee, headed by Peake, was delighted in 1972 that activities to keep the Fund in the news and raise money were extended. Such events as Group Captain Douglas Bader, the legless Battle of Britain fighter ace, presenting the sports cups and prizes at Vanbrugh Castle School speech day in July, the Vanbrugh boys visiting the RAF base at Akrotiri in Cyprus in August, and a Whirlwind helicopter from the RAF station at Thorney Island giving an air-sea rescue display off the beach at Princess Marina House, played their part in helping the Fund to accumulate a total of £431,013, or about forty per cent of 1972's expenditure on the relief of distress. Among other efforts to keep the Benevolent Fund in the minds of both the public and the service were pictures of Corporal Michael Buxton of RAF, Colerne, handing a cheque of $500 to the Controller, money his team had received for winning a mock Battle of Waterloo at Houston in Texas, and also of the Controller visiting the Thrift Shop at RAF Stanmore, after it had presented £250 to the fund from its profits. Further, Air Vice-Marshal Broom had been in action again. At the annual carol service at St Clement Danes he presented the church with a goblet dating from the Napoleonic Wars 'as a late payment of a debt owed since 1940'. The goblet had been engraved by Miss Honoria Marsh, a diamond-point engraver, after being bought with money donated by Broom's No. 11 Group of Battle of Britain renown.

In another gesture to help the Fund Miss Honoria Marsh also created a larger Royal Air Force goblet. On it the artist engraved the Churchill Statue in Parliament Square and Big Ben with the hands at 19.40. Around the base of the glass are symbolic smoke and flames with the inscription: 'This Was Their Finest Hour'. Nine aircraft, including the Hurricane, Spitfire, Lancaster and Mosquito, fly around the great goblet, which also includes the badges of the Royal Air Force and the Society of British Aerospace Companies. Miss Marsh signed an inscription on the base of the bowl: 'For All Those Who Did Not Fly Home – Lest We Forget'. The goblet was purchased by the SBAC with a donation of £5000 to the Fund and is on permanent display at the Royal Air Force Museum, Hendon.

The effectiveness of keeping the Fund to the fore with the service can be appreciated from the fact that of the 1972 contributions total of £431,013 almost £351,000 had been contributed by servicemen and women, representing more than £3.25 each. However, satisfactory though this was, the Fund was concerned that those who had served were not making a comparable contribution and it was thought desirable to reach out to them and seek to supplement their share of the Royal Air

Forces Association's contribution which, in 1972, was £22,065.

Possibly the most heartening part of McKelvey's first full year as Appeals Secretary was a big leap forward in legacies and capital donations, which at £252,003 were sixty-six per cent up on the previous year. This achievement was greatly assisted by the final payment from the Hattersley Bequest through which Mr R. E. Hattersley, an Ormskirk engineer and industrialist, who had died in 1949, left his fortune to the Fund. In a Council chamber ceremony on 20 April 1972, Mr Hubert Nicholson, a former chairman of Peglers (Holdings) Limited with which Hattersley (Ormskirk) Limited had merged, handed Peake a cheque for £25,000, bringing the total bequest to more than £700,000.

Very early spring had been propitious for the Fund in this year because, six days before Mr Nicholson's visit to Portland Place, the Duke and Duchess of Kent had attended the annual concert at the Royal Festival Hall, the Duke attending as guest of honour for the first time since succeeding his mother as President. It was a happy augury because more than ninety per cent of the house was sold before the box office opened in March and within thirty minutes of its opening bookings were closed, creating a record £1780 profit for a single RAF anniversary concert and bringing the total received from seventeen concerts to £17,222.

Spring is a time of reawakening and each year the early spring flowers in Regent's Park, where Fund staff take a lunch-hour stroll, confirm that yet another Appeals campaigning season is about to begin. Preparations for the summer's regular Battle of Britain and other outdoor activities must be well advanced, including those for the money-spinning *Royal Air Force Souvenir Book*, which in 1972 and 1973 made profits of £18,553 and £21,968, shared with the Royal Air Forces Association.

However, the problem, as ever, was to create or develop new sources of income and publicity. In the spring of 1973 Coles and McKelvey, with the help of Peter Taylor, whom Peake had now invited to join the Appeals Committee, began to take a more intimate interest in the Mosquito Memorial Museum at Salisbury Hall, the birthplace of the prototype de Havilland Mosquito, near St Albans in Hertfordshire. Since its opening in 1959 and its modest gate money contributions to the Fund, the Museum had been enlarged sufficiently to attract increasing numbers of visitors until it had been acknowledged at Portland Place as a regular source of money and publicity for the Fund. By now McKelvey had joined the Salisbury Hall Committee as the Fund's representative and on 23 July 1973, at a Salisbury Hall ceremony, Group Captain John Cunningham, Chairman of the Mosquito Memorial Museum Committee, later to become the de Havilland Museum Trust Limited, presented Coles with a cheque for £1000 with which to establish the Mosquito Memorial Fund as a subsidiary fund, to perpetuate the memory of the de Havilland Mosquito and of those who fought and died in the wooden aircraft whose exploits earned it the affectionate nickname of 'The Wooden Wonder'.

In 1973 the Fund's total income of £454,506, representing thirty-five per cent of the year's outgoings on the relief of distress, together with a record of £394,472 in legacies and donations – fifty-seven per cent up on 1972 – owed much to the drive of McKelvey and his staff and Peter Taylor's public relations activities. Among these was the unveiling by Coles at the Royal Air Force Museum, Hendon, of the Fund's own exhibit. The display includes the log of Winston Churchill's flight to Moscow in 1942 and a victory bell, one of many cast from the metal of destroyed *Luftwaffe* aircraft and sold during the Second World War on behalf of the Fund. It was also a year in which the flower bed scheme, hitherto adopted at Folkestone, Blackpool, Southport and Scarborough, blossomed, enabling Taylor to report to the Appeals Committee that a particular colourful floral rendering of RAF badge and wings had been planted in Calverley Grounds at Tunbridge Wells. Further flower beds were to be planted at Torquay and Hastings in 1974 and 1975.

Here it should be added that, although the flower beds brought much pleasure to Taylor, he took more pride in being a founder member, indeed the sole survivor, of the committee which launched the anniversary concerts, having produced twenty-five programmes.

The annual anniversary concerts produced some of the more moving moments of each Appeals year, the rousing music and the RAF march evoking so many personal memories among a predominantly service and ex-service audience. But in 1974 even the thunder of the stirring RAF march was stolen as the Dam Busters March was played. For, centred in the Chairman's box as guest of honour, sat Sir Barnes Wallis, creator of the dam-busting, bouncing bomb with which in 1943 Wing Commander Guy Gibson and his Lancaster crews breached the Mohne and Eder dams. As the music filled the Royal Festival Hall the entire audience rose to its feet in honour of Wallis, an audience which undoubtedly included men who owed their survival to Wallis's sturdy geodetic construction of the Wellington bomber, and men serving in the RAF whose education had been paid for at Christ's Hospital through the foundation created by the silver-haired inventor.

Presenting Sir Barnes that evening with the Fund's Battle of Britain poignard for outstanding services to the Royal Air Force Benevolent Fund, Sir Harald Peake reminded the gathering that in 1951, despite personal needs and a large family, the inventor had given his £10,000 bouncing-bomb award to launch the educational foundation at Christ's Hospital.

In terms of publicity it was difficult to compete with the pull of the name and reputation of Sir Barnes Wallis, but throughout 1974 the Fund fostered a round of activities to keep its work before the public and help to bring in £456,792, while legacies and capital donations for the year rose a further 26.5 per cent to just under £500,000.

Christmas card sales, so tentatively developed from the Brooms' do-it-yourself pilot scheme, had grown to the extent that the Fund was now selling eighteen different designs and, thanks to two designs featuring the Red Arrows and St Clement Danes Church, donated by Chris Wren, *Flight International*'s renowned cartoonist, was planning a further sales drive for the following year.

For all this, the emphasis of appeals still lay emphatically, if understandably, on the past exploits of the RAF. This did not, however, make the Fund any the less delighted with its share of the proceeds of Battle of Britain Week, for which the RAF's maintenance of the Flight of vintage aircraft is the essential element. In this respect annual surgery and convalescence is as imperative for the Flight Hurricane, Spitfire and Lancaster as for some of the former aircrew of those historic aircraft at Princess Marina House or Sussexdown. Consequently, in 1974 the Fund was indebted to the Silentbloc Holdings Group for making it possible to run the Merlin and Griffon engines in the Spitfire and Lancaster for a further ten years. At RAF Coltishall, the home of the Flight, Group Captain L. Swart, the Commanding Officer, received on behalf of the Fund a cheque for £250 from Mr R. A. Muir, Chairman of Silentbloc, the company's nominal charge to the Ministry of Defence for 100 essential couplings.

The following year's concert opening of the campaigning season, when Air Commodore F. M. F. West, the last surviving RAF holder of a First World War VC – he died in 1988 – was guest of honour, saw the beginning of Bill Coles's round of farewells, before his retirement in August 1975 closed the happy and fruitful partnership in the fund-raising business with Peake, Holloway, McKelvey and the staff at Portland Place.

Sadly Sir William was only able to enjoy four years of retirement. He died suddenly on 7 June 1979. A Thanksgiving Service was held in St Clement Danes Church on 31 July 1979, when the Church was crowded with serving and ex-serving members of the Royal Air Force, including those on the Staff of the Fund, and representatives of the Royal Air Forces Association, the 'Not Forgotten' Association, 194 Squadron Association and the Metropolitan Police.

CHAPTER 18

FOUR EVENTFUL YEARS

Any reader of this account cannot but have been impressed by the good fortune which has attended the Royal Air Force Benevolent Fund in its choice of Controller. Throughout the Fund's first seventy years the Council appointed the man for the moment. There had been Uncle Mac, later of *Children's Hour*, who had received King Alfonso's fiver; Squadron Leader Erskine-Lindop, who had been the Secretary of the Fund during the Second World War, when it expanded tremendously, before the Fund had a Controller; Air Vice-Marshal Sir Hazelton Nicholl, who found and equipped 67 Portland Place; Cordingley, with his Victorian attention to detail and attitudes to hard work and thrift; Whitley, who visited most RAF stations; Coles the extrovert sportsman who led the Fund into the 1970s, inspiring the forward moves towards two of the Fund's greatest goals; and now in mid-August 1975, just four years short of the Diamond Jubilee, entered Crowley-Milling.

If, as the former Battle of Britain fighter pilot arrived at Portland Place

Air Marshal Sir Denis
Crowley-Milling,
Controller 1975–81.

at the age of fifty-six, it was premature to describe Air Marshal Sir Denis Crowley-Milling as yet another man for the moment, the rapid developments and the new directions leading up to the celebration of the Diamond Jubilee were to demonstrate that Peake, who had urged the appointment of Coles, had picked another winner.

It is not easy to equate the quiet, compact Air Marshal in half-moon spectacles with the fighter pilot of 1940. Even Dowding, for all his immense regard for the very young pilots he called his 'chicks', was as surprised as he was delighted in his declining years how well some of them had done in the higher ranks of the service or in business.

To name but two survivors of the Few: Group Captain Sir Hugh Dundas, who enjoyed a distinguished business career, and was to serve on the Fund's Council and Finance and General Purposes Committee until May 1989; and Mr H. M. Stephen, who became managing director of the *Daily Telegraph.*

Denis Crowley-Milling, unlike so many of his fellow survivors of the Battle of Britain and of the Second World War, had stayed on in the RAF and joined the Fund after representing Britain at the Central Treaty Organisation – an appointment reflecting his flair for diplomacy which had marked three years in the late 1960s as Commander RAF and Principal Air Attaché in Washington. These appointments had been preceded by periods commanding the RAF in Hong Kong, directing air operational requirements at the Ministry of Defence, and commanding the RAF's Nos 38 and 46 Groups.

Thirty-four years after, the Rolls-Royce engineering apprentice received an attractive offer from industry as retirement in the rank of Air Marshal appeared on his horizon. In the event Crowley-Milling sidestepped industry and, encouraged by Marshal of the RAF Sir Andrew Humphrey, then Chief of the Air Staff, who had been his Commander-in-Chief when Crowley-Milling commanded Nos 38 and 46 Groups, he accepted Peake's invitation to succeed Coles.

Taking over from Coles, the new Controller knew that he had inherited a smooth-running organisation and it was not long before the salesman in him – in Washington Crowley-Milling had played an important part in selling the Harrier jump-jet to the US Marines – asserted itself. His chief role, he decided, should be to commit his talents to the complementary interests of publicising the Fund's work and bringing the money in. It was a policy of which Peake wholly approved. At a time of relentless inflation and ever-increasing demands on the Fund's resources Crowley-Milling's drive was precisely what was required.

The new Controller looked at the figures. Expenditure at the end of 1975 after his five months in office would be running at the rate of £1,818,484 a year against ordinary income of £1,833,599. Moreover, two of the most expensive and cash-consuming developments ever undertaken by the Fund were in the pipeline: the conversion of Woolpit into Duke of Kent School and the large-scale development of Princess

Marina House. The costs of each project, with furniture and furnishings, were eventually to rise to nearly £1 million at the school and over £1 million at Princess Marina House.

As the new Controller, guided by the Council and Finance and General Purposes Committee, saw it, the Fund had spent bounteously on the post-war resettlement and housing of servicemen and women and on the education of their children, but now, with the 1980s in view, the needs of veterans of the Second World War as they reached old age had to be paramount.

Statistics do not disclose the plight of the bedridden fitter who had serviced Lancaster bombers on frozen airfields in wartime winters, the arthritic air-gunners, the varicosed, overweight former WAAF or WRAF cook, but the Fund had to face a situation in which many such people would be numbered among its beneficiaries, with disabilities ranging between ten per cent and 100 per cent. In discussions with Sir David Lee, Crowley-Milling was especially alerted by him to the numbers in which twenty per cent disability cases of more than thirty years ago developed into disability of eighty per cent or more as ex-servicemen and women advanced from middle to old age.

Most of the war-time leaders had already departed: Dowding in 1970 and in the same year Thurso, who as Sir Archibald Sinclair had been a wartime Air Minister; Portal in 1971. In the Fund's Diamond Jubilee year, Dowding's 'chicks' were in their sixties. Thus, far from the needs of ageing veterans receding, survivors of the Second World War would require ever more costly care and succour as their war began to feature in the history lessons at Duke of Kent School.

Duke of Kent School differs in so many respects from Vanbrugh that in Diamond Jubilee year, three years after Vanbrugh's merger with Woolpit, it seemed almost invidious to make comparisons. Yet such were the heart-searchings from the smallest Vanbrugh boy to the most senior members of the Fund's Council that preceded the break and the move, that respect for them demanded a hearing.

Boys and grown-ups cross such chasms with differing perspectives and yet it was Arthur Rodgers, a former Vanbrugh pupil and later a master at Duke of Kent, Bill Jones, headmaster, and Michael Morton, the Fund's longest-serving schoolmaster, who produced a common outlook. It was this: they had exchanged one remarkable view for another; they missed the quaint passages and dungeons of the castle, and the school had gained much from the admission of girls.

Each of these points serves to exemplify an essential difference between Vanbrugh Castle and Duke of Kent. If Vanbrugh might have been custom-built to appeal to the romanticism of an eight-year-old boy writing in his first week of term from the heights of Blackheath, 'Dear Mummy, I live in a castle and can hear the ships on the river at night', Vanbrugh's stout main gates, broad grey walls and crenellation presented a stark, ancient appearance.

In contrast, Duke of Kent School set in forty glorious acres in the Surrey Hills and with a view which stretches to Chanctonbury Ring – and on a clear day a blue, pinpoint glimpse of the sea – is everything a fee-paying preparatory school can aspire to be. The country mansion built in the 1880s by Sir Henry Doulton, the ceramic tile pioneer, together with the modern annexe and hall built by the Royal Air Force Benevolent Fund, combine to remind the school's boys and girls of the stolid values of Victorian Britain, while providing them with a kitchen, dining-hall, science laboratory and dormitories as remote from that period as the moon might have seemed to Doulton.

Cementing the merger, the Fund respected Doulton's fabric and interior decoration – the headmaster's tiled ornamental bathroom is a museum piece – as it also respected the memory of Woolpit School, amalgamating its traditions with those of Vanbrugh. A quiet place of worship and altar to the left of the front hall remains in use, recalling that Woolpit was founded in 1949 by Dr Francis Brown, the Rector of nearby East Clandon. Dr Brown's wish was to educate the sons of clergy and the St Thomas's Church Schools Company was formed to manage the school as it moved to Woolpit House from its one-room start in the Rectory. Dr Brown gave up his living at East Clandon and was headmaster from September 1950 until leaving five years afterwards for Milton Abbey School.

From the moment of Coles's first inquiry, Dr Brown's successor, Mr John Hall and his wife, who had come to Woolpit from the Cathedral School at Wells, put their all into smoothing the merger, retiring only after Bill and Peggy Jones were as thoroughly at home at Woolpit as they had been at Vanbrugh Castle. However, even the Halls' departure did not break the link with Woolpit's excellent record. Mr Ingram Blenkarn, who had joined Dr Brown as a master at the school's inception, stayed on and took over, among other duties, the burden of collecting the fees as bursar. His colleagues also elected to carry on. Nor were any of the eighty-five Woolpit boys removed by their parents. The Fund was also delighted that several of Woolpit's Governors, headed by Mr Trevor Jones, joined the new Board under the chairmanship of Air Chief Marshal Sir Walter Merton.

At the outset, Duke of Kent's pupil population of 135, of whom forty were Vanbrugh pupils, or Foundationers as those assisted by the Fund are known, and ten other service-connected new boys, was imbalanced in favour of Woolpit. The Fund's policy was to increase the RAF presence gradually as Woolpit boys moved on to public schools. By Diamond Jubilee year, of a total of 157 pupils there were forty-three Foundationers, seventy-seven were fee-paying service children, twenty-one were fee-paying boarders and sixteen were fee-paying private day pupils. Of the total some twenty pupils were girls of RAF parentage.

In its second term the merged school had settled down sufficiently for the Governors to welcome the Duke of Kent's offer to visit it on 3 March 1977. He lunched with the boys, talked with many of them in the class-rooms and toured the grounds and MacRobert Playing Fields.

The school, as the Duke found it, was divided into four houses named Churchill, Whittle, Armstrong and Hillary. Much consideration had been given to the selection of these names. Those of RAF leaders and heroes were avoided deliberately because Duke of Kent School included non-service children (Whittle's name was used because of his jet engine, not because he was an air commodore). Nevertheless the RAF has received its due recognition throughout the school buildings. Just as the name of the Duke of Kent's air commodore father, who was killed on active service in 1942, is honoured in the title of the school, classrooms and dormitories are named after Trenchard, father of the RAF and founder of the Fund, Tedder, deputy Supreme Commander in Europe to Eisenhower, Guy Gibson VC, leader of the Dam Busters, and many others.

The memory of Sir Harald Peake, who before his death in May 1978 had done so much in Council and Committee to ensure removal from Vanbrugh Castle and promote the wisdom of spending generously on new buildings, is fittingly perpetuated in a hangar-size all-purpose chapel, hall, theatre and gymnasium which bears his name; as it is also at the swimming-pool which he made available in all seasons by paying for a convertible roof as a personal gift to the school.

Yet such excellent facilities and heavy investment do not of themselves constitute a successful school without one essential ingredient – the right spirit. Here the Duke of Kent was impressed by the happy, well-ordered routine, the simple rules based on common sense, and an overall insistence that courtesy, kindness and consideration for others is expected at all times.

Towards the end of the 1980s when it can be argued that such standards showed a national decline, Duke of Kent School set a meritorious example. In economic service phraseology, the Royal Air Force Benevolent Fund defined the school's objectives thus: 'To provide for the optimum development of character and intellectual ability of all pupils whilst fostering the qualities of integrity, unselfishness, leadership, self-discipline and self-confidence.'

It was fitting at a time of so much change in the Fund's leadership and outlook that Marshal of the Royal Air Force Lord Elworthy, a vice-president since 1964, who was shortly to return to his native New Zealand, should address the school as principal guest at the July 1978 Speech Day and describe it as 'one of the most imaginative creations of the RAF Benevolent Fund'. The departure of the Elworthys saddened all at Portland Place, where Lady Elworthy was to be much missed in Council, as a member of the Finance and General Purposes Committee and Deputy Chairman of the Grants Committee since 1974.

In March 1979 Air Chief Marshal Sir Walter Merton, who had been primarily responsible for the 'imaginative creation' of Duke of Kent School, retired as Chairman of its Board and handed over to Air Chief Marshal Sir Lewis Hodges. After previously chairing the Vanbrugh Board since 1967 and the Fund's Education Committee and serving on the Council and Finance and General Purposes Committee, Sir Walter could leave Duke of Kent in the knowledge that it was flourishing, paying its way and full to capacity.

Determination by the Royal Air Force Benevolent Fund to extend the facilities at Princess Marina House dovetailed happily with the philosophy which had diverted Crowley-Milling from industry after retiring from the service. If the Controller and ex-RAF colleagues at Portland Place, in the Fund's branches and among its hundreds of voluntary helpers, could find pleasure and satisfaction from working and associating in a familiar, well-ordered atmosphere, then it was a duty to attempt to provide similarly congenial surroundings among the convalescent, sick and disabled, and also their dependants.

Wherever possible, present and former members of the RAF and, accommodation permitting, the Army and Navy should be rescued from the wards of a much-stretched National Health Service and cared for among people whose shared memories, experiences and standards would accelerate a convalescent's restoration to health and comfort the long-term residents.

Crowley-Milling, ably assisted by Allan Scott, threw himself wholeheartedly into the executive task of creating the development at Princess Marina House – once not unreasonably described in the RAF *News* as 'the Savoy of the South Coast' – enabling fifty long-term residents, some in need of light nursing, to be cared for, while buildings going back to Mrs Newton Driver's days continued to provide convalescent accommodation for a further fifty men and women.

Late in 1976 the groundwork resulted in the Council's approval in principle of the construction of a building to accommodate about fifty partially disabled and aged people in the grounds of Princess Marina House at an estimated cost of £800,000 and, as Peake reported to the Council, £650,000 had been appropriated from the 1976 accounts to meet part of this expenditure.

In the following year the total of guests established a new record of 569, illustrating that the Rustington complex was already bursting at the seams. However, a new house for the manager was almost ready, making his former house, Adref – part of the original arrangement with Mrs Newton Driver – available for use as a club within the large development for which planning permission had now been received.

The specification for this building work had been put out to tender and Mr Donald Ensom of Debenham, Tewson and Chinnocks had been appointed Project Manager. In consultation with Allan Scott he co-ordinated the professional team and Scott acted as the 'link man' with the Committee. Supporting its desire to press forward speedily with the work the Fund appropriated an additional £700,000 in the accounts for 1977 towards its cost.

Any novelist, playwright, short story or documentary writer short of inspiration would be rewarded by a visit to Princess Marina House. Cocooned temporarily or permanently in its comfort are to be found people with as interesting and extraordinary reminiscences as are likely to be found in any such centre in Britain.

The stories are as varied as the ages and experiences of their narrators. Nursing his beer in the club one could find Ron, who, looking back from his late eighties, could remember helping de Havilland with ex-perimental work in 1913. He served in the Royal Flying Corps in the First World War and, after a civilian interval as a toolmaker, returned to the RAF as a flight sergeant, retaining his RFC service number of 981, such a low number that wherever Ron was stationed it was difficult to convince the squadron that it was correct. He was one of the early birds of the service and one of the first long-term residents in 1969.

Toni Turton flew – yes, flew – at Netheravon in 1918 and, at the age of forty-six, rejoined in 1941. She would have jumped back into uniform at the outbreak of the Second World War had she not been in a reserved occupation as a schoolteacher. Then, at forty-six, she was allowed to resign – in consideration of her age – and rejoin.

No less absorbing are the stories of the convalescents. Obviously these will depend upon who happens to be staying as a temporary guest. On a particular morning two men and two women are exchanging reminis-cences over coffee in the sun lounge. The men are widowers and the women are widows, but it is their association with the RAF, Army or Navy rather than their bereavements that has brought them together in Sussex-by-the-sea.

There is the Chinese lady from Lymington in Hampshire. When the Second World War broke out in 1939 she was the wife of a British busi-nessman in Singapore with two small children. Her husband packed his bags and returned home to join up. When Singapore fell and the Japanese marched in she slipped quietly out of town and into her family village as a bird might seek the protective colouring of its environment. Her husband trained to parachute into Malaya to join the anti-Japanese guerrillas and in the hope of making contact with his family. Becoming unfit while training, he was unable to carry out his plan and returned with the British Military Administration when Singapore and Malaya were reoccupied in September 1945.

Now he was dead, but his widow was eligible for the care and comforts of Princess Marina House; as was the former WRAF balloon operator whose husband, who had served in the wartime Air Force, had died recently of a heart attack. Unnerved by the stress and strains of losing her husband and contending with the problems of his business, she needed a change and a rest and here she was. And here, too, were the two widowers.

Each of the men had served in the Second World War yet their lives had run dissimilar courses until a common need of convalescence had brought them together in this sunny lounge within a hundred yards of the sea. Here was Bill, who had joined the RAF as an apprentice in 1930 and had helped to plan the invasion – eventually the peaceful reoccupation – of Singapore and Malaya as a staff officer in India. He had not retired from the service until 1968 at the age of fifty-five, when he started a civilian career as an executive working with the British Aircraft Corporation on the air-support system for Concorde. After six years with the company he had started a second civilian career as a works manager in the manufacture of exhaust systems. At sixty-six, after heart surgery and the loss of his wife, he was convalescing, improving his French and planning a third civilian career in the Common Market.

Andy, the second widower, rolls up the trouser leg of his recently amputated right leg and tells his story. He is sixty-four and wears a neat white beard, but his dark, deep-sunk eyes are as quick and sharp as in the days before the Second World War when he learnt to fly as a Civil Air Reserve pilot in his native New Zealand. He flew Fairey Battles with No. 103 Squadron in 1940 and his subsequent exploits as a Wellington bomber pilot with No. 108 Squadron in the Middle East are recorded in the official history of the Royal New Zealand Air Force. But the historians do not narrate how Andy converted to Liberators and fell asleep in the Liberator ferrying his crew from the Middle East to pick up a Liberator of their own. Andy was picked out of the wreckage of the ferry Liberator in the mountains of Mourne. His legs were badly damaged and burnt but he escaped to Northern Ireland from the Irish Republic and was sufficiently repaired to return to flying and to drop paratroops from a converted Whitley bomber after the invasion of Normandy.

Now, all these years afterwards, the old leg wounds had played him up – and they had lopped a leg off at the Queen Victoria Hospital in East Grinstead, the Sty of the Guinea Pig Club, it will be recalled. There he had encountered Lady McIndoe, widow of Sir Archibald McIndoe, and she had diverted Andy in the direction of Princess Marina House whence, after a rest, he returned to his self-employed business of making and selling sails for racing yachts.

The coffee trolley is wheeled away and Sister Christine Hall reminds Bill that it is time for his heat treatment; and as it is now midday, Wing Commander Arthur Carvosso, who had managed Princess Marina House since November 1973, suggests a visit to the club. Can it be more than a coincidence that, as with Bill Jones, Headmaster at Duke of Kent School, Carvosso is a former Second World War flying instructor, that Bill Coles as an instructor had examined Crowley-Milling in the Canal Zone of the Middle East for his routine pilot's instrument re-rating?

It must be a certainty that the patience and encouragement with which pupil pilots from such varied educational and social backgrounds were taught to fly to operational standards during and after the war had equipped Bill Jones and Arthur Carvosso for their respective responsibilities in their fifties. Carvosso flew with the RAF for twenty-eight years and had all but accepted a senior post with the Red Cross when Bill Coles invited him to manage Princess Marina House. The gravitational pull of the RAF way of life, as with Crowley-Milling and almost all who serve the Fund, had proved decisive and it was only when he was interviewed for the appointment that Carvosso discovered that the Chairman of the Princess Marina House Committee was Air Chief Marshal Sir Wallace 'Digger' Kyle, the Australian whom he had served recently as personal staff officer.

Flight Lieutenant Frank Smith, Carvosso's deputy manager, came to Rustington with similar sentiments and, although no ex-officer could be more suitable for the post, his recruitment owed everything to the chance that Coles was playing golf with a Ministry of Defence friend when he dropped the hint that he was looking for a retiring officer with a Princess Mary's nursing sister wife. Could he find somebody who would fit the bill? Coles's opponent had produced Frank and Berwyn Smith and it was only after the couple had joined the staff of the Royal Air Force Benevolent Fund that Frank encountered Paul Cutting, the Secretary (Administration) and a member of the Princess Marina House Committee. Smith and Cutting had joined the RAF on the same day in the 1930s at Ruislip, where a certain Group Captain Cordingley was their Commanding Officer.

Such coincidences and service relationships cannot but fuel the great warmth and friendliness which contributes to the convalescence and well-being of the guests and residents at Princess Marina House.

Throughout the Fund's offices and branches the spirit of the RAF in war and peace pervades its welfare work, but no more so than in the Princess Marina House club where, from behind the bar in this period, the silver handlebar moustache of Squadron Leader Gower Peachment and the steady hand at the optics of his wife Peggy, recalled that he fought in the Battle of Britain and she survived the bombing of Biggin Hill, where she had been one of Dame Felicity Peake's WAAFs.

Perhaps the best feature of the whole Princess Marina House complex is the care that has been taken to facilitate the self-propulsion, either on foot, crutches or in chairs, of disabled people. Lifts do not take off like rockets, nor do they open and shut at speed as if to suit their own convenience. They await the whim of the user with admirable patience in these times of high-speed technology. Passages, such as the link-way to the club in its separate house, have been designed to make wheelchair travel possible and comfortable. This is a consideration which was especially appreciated by Lady Burton, the wife of Air Marshal Sir Harry Burton, Kyle's successor as Chairman of the Princess Marina House Management Committee, and Crowley-Milling's former Commander-in-Chief. Lady Burton, who was a polio victim and in a wheelchair, was to be a source of much practical advice.

The club was opened on 24 July 1978 by Lord Catto, shortly after his succession to the late Sir Harald Peake as Chairman of the Royal Air Force Benevolent Fund. In the course of the ceremony Catto unveiled a portrait of Marshal of the Royal Air Force Sir Andrew Humphrey, who was Chief of the Defence Staff at the time of his death at the age of fifty-six. Henceforth, the bar has been known as the Andrew Humphrey Room. It is furnished from donations received by Lady Humphrey, who is a member of the Fund's Council and Finance and General Purposes Committee, and advised on the furnishing of the development.

'There is a cosy, well-stocked and friendly little bar,' wrote Mrs Newton Driver in the post-war brochure for her Services' Club at Rustington. Although Mrs Newton Driver would not recognise the much larger Andrew Humphrey Room as it is today she would be as much at home with its users as in her wartime London club or indeed its 'cosy' pre-decessor. Nor would she fail to find the occasional familiar face. Rose Jackson, looking after the linen, was at Rustington from the start; as also was Topsy, Mrs Newton Driver's black cat. Topsy, until her death in 1979, was fed and cared for by the RAF Benevolent Fund under the terms of its acquisition of the property and Mrs Newton Driver's bequest.

Among the Fund's reasons for launching its large-scale development at Princess Marina House was a desire to overcome the problem of burdening its Storrington neighbour, the Royal Air Forces Association's home at Sussexdown, with patients suffering from extreme disability and requiring constant nursing. There will, no doubt, continue to be people for whom the Fund will seek and pay for places at Sussexdown while, reciprocally, the Royal Air Forces Association will recommend con-valescents for Princess Marina House as one of the many two-way arrangements between the organisations.

Here it should be emphasised that never in their long relationship has the rapport between the Fund and RAFA been so harmonious and it helped in recent years that Coles, Crowley-Milling's predecessor, had been the Fund's representative on RAFA's Council and that Crowley-Milling was a close personal friend of long standing with RAFA's President, Air Chief Marshal Sir Augustus 'Gus' Walker. It was particularly helpful that the one-armed Air Chief Marshal served as RAFA's representative on the Fund's Council and was a vice-president of the Fund.

With its network of clubs and representatives throughout the country, the Royal Air Forces Association gives enormous assistance by investi-gating cases on behalf of the Welfare Secretary of the Fund and his staff.

While RAFA has Sussexdown and its own convalescent home, Richard Peck House at St Annes-on-Sea in Lancashire, the interdependence of the organisations was never so evident as in Diamond Jubilee year. In the simplest terms, the apparent contradiction of there being two such organisations, with what would appear to be many similar objects, can be explained thus: their efforts are complementary. The Royal Air Forces Association normally turns to the Royal Air Force Benevolent Fund for grants and loans when it wishes to relieve the distress of its members. Through its clubs and its Battle of Britain fund-raising activities it contributes generously to the Fund. It also helps where cases are outside the Fund's scope, for example by assisting pilgrimages to war memorials and providing an advice service on pensions, disability awards and job-seeking.

The Fund, for its part, is so indebted for the assistance it receives from the Royal Air Forces Association that it will listen sympathetically to any request for special expenditure involving a large sum of money. As an example, in 1974 the Fund, after being approached by Air Vice-Marshal Sir Ben Ball of RAFA for a loan of £60,000 towards building a new wing at Sussexdown, offered an interest-free loan for the total with repayment spread over five years. In the event the RAFA repaid £30,000 and the Fund converted the balance of £30,000 to a donation, which was used to name three beds at Sussexdown in memory of Peake, Bandon and Cordingley, making a total of six beds endowed by the Fund.

Towards the end of his first six months as Controller, Crowley-Milling was as impressed as Coles had been by the sheer volume of work processed at Portland Place. In his Chairman's report for 1975, Peake, making the point that the new Controller had taken over 'a highly

The Council in session in May 1976, during the Controllership of Air Marshal Sir Denis Crowley-Milling. The President, HRH The Duke of Kent, and on his left, the Chairman, Sir Harald Peake, listen attentively as Sir Denis delivers his annual report.

efficient and dedicated staff of eighty-five men and women', said that, 'at first sight this might appear to be on the large side'. However, it had not taken Crowley-Milling very long to appreciate that, quite apart from the Fund's many other activities, servicing the Grants Committees required painstaking hours of work, often involving lengthy and detailed negotiations to provide housing, education, transport or domestic help. In 1975, not only had 7368 awards been made at a cost of £1,494,033, but 902 applications had been declined mainly due to the absence of any degree of distress. Refusals were as time-consuming as acceptances and, because it is less easy to say no, often more testing of the staff's emotional resources. It is not difficult to imagine, for example, the work involved before the following case was presented to a Committee chaired by Lady Elworthy, who in 1970 had become the first lady member of the Finance and General Purposes Committee and who was then Deputy Chairman to Air Chief Marshal Sir David Lee, Chairman of the Grants Committee.

The wife of a sergeant with seventeen years' service had died from cancer. She had been in considerable pain for some time and could not cope with their four young children. The Fund found boarding schools for the children, bought their uniforms and paid the fees after taking into

After business the annual Council meeting offers an opportunity for an informal get-together of old friends. Here the President, the Duke of Kent, talks with the Chairman, Lord Catto (facing), the then Controller, Air Chief Marshal Sir Alasdair Steedman (left) and his two surviving predecessors, Air Marshal Sir John Whitley (centre) and Air Marshal Sir Denis Crowley-Milling.

account the service educational grant. But this was only part of the Fund's involvement. The sergeant was buying a house on mortgage and, with only a short time left to serve, a move into quarters would be unsettling. The sergeant's case was strongly recommended by his station commander and the Committee sanctioned assistance which went far beyond the school fees and uniforms, taking in funeral costs and debts.

Among the year's awards there were many such considerable undertakings, but the spending of smaller sums can often involve more investigation, care and discretion. A sergeant observer had been killed in 1941 on flying operations and his mother had died soon afterwards. Now his father, aged seventy-eight, lived alone. The Fund would not have heard of this elderly man's distress and lack of interest in life had it not received an anonymous letter from a sympathiser. Because the old man's son had served and died in the RAF, the Fund made a grant to buy a new radio and other necessities.

A flying officer of the Second World War had died of cancer in December 1974, leaving a severely disabled widow suffering from osteoarthritis. She had an invalid car, but could move in her cottage only with the aid of sticks or a frame. She had lived there for some years and it was considered best that she should remain among friends, but there was the problem of meeting mortgage repayments from a very limited income. The Fund took over her mortgage with repayments delayed indefinitely.

It merits note, incidentally, that despite inflation 1975 witnessed a small reduction in cases and the cost of relief, reductions which Sir David Lee attributed to a drop in requests for house purchase loans and to increased war pensions, supplementary benefits and other pensions and allowances. It seemed, also, that the benefits of the Insurance Advisory Service and RAF Dependants Fund and Income Trust were beginning to reduce the demands on the Benevolent Fund.

In 1976 the upward trend in relief expenditure resumed, 7859 people receiving assistance totalling £1,759,626. The Fund's surplus of ordinary income over expenditure was £32,761 compared with £15,115 in 1975.

But 1977 was a very much better year. While relief of distress was as ever the first priority in spending income, the Council was much encouraged that welfare spending had dropped from 7859 cases to 6916 and the overall cost, including administration, was down to £1,689,141. Moreover, the surplus of ordinary income over expenditure had soared to £579,494. Possibly with some of the Fund's less provident beneficiaries in mind, Peake told the Council: 'It is always prudent to live within one's income and this we have again succeeded in doing.' He warned, however, that it seemed unlikely that the lower trend in the cost of relief would continue in 1978.

It fell to Lord Catto to bear out Peake's warning. Reporting to the Council on the Fund's activities in 1978, the new Chairman disclosed that expenditure of £2,023,322 on the relief of distress had exceeded

£2 million for the first time, bringing total annual expenditure to almost £2.5 million. Fortunately, however, increased income at £532,069 from the RAF and from investments – up from £1,033,239 to £1,099,637 – and a marked increase in legacies had enabled total income at £2,493,793 to exceed total expenditure of £2,488,261, if only just. At the end of the year, investments at book value stood at £9,030,796 compared with the 1977 figure of £8,617,964. In all the circumstances the Chairman regarded the results as 'highly satisfactory', a further £500,000 having been appropriated to the Development Fund which had now financed the expansion at Duke of Kent School and was financing the Princess Marina House development. Such results, Catto told the Council, were 'a great credit to his predecessor, Sir Harald Peake, who in the last few years of his life had devoted himself wholeheartedly to the Fund's interests'.

Such results, as Catto, a merchant banker, was only too well aware, could not be achieved without much painstaking work before the balance sheets could be prepared for the Finance and General Purposes Committee and the Council. Since succeeding Jack Cairns as Finance Secretary six years earlier, Ted Holloway had expanded the scope of the Finance Department considerably so that the Secretary and his staff had become much more closely involved with investment decisions and procedure. Ted Holloway accompanied the Controller at the routine meetings with Morgan Grenfell and took a leading role in the preparation of proposals for the purchase and sale of stock.

Another important aspect of the Finance Department's role in maintaining the Fund's income and capital was the persistence – and compassion – with which in this period it recovered loans. Here the Finance Secretary was much assisted by a number of ladies, each of whose length of service at Portland Place was such that their knowledge of cases stretching for many years helped them to interpret debts in human terms. It would be ungallant to the ladies who staff the department to total their combined years of service, but suffice it to say that the aggregate provides invaluable continuity, especially where loans and their repayment are concerned.

Notwithstanding the fact that in 1975 reduction in welfare cases and the cost of relief had proved short-lived, Sir David Lee, in suggesting that the Insurance Advisory Service, Royal Air Force Dependants Fund and Income Trust may have contributed to this bonus, had put his finger on a vital element as the Fund approached the 1980s, with all the threat to its financial defences an ageing ex-service population implied.

Crowley-Milling followed Coles's example of driving home the benefits of these three additional arms to the Benevolent Fund. He was ably assisted by Ginger Murray, another Battle of Britain pilot, who had now become the senior executive of the Insurance Advisory Service, and by Wing Commander Freddy Tame who, in addition to running the Dependants (Income) Trust, had taken over the secretaryship of the

Dependants Fund from Innes Westmacott, who had to leave due to the effects of injuries sustained in an aircraft crash many years previously. By the end of 1978 the Royal Air Force Dependants Fund had only to reap the remaining five per cent of servicemen and women to produce a 100 per cent membership – a prime target for the Diamond Jubilee year. It was highly telling that up to October 1978 the Trustees had made 1271 grants totalling £807,905 with each grant since the beginning of March 1977 being £900. Membership of the Royal Air Force Dependants (Income) Trust had reached some twenty per cent of Dependants Fund subscribers by 1978 as a result of an increase of 2000 in the first six months of the year. Many of the subscribers to the Income Trust had taken additional units of benefit which would have provided their beneficiaries with a greater income than the £440 per year cover provided by the basic membership benefit. On leaving the service, subscribers may without any evidence of health continue the cover provided under the Trust into civilian life as a direct policy with the underwriters. This can be in the form of an endowment or whole life cover or as similar benefits as provided under the Trust while in the service.

Meanwhile, life and other policies resulting from the counsel of the Insurance Advisory Service continued to multiply and by the end of 1978 impartial advice had – with much help from Mr R. L. Jones, the Fund's insurance consultant, and in retirement its honorary consultant – been given to 13,470 members of the RAF, the sums assured amounting to almost £21 million.

An extremely satisfactory aspect of the increasing use of the Insurance Advisory Service, RAF Dependants Fund and Income Trust was that, in the 1970s, service people were so ready to take advantage of them in addition to giving half-a-day's pay a year to the Royal Air Force Benevolent Fund and contributing through a range of activities at RAF stations. As did his predecessors since Dowding's insistence on the scheme shortly before he fought the Battle of Britain, Crowley-Milling, from the beginning of his controllership, kept a weather eye on income from the service, an income which rose to £466,733 in 1976 but dropped back slightly to £465,744 in 1977. Despite the setback Peake felt it was still a creditable achievement, taking into account a diminishing RAF and the effects of inflation. He told the Council: 'A service which helps itself to this extent need not feel ashamed of appealing for public support.'

The Controller's instinct, however, was that the service could do better and he launched a drive to secure more covenanted subscriptions, introducing the simple expedient of making it necessary to opt out of a covenant rather than into one when undertaking to subscribe to the half-a-day's-pay scheme. In 1978 of some eighty-three per cent of serving subscribers thirty-three per cent had signed covenants, contributing towards a total income from all RAF sources of £532,069.

In his early weeks at Portland Place there were moments when

Crowley-Milling, the *Financial Times* at his elbow as he settled down behind the desk in the corner of the Council chamber, must have wondered whether after all he had not opted for a career in business. He relished his share of the responsibility for the Fund's investments and power to sanction market deals within certain limits. He was most ably assisted by Ted Holloway. Indeed, he was working and living much in the style of the managing director of a fair-sized company – his 'company' had accumulated funds at the end of 1975 of about £10 million – and it helped that he was fortunate in being the first Controller to make his London home, at Peake's request, at 8 Clarendon Close in West London, a mews house which had formed part of Mrs Newton Driver's bequest. The availability of Mrs Newton Driver's London home greatly assisted Crowley-Milling's energetic pursuit of all aspects of the Fund's welfare, investment and fund-raising activities. It was a place where he could entertain Fund supporters. It was almost as if he were living 'over the shop'. His successors at Portland Place, Steedman, Kennedy, Palin and Cousins were also to make a London home there.

Peake, the banker, Catto, the merchant banker investment consultant, and Crowley-Milling, supported by an array of expertise in Council, Committee, and among the staff, presented a formidable money team behind, as Peake told the Council in 1976, his 'determination to maintain the present strong financial position of the Fund'.

In 1976 income from investment was up from £814,863 to £887,131 and ordinary income was £2,156,122 compared with £1,833,599 in 1975. One particularly satisfying aspect was the rate at which loan repayments were rising, amounting to £630,271 in 1976 against £449,259 in the previous year. Peake noted that this was partly due to the fairly recent policy of making short-term loans to members of the RAF within the last two years of their service to help them to adjust to civilian life and thereby diminish a potential source of distress. As an example, a WRAF corporal, leaving the service after twenty-two years and wishing to buy a caravan for her retirement, received a loan against her terminal gratuity so that she could have the caravan ready to move into from service quarters.

Working closely with Morgan Grenfell, the Fund kept investments under close and constant review in the years leading to the Diamond Jubilee and, while Peake's death in June 1978 was an irreplaceable loss, the election of Lord Catto, the investment consultant, to the chairmanship – he was now also chairman of Morgan Grenfell – was a considerable compensation. By 1977 accumulated funds had risen from £10,651,587 to £11,714,954. In 1978 they were £12,710,102. Investments in 1978 at book value were £9,030,225 compared with £8,617,964 in 1977 and a gratifying increase was achieved in Diamond Jubilee Year.

Legacies and capital donations were sources of addition to capital which also closely engaged the Controller's attention. The occasional windfall, such as the Hattersley bequest or a legacy of £242,000 received in 1975 from Mrs M. E. M. Lousada, whose only son Ormond had been killed as an air-gunner in November 1944, make legacies something of a lottery in the annual accumulation of capital. Donations and their sources are just unpredictable. Over the years Mr Ian Smith, the Rhodesian politician who served in the RAF as a fighter pilot during the Second World War, has remembered the Fund and its needs by passing on fees for his articles published in British newspapers. It will be recalled that when McKelvey took over from Arbuthnot in 1971 legacies had nose-dived by twenty-seven per cent to £151,691, making them nearly £100,000 down on Golden Jubilee year. Subsequently, in McKelvey's early years as Appeals Secretary, they had recovered substantially, rising from £474,357 at the end of 1975 to £493,305 at the end of 1976, Crowley-Milling's first full year. A drop to £279,786 in 1977, the year of McKelvey's retirement from full-time employment, impressed the Fund with the urgency for a special effort in this direction. Crowley-Milling therefore sought to regularise the likelihood of legacies so far as might be possible by inviting McKelvey to carry on part-time as Legacies and Trust Officer. After his experience as Appeals Secretary no one was more conscious of the needs of contact-keeping with potential benefactors and their legal and accountancy advisers, of chasing bequests in the pipeline, and hunting for new legacies. McKelvey gladly accepted the new appointment

There was the difficulty, however, with the Portland Place offices bursting at the seams, of finding suitable accommodation there. But legacy hunters are not easily daunted and McKelvey, displaying the enterprise which had brought him from boy-apprentice to air commodore, took possession of what used to be a tiny attic bathroom and very soon the results of his labours in this specialist field were apparent.

It is fitting to close this chapter with what proved to be a particularly prof-itable money-raising operation.

The Controller had long admired the wildlife and aircraft paintings of David Shepherd when the artist, grateful to the service for flying him to Aden and Nairobi, asked, 'Can I do something for the Royal Air Force?' The question, first put to Air Marshal Sir Maurice Heath, who had arranged the Aden visit, was referred to the Fund where Crowley-Milling said: 'Why not paint the last Lancaster for us?' Basically, the proposal was for a portrait of the RAF's most illustrious Second World War four-engined heavy bomber. No more than 850 signed and numbered prints were to be sold at £150 each on behalf of the Fund. Donation of a further £100 would secure one of a limited number of 176 prints signed by Marshal of the Royal Air Force Sir Arthur Harris – Bomber Harris – and by Sir Barnes Wallis, whose bouncing bomb had been carried by Wing Commander Guy Gibson's Lancaster force in the breaching of the Mohne and Eder dams.

But David Shepherd's great enthusiasm considerably broadened the project. He explains:

> I owe a very great debt of gratitude to the Royal Air Force, for it was through their flying me to Kenya in 1960 that I became a wildlife artist and it seemed only reasonable, therefore, to accept their invitation to paint a picture to raise funds for the Royal Air Force Benevolent Fund. Moreover, it was a marvellous opportunity to return to one of my first loves which I had almost totally neglected for several years, aviation art, and paint a Lancaster bomber, my favourite aircraft.
>
> I hope I have been able to evoke, in my painting, the memories and feelings which must still be fresh in the minds of thousands of ground and aircrew, now dispersed all over the world, who flew 'Lancs' with the Royal Air Force during those momentous days of the Second World War. How many must still remember 'their' Lanc at far-flung dispersals; a watery sun casting long shadows on a chill autumn evening; the leafless elms of a countryside 'somewhere in England'; the wet runway and the mud; and all the untidy clutter of last-minute preparations before take-off; final adjustments to an engine – 'the revs were a bit low on the port inner last

Air Marshal Sir Denis Crowley-Milling and David Shepherd with Sir Barnes Wallis, the airship and aircraft designer, famous for his invention of the dam-busting bouncing bombs, and benefactor of the Fund, as he signs copies of the limited edition of Shepherd's celebrated Lancaster bomber scene, *Winter of '43, Somewhere in England*, sold in aid of the Fund.

night over Essen, Fred – it's Cologne tonight, so get 'em right' – and the inevitable bicycles. I hope it is all there, the feeling of those historic times.

As the illustration of the painting shows, it was – but not before a painstaking search for period vehicles and other bomber airfield para-phernalia had authenticated the setting. On the last day the last Lanc sat for its portrait it refused to rain and water was sprayed around the dispersal point to catch the reflection of the sky.

Once the painting was ready the Fund adopted the limited-edition formula Shepherd had followed with his paintings 'Tiger Fire' and 'African Afternoon', which raised more than £200,000 between them for the World Wildlife Fund.

A reception was held in the RAF Museum, Hendon, in the spring of 1978 for the buyers of the numbered prints of 'Winter of '43, Somewhere in England'. The winner of the draw for the lucky number was offered the opportunity of commissioning the artist to paint free of charge a canvas measuring up to thirty inches by twenty inches, framed, of any aircraft in flight or any wildlife subject.

The net proceeds of £91,000 were devoted to Princess Marina House, the development of which and the care of its residents owes so much to the generosity of David Shepherd.

The International Air Tattoo, staged first at RAF Greenham Common and more recently at RAF Fairford, has proved a magnificent fund-raising attraction.

CHAPTER 19

THE INTERNATIONAL AIR
TATTOO IS INTRODUCED

For some while before Crowley-Milling's appointment as Controller, his predecessor, Air Marshal Sir William Coles, and Air Commodore McKelvey, the Appeals Secretary, had been nurturing an idea. It has been seen how in Coles's time the Appeals Committee had started to seek ways of bringing in money and publicising the Fund which would free it of excessive reliance upon the RAF's glories and in particular the events of 1940. In mid-summer 1975, McKelvey, recognising the salesman in the new Controller and confident of an enthusiastic response, said: 'Why don't we go back into the business of airshows?' After all, if flying was what the RAF was all about and peacetime conditions had reduced the operational opportunities of a much-contracted service, then – as the Society of British Aerospace Companies spectacular exhibition and flying displays, mostly of civilian aircraft, at Farnborough had shown – the Fund's own airshows of service aircraft ought to be capable of providing the complementary benefits of bringing in money and generating useful publicity.

Making his submission, McKelvey played the trump card that a fund already existed within the Royal Air Force Benevolent Fund for the specific purpose of organising air displays. This was the Royal Air Force Benevolent Fund Development Trust, which had been formed twenty-five years earlier with a grant of £30,000 from the Air Council and which, when the Appeals Secretary approached the Controller, had reached almost £100,000.

Crowley-Milling was immediately attracted by the proposal. Having joined the Fund within a month of retiring from the service he was only too well aware that RAF cutbacks had reduced the fund-raising 'At Home' days at its stations. Thus, when the Royal Air Forces Association, which for the past five years had run a series of volunteer-organised Embassy Air Tattoos supported by W. D. and H. O. Wills, abandoned its plan for a 1975 air tattoo after withdrawal of the tobacco company's overall support – the financial risk was unacceptable – the Royal Air Force Benevolent Fund decided to step in.

Confronted by the risk element Peake brushed it aside: 'Find the man to run it and go ahead.' McKelvey already had his man and he returned to Paul Bowen, the acknowledged expert in the air tattoo business, who had just seeded the idea with the Appeals Secretary for a two-day International Air Tattoo at RAF Greenham Common near Newbury in Berkshire.

When it happened on the weekend of 31 July and 1 August 1976, fifty-six years after the Fund's first tentative Aerial Pageant at Hendon in 1920, the International Air Tattoo was a vast success.

Organised on a scale beyond the wildest dreams of Air Vice-Marshal Sir John Salmond – who, having been over-modest about possible takings in 1920, had sent six officers' wives home with £1000 each to put under their pillows for the night – it yet retained at least one link with Hendon's glorious past: presiding over the organising committee was the legless Battle of Britain air ace, Group Captain Sir Douglas Bader, who, as a very junior officer, had flown in some of the pre-war air displays.

When Crowley-Milling, as Chairman of the Tattoo, McKelvey, Bowen, Tim Prince and Frank Windle, the directors of flying and administration respectively, and their committee colleagues immersed themselves in preparations there must have been moments when they were appalled at the magnitude of what they had set out to achieve. Never before in Western Europe had such an ambitious air display been attempted. Detailed planning was required to accommodate and fly more than 200 aircraft from twenty air forces.

Sir Douglas Bader, the then President of the International Air Tattoo, greets the Duke of Kent at RAF Greenham Common on the occasion of the 1981 event.

Naturally, the RAF provided the centrepiece of the tattoo. Led by the Red Arrows aerobatic team it thrilled crowds of an estimated 120,000 people over two days with the Gazelles helicopter team, its Falcon free-fall parachutists, and Harrier, Phantom, Lightning and Vulcan displays. Since no such show would be complete without the Battle of Britain Flight, the Lancaster, Hurricane and Spitfire received an ovation which owed as much to their presence as to the knowledge that presiding over the proceedings was the legless ace who in September 1940 had led the wing of sixty Hurricanes and Spitfires from five of No. 12 Group's squadrons stationed behind London to give *Luftwaffe* aircrews a 'pasting' over the capital. Not until this surprise deployment of Air Vice-Marshal Leigh-Mallory's Big Wing tactic had the *Luftwaffe* encountered so many RAF fighter aircraft at one time over London and south-east England in daylight.

But this was history, better left perhaps to Bill Jones and his staff at Duke of Kent School, because also here at Greenham Common were NATO aircraft and crews, possibly including the sons or grandsons of the German pilots who had jousted with Bader's wing of British, Canadian, Czech and Polish squadrons in the summer of 1940.

Here, too, was the United States Air Force, sympathetic but neutral in 1940, but with a Flying Fortress at Greenham to remind spectators of its part in destroying Nazi Germany's industrial war machine and a fly-past of its swing-wing F-111s to emphasise its predominant role in the West's NATO shield. As Paul Bowen was to note, without the enthusiasm and unstinting support of General Ellis, Commander, United States Air Force, Europe, Major-General Evan W. Rosencrans, Commander 3rd Air Force, USAF, his staff at RAF Mildenhall and the commanding officer, officers and men of the USAF based at Greenham Common, the tattoo would not have been possible.

Much financial assistance and practical help in kind was received also from the great commercial enterprises which in the past had built Britain's air power, often with private venture aircraft such as the Spitfire, Wellington and Mosquito. For instance, Hawker Siddeley, apart from making a donation of £5000 through an advertisement for the programme, had helped to create an International Hunter Meet, a gathering of twenty-five Hawker Hunters. Sponsors were many and generous and especially welcome was W. D. and H. O. Wills whose withdrawal of support had ignited the Fund's determination to go it alone, yet who nevertheless participated, supplying a £1000 silver Embassy Jet Aerobatic Trophy to award to Europe's best aerobatic pilot; while Shell provided a trophy for the best individual effort.

After the weekend, when the money had been counted, Crowley-Milling was tempted, in honour of Salmond, to put £43,292 under his wife's pillow for the night. But the Fund had moved on since 1920 and Wing Commander Holloway, the Finance Secretary, might have been appalled. In the event, the Royal Air Force Benevolent Fund kept

£35,622 after making payments to local charities and the funds of the other services in recognition of their contribution to the success of International Air Tattoo '76.

Despite the success, it would have been understandable if, upon reflection, the Fund had refrained from organising further tattoos. Behind the achievement lay a mountain of administrative detail during which many lessons had been learnt, not least that where aerobatics are concerned local farmers appreciate more than two weeks' notice.

No such undertaking is likely to be without its crisis. There was very real alarm in the week before the Tattoo when contractors warned that they could not lay cables to the exhibition site and catering tents because cable supplied by the Army was unsuitable. Yet such is the Fund's rapport with industry that McKelvey telephoned the managing director of Sterling Cables, who had the correct cable delivered the same day – and with the compliments of the company.

The International Air Tattoo was here to stay, a new concept in aviation celebration pioneered by the Royal Air Force Benevolent Fund in partnership with Paul Bowen, its Tattoo Director, Bowen's small permanent staff and many volunteer helpers.

After the experience of 1976 the 1977 International Air Tattoo was even more successful, 120,000 visitors and impressive donations and assistance from industries and individuals contributing towards a profit of £80,000, every pound of which was earmarked for the Princess Marina House development.

The entertainment provided by the 1976 and 1977 Tattoos and their financial success had more than justified the more aggressive fund-raising posture which Crowley-Milling, jet-propelled by Peake's ready-to-have-a-go philosophy, had introduced.

Such was now the recognition of the Royal Air Force Benevolent Fund's Tattoo as the international meeting place of so many air forces and as an exhibition centre for companies in the aerospace sector of industry that, after its further success in 1977, the Fund decided to make the event biennial. The chief reason for this was an earnest desire not to compete with its generous supporter, the SBAC's biennial Farnborough Air Show.

Therefore, airshows were organised in the fallow years, like the Anglo-American Air Festival which Paul Bowen's team fielded at Bassingbourn on 27 and 28 May 1978 at the invitation of Lt-Col H. M. du V. Lohan, Commanding Officer, Depot, The Queen's Division. Although attendance at 50,000 was less than half that at RAF Greenham Common, the effort was rewarded by profits of about £32,000, half of which came to the Fund, the other half being shared between the Army Benevolent Fund and the Ex-Services Mental Welfare Society. Moreover, it combined the merits of enabling the Tattoo team to sharpen its edge for Diamond Jubilee year and providing a baptism for Air Commodore Rooney who, after McKelvey's retirement in July 1977, was now the

Prince Michael of Kent was on hand to congratulate five winners of Sir Douglas Bader Flying Scholarships at the 1983 Tattoo. Left to right: Mr A. Barratt; Miss T.J. Mattinsley; Mr T.R. Leonard; Mr G.J. Rann and Mr P.J. Lowe.

Appeals Secretary and would very soon be involved with the arrangements for the Tattoo of Tattoos on the weekend of 23 and 24 June 1979. Sadly Rooney died on 17 March 1979, after a short illness.

To visit RAF Greenham Common in March twenty years ago was to gain an insight into the build up of successive June Tattoos. Dark rain clouds shrouded the Berkshire Downs in the direction of Highclere, where the Queen's horses exercised for the approaching flat-racing season. The air base with its runway and taxiways – their wide acres gave away that they were built to accommodate the B-52 – was empty and silent and it was a relief to see a patrolling police car. Yellow petrol bowsers stood despondently at dispersal points as though forgotten after some long-past emergency. It was eerie, but in the stillness of this vast air base in deep-freeze search for life ended at two tall flagstaffs which flew the RAF and United States colours outside an office building. Inside a coloured US Air Force sergeant, scarred and decorated, a man who had known Saigon, answered: 'The International Air Tattoo? Sure, Hut 91.' He belonged to the 7273rd Air Base Group, USAF, which maintained this ghost air base as a stand-by for NATO reinforcement. Thanks to the Americans this Second World War glider base was in mint condition and its runway had been resurfaced recently. Two miles south of Newbury and midway between London and Bristol on the M4, it was the ideal venue for the biennial International Air Tattoo, presented in aid of The Royal Air Force Benevolent Fund in association with Nationwide Building Society. There was the extra advantage that rail and light civil aircraft visitors could arrive at the adjacent race-course's railway station or landing strip. The racecourse also provided a campsite. Fees received by the racecourse were devoted to the Injured Jockeys' Fund.

Hut 91 was more reassuring than its avenues of deserted neighbours. There was the tap of typewriters, the ringing of telephone bells, a clinking of coffee cups. Paul Bowen, the Tattoo Director, was speaking to Amman: 'Yes, we'd love to have the Royal Jordanian Air Force. Will the King be attending himself? Well, we have to ask such questions.' Tim Prince, the Flying Director, called Switzerland. He understood the Swiss Air Force never left home, but hoped to send a team in June. Excellent, but what back-up aircraft were available? There was a silence and some embarrassment. It seemed that the only support aircraft available were two Ju 52s received as a gift from Adolf Hitler before the Second World War and the Swiss did not wish to offend any sensibilities. It was difficult to explain to them that, a Ju 52, would of itself make a star attraction for the Tattoo.

While Bowen and Prince were processing inquiries from some twenty air forces and several companies offering teams for the Fund's Diamond Jubilee year Tattoo, permanent and volunteer staff acknowledged the daily receipt of cheques in payment of advance bookings which provided an all-important cash flow. Bowen picked a cheque from the pile. It was drawn on a bank in Melbourne and it was from an Australian who had booked through the Melbourne Tourist Office and was bringing his family. Sensibly, the Australian had applied for club memberships of Friends of International Air Tattoo '79. It was open to adults aged seventeen or over at £10 and at £5 for children from the age of twelve. It provided a family season ticket for the two-day event and included such additional services as mailed news sheets and a ten per cent discount on all official souvenir items.

Hut 91 was deceptive. Its bright decor, fitted carpets and busy type-writers were out of dimension with the arena within which it organised an International Air Tattoo for two days every two years and possibly an intervening but smaller air show elsewhere.

Paul Bowen thus builds up a picture of International Air Tattoo '79, but it could as readily be that of '76 or '77 – before the decision was taken to go biennial – or of '81, and even '89.

As spring moves into summer 100 soldiers will arrive from Army barracks at Bassingbourn in Hertfordshire to move stored bedding into the village of empty barrack blocks. Civilian contractors will transform the bleak grass verges of the runway with instant chalets, enclosures, tents and gardens for the banks, aerospace and other business enterprises which invite guests and parties to this Derby-week event of the world of international aviation. The President's enclosure, sponsored by Nationwide Building Society, and the pilots' enclosure, sponsored by Wilkinson Match Safety Division will be prepared and the ground exhibition contractors will move in.

The loss of tranquillity on this giant air base is a gradual thing from the first spasmodic hammering until all is built, all is ready, and there is a momentary return to silence.

By now Bowen, Prince and their small permanent staff are being re-inforced by an army of dedicated volunteers – dogsbodies as they self-deprecatingly call themselves – who take service leave or civilian holiday to help the Fund. Frank Windle, a captain in the 28th Amphibious Engineer Regiment, arrives from West Germany as director of administration; Kit Townend, an aviation scientist who has arranged publicity throughout the run-up, arrives from Bournemouth; and among many others with specialist volunteer posts Annette Hill, who as a wartime Air Transport Auxiliary pilot logged 1200 hours in Spitfires and similar types, is information officer.

More than 200 flying aircraft and some 140 static exhibition aircraft require considerable turn-round expertise in support of air force or company groundcrews. To supply such technical services, including refu-elling, twenty-five ground staff come in from the Aircraft and Armament Experimental Establishment at Boscombe Down, where the RAF's cele-brated Empire Test Pilots' School retains its honoured pre-Commonwealth title.

The prerequisite of any flying display is safety. In the run-up Duncan Simpson, former chief test pilot for Hawker Siddeley, later deputy director of the Society of British Aerospace Companies, selects and chairs his team of test pilots and others with experience of Farnborough, Paris and previous International Air Shows. Painstakingly Simpson and his Flight Safety Committee vet every visiting pilot, team and 'act', and where necessary reject performers even if their aircraft and crews have arrived.

By now a ghost air base has been transformed into a ghost airshow until in the silence the first approaching aircraft is heard. From this moment the International Air Tattoo is truly in business to bring money into the Royal Air Force Benevolent Fund. For a year the control tower has been a shell. Now five volunteer Civil Aviation Authority air traffic controllers who have given up holiday time begin to work to the tight schedule which Bowen and Prince – themselves former air traffic controllers who resigned from secure civil service posts to become International Air Tattoo and Aviation Consultants – have prepared in the past months.

Perhaps the first aircraft to touch down is *City of Ardmore*, the first production C-130 still in service with the United States Air Force, the first of some twenty-five Hercules transport aircraft flying in for the Hercules Meet, the feature of the 1979 Tattoo. For not only is it the Royal Air Force Benevolent Fund's Diamond Jubilee year, but it is also the twenty-fifth anniversary of the introduction of the western world's air force and civil air freight Hercules fleets. Twenty-five years after the second Lockheed prototype C-130 flew in California, and with more than 1500 Hercules aircraft in use, the Hercules Industry Team, comprising twelve companies involved in the aircraft's production and components, has made the Fund's Tattoo the venue of its own celebration.

Although the Hercules Meet was the feature of the 1979 Tattoo, anniversaries can sometimes accumulate in embarrassing numbers, as happened in the Fund's Diamond Jubilee year. The Tattoo staff were

Disabled and disadvantaged children receive VIP treatment as guests in the Fund's enclosure at the International Air Tattoo.

stretched to accommodate them. However, it was not overlooked that on 15 June 1919 Captain Alcock and Lieutenant Brown, flying a Vickers Vimy, completed the first non-stop trans-Atlantic flight from Newfoundland. Consequently, as it also happened to be the twenty-first birthday year of the McDonnell-Douglas F-4 Phantom, a trans-Atlantic west-east flight was arranged for Press day. Appropriately the Phantom was crewed by Squadron Leader Alcock, a nephew of Captain Alcock, sponsored by Rolls-Royce, whose engines powered the Vimy and the Phantom, and a fellow officer named Browne.

Other anniversaries commemorated at the International Air Tattoo '79 were the maiden flight twenty-five years earlier of the English Electric (BAC) Lightning and the thirtieth birthday of the English Electric Canberra; each aircraft was still in RAF service. Finally on 5 April 1979, it was also the thirtieth anniversary of the fifteen member countries of the North Atlantic Treaty Organisation, in the absence of which RAF Greenham Common would probably not be available for such a magnificent fund-raising opportunity.

Such is the variety of the types and nationalities of the aircraft and their crews as they arrive that the skilled Civil Aviation Authority volunteers in the control tower can expect surprises. The mix is almost unbelievable. Here comes a Hercules, now a torpedo-carrying Swordfish biplane, a Dakota, a Lancaster, the Red Arrows, a Spitfire, a Tornado, a Hurricane, a Tomcat, yes and here are the teams from the Royal Jordanian and Austrian Air Forces. Truly an aviation cocktail of high-octane ingredients.

As the aerobatic and display teams of at least twenty air forces and several civilian companies fly in in Marlboro and Rothmans Pitts Specials, and the Goodyear airship arrives, the Flying Control Committee meets.

In the past months there will have been many meetings, of which the most important have been regular progress committees, but now the Flight Safety Committee's deliberations and recommendations transcend all other considerations. With so many air forces, so many teams and individual competitors of so many nationalities and languages exhibiting their pilot skills above many thousands of spectators in this international meeting-place of the air, the Royal Air Force Benevolent Fund takes the realistic view that safety is the critical factor. An Army field hospital has been staffed and casualty evacuation helicopters stand by, but every precaution is taken to see that they will not be required.

Never in the field of aviation, as Winston Churchill might have said, was so much tact and diplomacy called for. Pilots who do not measure up to the Committee's standards are forbidden to fly. Pilots who deliberately flout its rules are sent home. There are heartaches, but poor rehearsal does not preclude below-standard performers from practising and improving in time for reassessment before the Tattoo opens.

While the Lockheed-Georgia Company's award of the Hercules

Concours d'Elegance Trophy for the best turned out Hercules attending the Meet presents no such problem, the Flying Control Committee is much exercised to preserve a balance between the brilliance required to win the flying trophies and its requirements.

The principal trophies at the Diamond Jubilee year Tattoo were the Embassy Trophy, presented by W. D. and H. O. Wills for the winner of the international jet aerobatic competition – the pilot who gives the best solo jet performance; the International Display Sword presented by Nationwide Building Society for the best flying display by an overseas competitor; and the Shell-UK Oil Trophy for the best overall flying display.

Each International Air Tattoo has its special features – the Hunter of 1976, the Tiger Meet of 1977 and the Hercules Meet of 1979 – but pervading the two-day event is its central theme, which as its late president, Sir Douglas Bader, stated, is to foster friendship among participating nations, to allow NATO and other armed forces to demonstrate their roles and above all to help the Royal Air Force Benevolent Fund keep pace with the continuing inflation which ever increases the cost of relieving distress.

All too soon the two days have passed and the last of the farewells have been said, but friendships have been forged which will be renewed in two years' time, possibly earlier at Farnborough or in Paris and in service or business exchanges. The last visiting aircraft departs, the instant gardens wither in the skips of their removal, the tents, chalets and enclosures disappear and local farmers breathe 'Thank God'.

As RAF Greenham Common resumes its bleak appearance there is a big smile on the face of Sheila Pinnegar, Deputy Secretary Finance to Wing Commander Holloway and finance manager of the International Air Tattoo. Yet again the takings are up and, after donations to other service and local charities in recognition of their help, the Fund has done well, with every penny earmarked for the Princess Marina House development.

After the event, Paul Bowen, Tim Prince, their staff and volunteer dogs-bodies experience depressing withdrawal symptoms. After so many months of so much effort it would be surprising if in the emptiness of the air base and the stillness of Hut 91 there were not a sense of loss and deprivation, a feeling of 'that was the Tattoo that was'. The psychological factor is recognised by the current Controller and this is why the next Tattoo begins where the last one ends.

CHAPTER 20

THE STEEDMAN YEARS

Alastrean House –
'A place of honour by the hearth for the winged ones.'

Lady MacRobert

When Air Chief Marshal Sir Alasdair Steedman was appointed Controller in 1981 he was already well acquainted with Portland Place. The Commandant of the RAF Staff College served as an ex-officio member of the Fund's Finance and General Purposes Committee and, holding this appointment from 1972 to 1975, he had attended committees under Peake's chairmanship. Since the Commandant's wife is a member of the School committee, Dorothy Steedman also had a head start. Aged eighteen, and just finishing his education at Hampton Grammar School, in 1940 Steedman saw the

Air Chief
Marshal Sir
Alasdair
Steedman,
Controller
1981–88

condensation trails of the Battle of Britain, heard the rattle of gunfire and wished he was up there. He volunteered, learned to fly near Stoke-on-Trent and got his wings under the Empire Air Training Scheme at Swift Current in Canada. He was to have been a fighter pilot, but learning that there was a six-month wait, he volunteered for an Army Co-operation squadron. He never regretted it.

Inevitably Controllers arrive at Portland Place conditioned by their service careers and, being human, not without a prejudice or two in their outlook. Steedman, privately a compassionate man, came in at a time when the crescendo of need for which his predecessors, 'the building Controllers', as he describes them, had prepared was beginning. Circumstances dictated his self-declared role as a spending Controller. The figures speak for themselves. In 1980 the Fund paid out £2.709 million on 8128 awards. In his last full year (1987) 14,777 cases were assisted at a total of £8.56 million.

A natural evangelist and fluent speaker, Steedman was a tireless traveller, spreading the Fund's message at home and overseas. Rapt gatherings at RAF stations were astonished. To many the Fund had been a mysterious treasure chest into which they dropped their annual donation of half-a-day's pay and which distributed it to the needy survivors of two wars. Now here was a forceful and compassionate man who probed the needs of serving men and women and their dependants; who explained that its most costly cases are very often those of men or women who die, suffer accident, disablement or disease while serving; that the Fund helps families rebuild their lives; that it buys more houses for widows than it sells.

Of all the Controllers, Steedman came closest to succumbing to the occupational hazard of letting his heart rule his head. To his inherently compassionate nature was added an imaginative tendency to identify with those the Fund was helping. The buff folders at Grants Committees were people not cases and never more so than when applicants were members of the Guinea Pig Club. Burned on the legs and arms in Italy as a No. 241 Squadron Spitfire fighter pilot, he felt a special affinity with 'McIndoe's Army', in the words of the Guinea Pig anthem in which he joined heartily as a guest at East Grinstead reunions.

Peake's death in 1978 was a paramount influence on the swift, almost abrupt imposition by Steedman of his style on the conduct of the Fund's affairs. While Peake, perhaps the Council's most energetic chairman, probed detail and liked to maintain a strong grasp through his chairmanship of the Finance and General Purposes Committee, his successor, Catto, while no less dedicated, preferred to keep Steedman on a very long rein. This suited each man's *modus operandi* perfectly and Steedman remained indebted to the chairman for his trust and confidence. As station commander at RAF Lyneham during Air Chief Marshal Sir Edmund Hudleston's period as leader of Transport Command, he had admired the Commander-in-Chief's talent for briefing subordinates and then letting them get on with it. It was a lesson Steedman applied as he himself climbed to Air Rank and which he carried with him to Portland Place.

Personal initiatives on the part of Controllers, as with Coles's seizure of the opportunity to move Vanbrugh to Woolpit and evolve the Duke of Kent School, have inspired some of the Fund's most fruitful decisions. Steedman, a Scot, was perhaps more aware than his predecessors of the disparity between north and south in the provision of convalescent and residential care. When he heard that Alastrean House, formerly House of Cromar, a seat of the Aberdeens, and more recently belonging to the MacRobert family, might be available, he moved fast. MacRobert benevolence towards the RAF had not ceased with MacRobert's Reply, the Stirling bomber, and Sir Roderic, Sir Alasdair and Sir Iain, three of the four Hurricane fighters presented to the RAF by Lady MacRobert in memory of her baronet sons during the war.

The house had since been a convalescent home and then a leave centre for officers. Ending that role for Alastrean, the MacRobert Trusts were obliged by the deeds to offer Alastrean to the Fund. It must have helped though that Air Marshal Sir Richard Wakeford, chairman of the Trusts, was also the Fund's director in Scotland. So Air Vice-Marshal Frank Dodd, the Trusts' administrator, called Steedman from Scotland: 'You don't want it do you?' Dodd was both surprised and pleased when Steedman, after a quick staff study, said enthusiastically, 'Yes please.' A £5 a year peppercorn rent was agreed. Additionally the Trust provided £120,000 for conversion to accommodate the disabled, and a further £360,000 towards the £500,000 cost of an extension. There could have

Alastrean House residents enjoy a round on the putting course.

been no more satisfying farewell in Steedman's last week as Controller than to attend the opening on 27 July 1988 of the Care Wing by the Duke of Kent, the occasion of the President's first visit to Alastrean.

Situated near the village of Tarland in the scenic rolling foothills of the Grampians, Alastrean, attractively fashioned in pink granite, is somewhat reminiscent of a small chateau. It has established itself with so much popularity as a retirement home since it opened in 1984 that there is always a waiting list for residential beds. But Mrs Maureen Robertson, its bustling manager, accepts that this does not imply Alastrean is suitable for every applicant. Its peaceful seclusion, while attractive to many elderly people, is not universally so. Thus great care over selection of applicants is taken at Portland Place and the Fund's Scottish branch in Edinburgh, and every prospective resident lives in for a trial period of eight weeks. But once happily settled, a resident slips contentedly into a cosy, if cocooned routine of comfort. The standard of accommodation and meals is that of a good country hotel, with the assurance that in the event of illness or serious disability matron will cosset one in the care quarters. There are eight double and twenty-four single rooms, and most have an *en suite* bathroom. Inability to pay does not exclude, but those of sufficient means contribute £98 weekly towards the £180 a week cost (subject to change), which is excellent value.

Tasteful conversion has created a retirement home, but the grounds are much the same as when the Aberdeens, the *Wee Twas* as they were affectionately known by their Balmoral neighbours, inhabited the House of Cromar. The Chinese Rowan tree planted by the Duke of Kent to commemorate his visit sustains a tradition, an avenue of royal trees dating back beyond Queen Mary and to the turn of the century when the house was built by the seventh Earl of Aberdeen. Created Marquis of Aberdeen and Temair in 1915 after being Viceroy of Ireland, he died in 1934 and the house passed to Lady MacRobert, widow of Sir Alexander who had made a fortune in India and who owned the neighbouring estate of Douneside. It is fascinating to reflect that had not MacRobert, who left school in Aberdeen at thirteen and rose from clerk in Cawnpore to founder of the giant British India Corporation, secretly paid some of Aberdeen's considerable debts, Alastrean's present residents would not be living there. MacRobert had eased Aberdeen's problems knowing that under a settlement agreed in 1919 the house would some day pass to his family.

Another chance circumstance also contributed to the Fund's eventual good fortune. MacRobert's wife, Georgina, had died in 1904, and in 1911 he married Rachel, daughter of the American-born Himalayan explorers, Dr and Mrs William Hunter Workman. Rachel's eldest son having been killed in a flying accident in 1938 and her husband's brothers having been killed in the war in 1943, as has been described earlier, she endowed the House of Cromar as an RAF aircrew leave centre and renamed it Alastrean. The name is a compound of *alar*, a wing or winged one, *astre*, a hearth or home, and *astrean*, belonging to the stars. Though many have surmised that the name is an amalgamation of her sons' christian names, Lady MacRobert regarded it as representing 'a piece of honour by the hearth for the winged ones'.

She died in 1954, but Alastrean's management committee chairman, Air Marshal Sir Peter Bairsto, Dodd's successor as the Trusts' administrator, Lieutenant-General Sir Robert Richardson, Colonel of the Royal Scots, and their colleagues perpetuated her sentiment. Certainly her presence remains pervasive. She is buried at the foot of a massive piece of red granite in her Douneside garden and the ashes of her eldest son, Sir Alasdair, lie in a great cairn in the grounds of Alastrean.

Alastrean exudes an atmosphere of quite contentment. The eight-week trial period normally eliminates applicants who find it too reclusive. This is not to say that residents opt out totally, but for a man like James, an octogenarian former prisoner-of-war of the Japanese who escaped from Singapore in 1942 only to be recaptured in Rangoon, or his friend, an RAF widow in her eighties, it is a rest home second-to-none. As with Princess Marina House, any balance of Alastrean's fees, after private and DHSS deductions, is paid from Portland Place, where Group Captain Don Starkey looked after the paperwork for both homes. Fortunately, the conversion of the Aberdeen family's House of Cromar has been so discreet that there is no suggestion of institutional life, a happy circumstance which was much assisted by the cheerful and totally unstarched manner of Maureen Robertson, the manager, Kathleen Diack, the matron, and the nursing and domestic staff who cared for forty residents. Moreover, Mrs Robertson, always aware of the possibility of problems arising from Alastrean's remoteness – though Tarland village is but a step away – arranged shopping trips to Aberdeen, twenty-five miles distant. She also encouraged hobby activities – there is a well-equipped workshop – and arranged games nights.

Stages in Alastrean's development, from the moment of that twinkle in Steedman's eye when Dodd offered the MacRobert Trusts' property to the Fund, reflect the alacrity with which it was gratefully accepted and converted from its previous role as a leave centre for RAF officers, dating as far back as 1943. In 1984, after the changeover, the central heating system was replaced and upgraded. To supervise the work, the Fund appointed a Board of Management under the chairmanship of Bairsto, a former fighter pilot and at the time only just retired as Deputy Commander-in-Chief, Strike Command. One of his first actions was to ask Maureen Robertson to stay on. Such was Bairsto's expedition that on 20 May in the next year the Fund's residential home for the north of England and Scotland was functioning. Then, on 27 September the Queen Mother, recalling memories of visiting Lady Aberdeen there with Queen Mary and the future King George VI in 1924, was welcomed by Air Marshal Sir Richard Wakeford, as Chairman of the MacRobert Trusts, and Catto.

By 1986 Alastrean was well established as Princess Marina House's northern counterpart in most respects but one. It lacked a care wing, an omission which Steedman moved swiftly to make good. The Fund's Finance and General Purposes Committee gave its blessing and with the sanction and financial help of £360,000 from the MacRobert Trusts, an extension (which includes six single hospital rooms on the ground floor and nine first floor rooms adaptable as singles, or doubles for married couples, and also as nurses' accommodation) was operational that June. Opened formally by the Duke of Kent on 27 July 1988, its popularity has since produced a waiting list.

There is also a waiting list for Princess Marina House, a reversal of the situation at sunny Rustington early in Steedman's career as Controller. Much had happened at the Sussex home since an active year in 1978 when Catto had opened the Andrew Humphrey Room and Crowley-Milling had signed the contract for its £1 million development. Building the new North Wing went ahead in the next year while Newton Driver House was converted into nurses' flats. Meanwhile, Lady Humphrey chaired a committee to furnish the new wing. Despite the inevitable disruption during construction, Princess Marina House accommodated 539 convalescent guests at a cost of £100 each, though no guest was asked to contribute more than £50 a week, nor was anybody unable to afford the sum turned away. On 9 July 1980, the North Wing, named after the President's mother, was opened by the Duke of Kent.

Assessing occupancy at Princess Marina House shortly after arriving at Portland Place in 1981, Steedman noted that it was building towards 100 per cent, but was concerned that the rank balance favoured officers and their widows. He urged an increase in its use by NCOs and airmen, or their dependants. Next year the benefits of the major development were more evident and satisfying. The North, or Care Wing, contained forty-nine residents, each of whom was eligible to remain for life, while the numbers of guests, mostly fortnightly convalescents, accommodated in the South Wing, continued to rise. Elderly, frail, or just lonely people unable to afford a change were also welcomed.

As the Care Wing settled down, lessons were learned, one of which was that the incidence of infections and illness rendered its four-bedded wards unsuitable. Consequently, in 1983 one such ward was divided into three single rooms, facilitating private nursing care where necessary. By 1984 the number of convalescent holiday visitors had climbed to 1000 and produced a waiting list. In the next year, need, always the decisive factor in accepting applications for both wings, was more than ever the imperative of a 'passport' to Princess Marina House. The South Wing received 1010 guests and at the North Wing, full the year round, vacancies were filled immediately from the waiting list. Much the same situation pertained in 1986, and in order to achieve Steedman's desired rank balance a temporary embargo was placed on applications from former officers and their dependants.

Taking stock of Princess Marina House's physical inability to cope with an ever increasing demand, the Fund's Finance and General Purposes Committee sanctioned an extension to the South Wing to contain one single and seven double rooms capable of accommodating convalescent or long-stay guests. Similar 'house full' conditions prevailed throughout 1987, providing a high note of success to coincide with Wing Commander Arthur Carvosso's retirement after fourteen years as manager; and a challenge for his successor, Group Captain Eric Goodman. However, availability of the South Wing extension from 17 July 1988 helped Goodman to get off to an encouraging start and the extension was opened officially by the Duke of Kent on 26 September. This additional accommodation permitted Princess Marina House to raise its 1988 guest numbers to 1041, and enabled Portland Place to lift the embargo on former officers and their dependants. This decision had not long been made when, yet again, the Care Wing had a considerable waiting list.

In the Fund's seventieth anniversary year, it was salutary to be conducted through the Duke of Kent School by Alison and Robert, each of whom had lost a pilot father. The corridors may display household names of the 1939–45 War, but their scurrying, book-laden denizens denote, as with Alison and Robert, losses of life and limb in the less desperate if equally sacrificial business of deterring war. No one can be more aware than Roger Wilson, the head, of the perils facing peacetime aircrew. His son is a helicopter pilot.

Some children have lost mothers. Others, of course, represent the school's dual role as the educator of families of service and civilian parents who are in no distress, but value its style and record. The group captain's son – his father is serving in Bangladesh – encountered whilst tucking into a pork chop in the dining hall, is an example of service children of fee-paying parents who are assisted by the Ministry of Defence boarding school allowance. That an NCO's son is at the same table demonstrates that rank is irrelevant.

Responsibility for selection of Foundationers and the making of grants rests with the Education Committee which meets at Portland Place, then under the chairmanship of Air Marshal Sir Charles Ness. A member of the Fund's Council and Finance and General Purposes Committee, he chaired the Duke of Kent School's Board of Governors, responsible for an average total of 176 pupils, of whom forty-one were Foundationers – all paid for by the Fund – 101 service boarders, eleven civilian boarders and twenty-three local civilian day boys and girls.

Although he flew in Bomber Command towards the end of the war, Ness, Air Member for Personnel from 1980 to 1983, brought recent Air Rank experience to his voluntary posts. As he fashioned the Fund's education policy for the 1990s he moved forward from the firm ground established by his predecessor, Air Chief Marshal Sir Lewis Hodges, renowned as a wartime escaper and Special Operations Executive pilot, whom he succeeded in 1985.

Sadly, another change at the top was necessitated when Bill Jones, the head who had achieved the move from Vanbrugh so successfully in 1976, died unexpectedly towards the end of the 1980 spring term. Michael Morton, the deputy head and an old Vanbrugh hand, breached the gap until Roger Wilson, the present head, took over. Morton stayed on until 1982 when he retired after seventeen years' dedicated service to the Fund, first at Vanbrugh and then at Duke of Kent. He was succeeded as deputy head by J. H. Day.

The new head's period of sixteen distinguished years at Christ's Hospital has been noted earlier. Educated at King Edward's School, Birmingham, and Corpus Christi College, Cambridge, he was to maintain the Vanbrugh and Duke of Kent Schools' reputation for all-round excellence. That year there were also important board changes. Following the resignation of Trevor Jones who had done so much to effect the transfer of the former Woolpit school to the Fund, and F. M. White, another Vanbrugh veteran, the appointment of L. G. D. Baker, headmaster of Christ's Hospital, strengthened the Duke of Kent's association with that school.

The past decade at the Duke of Kent had seen a steady improvement in buildings and facilities. In 1979 further gifts from the Variety Club of Great Britain enabled a changing room for girls to be built at the swimming pool and also provided full-fee bursaries for four Foundationers for five years. The Variety Club helped again in 1982 when a music centre, comprising a large room for orchestral rehearsal and ten practice rooms, was opened by the Club's chairman, Tom Nicholas. Among further changes on the education front, Air Commodore A. P. Vicary, who had masterminded the transition from Vanbrugh to Duke of Kent, retired as the Education Secretary at Portland Place, being replaced by the Welfare Secretary, Air Vice-Marshal Michael Robinson.

Next year, the name of Sir Harald Peake being so intimately associated with the school – Peake Hall speaks for itself – it was particularly appropriate that his widow, Air Commodore Dame Felicity Peake, as principal guest, should have presented the prizes and trophies at Speech and Parents' Day. Examination results in 1984 reflected the school's annual success in obtaining scholarships and places in a range of senior schools. Scholarships were obtained at Oundle and Trent College while a girl Foundationer was awarded a bursary place, partly financed by the MacRobert Trusts, at Gordonstoun. Fittingly, Guy Dodd, the headmaster of Lord Wandsworth, a college with a long record of accepting Foundationers, and now as Duke of Kent governor replacing Baker, did the Speech Day honours as principal guest.

The Gordonstoun bursary for a girl Foundationer was evidence of the increasing demand for girls' boarding places and, taking note, the

governors reaffirmed the board's opinion that an ideal balance should be
130 boys to fifty girls. This ought to retain the school's overall character
and its sporting competitive edge. Therefore, steps were taken to accommodate up to fifty girls, and in 1985 two all-weather areas were provided
for their netball and tennis. Here, again, the Variety Club gave generous
help, providing £6500 towards the £17,000 cost.

By 1987 it did not need the newly-installed teaching computers to
discover that popular demand for girls' places had over-run the ideal
balance. Air Chief Marshal Sir David Craig, Chief of the Air Staff, and
Lady Craig as principal guests at the summer Speech Day, noted that
of 173 pupils fifty-nine were girls. In 1988 the total population had risen
to 176 of whom sixty were girls. But the prime consideration, priority of
admission for Foundationers, remained sacrosanct and forty-one
Foundationers, twenty-six boys and fifteen girls, were assisted as necessary by the Fund. At Speech Day it was again the Christ's Hospital head's
turn to present the prizes. In a particularly good year for sporting achievements, Richard Poulton, successor to Baker as head at Christ's Hospital,
had what must surely be the unique experience of being confronted by
a youthful captain of cricket – Alexander Earl – with a batting average
of 113.

CHAPTER 21

A SHARP FOCUS ON THE 1980s

'Unthinkable not to help.'

Lord Catto

As will have become plainly apparent from the account of preceding years, the Fund's activities form an annual pattern of spending and receiving – spending always comes first in the Fund's philosophy – a consistency which, irrespective of individual Controllers' inclinations, is confirmed in the chairman's annual reports to the Council.

Since the exits, the entrances and the pats on the back are also there, selection from and comment on Catto's reports of the 1980s – other than news of developments at the International Air Tattoo, the Duke of Kent School and Princess Marina and Alastrean Houses which have been described separately hitherto – provides an overall view of how the Fund fared in the period.

 In 1980 total expenditure exceeded £3 million for the first time. Of this, spending on relief of distress of £2.5 million set another record. This was largely due to more homes being bought by the Housing Trust and the doubling of the cost of running Princess Marina House following its extension. The variety of appeal sources outside such routine events as the Royal Air Force Anniversary Concert and displays put on by the International Air Tattoo organisation was maintained by Air Commodore Mike Stanton, Appeals Secretary, and his staff. Advantage was taken of the fortieth anniversary of the Battle of Britain to hold a dinner in conjunction with the Variety Club of Great Britain at the Battle of Britain Museum, Hendon. The Duke of Kent attended and was received by Marshal of the Royal Air Force Sir John Grandy, successor to Marshal of the Royal Air Force Sir Dermot Boyle, as Deputy Chairman. Grandy had commanded No. 249 Hurricane Squadron, during the Battle. A handicrafts centre at the Duke of Kent School benefited from £5314 of the money raised by the event. The enduring sense of national deliverance by the RAF in 1940 was reflected in numerous donations, not least £10 received anonymously 'with thanks for a free life since 1940'.

If total expenditure at £3 million had astonished in 1980, the next year's advance of nearly £41,000 on that figure on welfare alone indicated the likelihood of ever increasing annual distress benefits. But net

International Air Tattoo Organisation proceeds of £170,000, surpassing those of all previous air shows, were an encouraging sign on the other side of the balance sheet, and particularly gratifying in his retirement year to Crowley-Milling who had nursed the Tattoo Organisation since establishing it in 1976. It was a flourishing legacy for Steedman, latterly United Kingdom Representative to the North Atlantic Treaty Organisation, who succeeded him shortly afterwards. Support from other sources was up, receipts from Ministry of Defence, commands, stations, and units topping £1 million, a tribute to the effectiveness of the half-a-day's pay a year and covenant scheme. Figures representing those other important arms of the Service's self help, the Royal Air Force Dependants Fund and (Income) Trust were also encouraging, grants made by the former since inception in 1967 now totalling £1,116,600.

Meanwhile, the Dependants Trust, to which members of the Dependants Fund had subscribed since 1971 to provide additional tax-free income or lump sums for nominated dependants, now made annual awards to beneficiaries totalling more than £186,000 a year. That 960 cases – another increase – were advised by the Insurance Advisory Service was another indication of service people's readiness to provide for themselves.

Yet there will always be those who, however provident, will face unexpected calls on their resources, a factor emphasised by the nomination of 1981 as International Year of Disabled People. As its contribution the Fund gave £272,961 to forty-five organisations which help disabled members of the RAF. Another reminder of the Fund's generous reputation as a donor was the presentation of £50,000 to the Royal Air Forces Association to endow three beds at Sussexdown in memory of Marshal of the Royal Air Force Sir John Slessor, a vice-president; Air Marshal Sir William Coles, Controller from 1968 to 1975; and the Guinea Pig Club.

Statistics prepared for the chairman's 1982 report showed that welfare spending of almost £4 million out of a total expenditure of £4.85 million had almost doubled over four years, giving a deficit on ordinary income of £865,777. However, other income, including legacies, totalling £1.136 million – welcome but uncertain by their very nature – brought receipts of £6.36 million to provide a healthy surplus. Some measure of the burden carried by the dedicated welfare team of Air Commodore Roy Dutton and his assistant, Jean Ashton, can be appreciated from the chairman's acknowledgement on Dutton's retirement as Welfare Secretary that over eleven years he had administered the disbursement of more than £19.5 million.

Dutton's retirement and succession by Air Vice-Marshal Michael Robinson shortly preceded other retirements which indicated that age and service was gradually claiming members of the old guard, who seemed to have been at Portland Place forever. In 1983 Wing Commander Ted Holloway, who had implemented the Fund's financial policies for nearly seventeen years laid down that particularly onerous burden, while Wing Commander Freddie Tame who had looked after the Dependants Fund and Dependants (Income) Trust said goodbye after fourteen years. Long service is customary at the Fund and not only among its salaried staff. In Council the Duke of Kent, the President, thanked Catto for his fifteen years of service, especially for the past five years as chairman.

Figures prepared for 1983 by Holloway's successor, Wing Commander Jack Connell, showed welfare spending of over £4 million, but once again public support saved the Fund from what would otherwise have been a deficit of £700,000. It was noted that a new and expanding part of the Fund's work was the provision of accommodation through the acquisition of nominations for units with housing associations and provision of a comprehensive advisory service for needy applicants seeking somewhere suitable to live.

Looking ahead in the conclusion of his 1984 report, the chairman remarked that more than £5 million had been spent on the direct relief of distress and that demands made on resources showed no signs of abating. The Fund, he emphasised, must expect the numbers of welfare cases and the sums expended on them to increase until at least the turn of the century. He also stressed that some forty per cent of men who served with the RAF during the 1939–45 War were born between 1920 and 1924, creating an expectancy of a high level of claims for fifteen years or more.

With key members of the Fund's old guard belonging to the same generation, the year inevitably yielded further retirements. Wing Commander Allan Scott, Secretary, Homes and Princess Marina House, who had been at Portland Place since 1975, made way for Group Captain Don Starkey, and Paul Cutting handed over as Secretary, Administration, to Group Captain Ken Hebborn. Cutting's retirement after thirty-nine years with the Fund left a void impossible to fill. Sensibly, his successor recognised this and, while supported by the Cutting tradition, updated the role and set a new style compatible with the introduction of computer technology. Cutting, as will be recalled from an earlier chapter, was part of the Cordingley legend, an attribute which greatly assisted his task as editor of earlier editions of *The Debt We Owe*. He was awarded the OBE, a richly merited honour.

The chairman's financial fears for the future were confirmed by events in 1985. Welfare cases was 7.5 per cent up at 13,044, calling for expenditure of £7.13 million, an increase of more than thirty-two per cent. Total expenditure of £8.53 million exceeded income from donations and fund-raising, repayment of welfare loans and return on investments, which the Fund regards as dependable income, by £2.92 million. Legacies of £1.15 million, as ever unpredictable, failed to close the gap which was met by realisation of assets and reinvestment, leaving a net cash gain and minimising the need to erode capital.

The RAF coach crash in Germany affecting the lives of the families of

many victims was a reminder that heavy calls on the Fund do not necessarily involve its ageing beneficiaries or aircrew families. During the year,
110 serving personnel died as a result of accident or illness. Inevitably,
however the deaths of 1756 former service people reminded Welfare of
the ageing factor. Help was given when needed. It would, in the
chairman's own words, have been 'unthinkable' not to have helped any
case whether serving or non-serving. In response to the Fund's ever
growing welfare commitment, two retiring Assistant Secretaries in the
branch, Wing Commander E. L. Macro and Wing Commander H. T.
Williams were immediately replaced by Air Commodore April Reed, a
former Matron-in-Chief and Director of RAF Nursing Services, and
Squadron Leader Sheila Joy, another former member of Princess Mary's
Royal Air Force Nursing Service.

Surveying events of 1986 the chairman felt obliged to view the
increasing scale and cost of the Fund's welfare activities 'with a sense both
of satisfaction and apprehension'. The Fund was achieving its prime
purpose of relieving distress, but in doing so was putting considerable
strain on its financial resources. Profits had been 'creamed off' from the
sale of investments, while maintaining the book value of the investment
portfolio to bridge the gap yet again between income and expenditure.

Air Commodore Freddie West, the 1914–18 War Royal Flying
Corps VC, and Air Chief Marshal Sir Alasdair Steedman,
Controller, watch Marshal of the Royal Air Force Sir William
Dickson cutting a cake at the Royal Air Force Club in 1983 to
mark the publication of the book, *A Lifetime of Service*, in aid of the
Fund.

Princess Alexandra presents the 1984 Wilkinson Sword to Group
Captain A.C. Tolhurst of RAF Finningley in recognition of the
station's efforts on behalf of the Fund.

But the chairman warned that this could not go on and new sources of
income would have to be explored.

Welfare spending rose to 'the staggering sum' of £8.16 million, a new
record which signified the Fund's indebtedness to Air Chief Marshal Sir
David Lee, chairman of the Grants Committee. Certainly, its new
members, Lady Harcourt-Smith, Air Vice-Marshal H. A. Caillard, Air
Commodore D. F. Rixson, Lady Jones and the Polish Air Vice-Marshal.
A Maisner, had been plunged in at the deep end. Support from the Royal
Air Forces Association and the Soldiers', Sailors' and Airmen's Families
Association, frequently the link between the Fund and its beneficiaries,
assisted it in dealing with forty per cent of cases and in disbursing the
Fund's money. However, a change at the top of the Insurance Advisory
Service when Wing Commander A. J. Webster, handed over after ten
years to Group Captain C. S. Jackson, served as a reminder of its contri-
bution to narrowing the long-term drain on resources. Another departure
was that of Group Captain S. J. Perkins who had served nearly eleven

years as an Assistant Welfare Secretary and was replaced by Wing Commander A. J. Schollar.

Although the Fund fared better than many investors in the Stock Market crash of October 1987, a 19.6 per cent fall reduced its investments' market value to £24,282,816 and reinforced the chairman's call for new sources of income. But the Fund's escape from an investment fate that might have been far worse owed much to the counsel of Morgan Grenfell, its advisers, and its own cautious approach to risk, twenty-eight per cent of its investments being in gilts. Even so, at such a time, the importance of the £1,882,815 of self-help from the RAF's voluntary half-a-day's pay, and after fund-raising, shone through the accounts, as did receipts from station and wives' functions, public support through the International Air Tattoo and other events and individual donations ranging from fifty pence to £25,000. All very necessary set against stock market volatility and the continuing rise in welfare spending. Up 4.8 per cent at £8,556,972, it set yet another new record and marked the retirement of Air Chief Marshal Sir David Lee after more than sixteen years as Chairman of the Grants Committee. He was succeeded by Air Chief Marshal Sir John Aiken.

Other retirements included two long-serving Council members, Lord Ward, Honorary Treasurer from 1969 until the end of 1986 when he was succeeded by Mr F. W. Crawley, and Mr E. de Rougemont who had been involved with the Fund for forty years. With the death of Lord Trenchard, whose father had founded the Fund and who had been a vice-president since 1970, the Fund lost another valued member of the Council and Finance and General Purposes Committee. Another distinguished vice-president, Marshal of the Royal Air Force Sir William Dickson, died during the year. But recruitment of Sir Kenneth Durham brought additional business expertise to the Council and Finance and General Purposes Committee. After a succession of changes in the Fund's staff in recent years, there was less movement in 1987, though Wing Commander Arthur Carvosso's retirement as manager at Princess Marina House, since managed by Group Captain E. J. Goodman, was a reminder of how much he had achieved there in fourteen years.

Once again, 1987 was a year in which self-help among the serving was such that it should not be seen to be eclipsed by the massive expenditure on welfare. Ninety-six per cent of service personnel subscribed ten pence a month to the Royal Air Force Dependants Fund which raised to £1200 its immediate tax free grant made to nominated beneficiaries of subscribers who die while serving. In 1987, too, that other fine example of self-help, the Royal Air Force Dependants (Income) Trust, which pays an increasing tax free income to beneficiaries of subscribers – basic subscription £1.30 a month for an income of £440 a year until what would have been the subscriber's fifty-fifth birthday – paid out £380,000.

In 1988 there was a welcome deceleration in the rate of welfare expenditure, the total of £8.664 million being but one per cent up on 1987.

Moreover, possibly reflecting an early result of Kennedy's 'tighter ship', of which more later, the rise, historically infinitesimal, was almost entirely accounted for by awards associated with donations to other organisations that assist the Fund in its welfare work. In view of long-term concern over the call of the 1939–45 War 'bulge', it seems more likely that careful stewardship rather than reduction in demand was responsible. Financial support from the Service at £1.98 million, and £2.46 million from the public, was strongly boosted by a grant-in-aid of £418,000 from the Ministry of Defence. This related to a Retail Price Index-linked adjustment to pensions paid to Service pensioners and an outstandingly generous personal donation of more than £1 million from Mr J. W. Greening, one of the Fund's honorary helpers.

Evidence that over the years the Fund's costly help on housing was not always one-way can be found in figures featuring repayment of loans, and gains from the sale of Housing Trust properties no longer required by beneficiaries. Taking in payments made by residents and guests at Princess Marina and Alastrean Houses and rentals from Housing Trust properties these amounted to more than £2.8 million. Total expenditure of £10.26 million against income of £11.59 million produced a welcome surplus, though but for Mr Greening's donation and the Ministry of Defence's grant-in-aid there would have been a small deficit. The Fund's three financial services, the Insurance Advisory Service, the Royal Air Force Dependants Fund and the Royal Air Force Dependants (Income) Trust, continued to flourish.

Among the exits and the entrances of the year, the Chairman in Council welcomed Steedman, the retiring Controller to its ranks and his successor, Kennedy, to the various committees on which the Controller sits. Among staff retirements, Air Commodore Mike Stanton's departure from Appeals lost the Fund its most talented fund-raiser ever – so much of the success of IAT and its burgeoning activities was due to his persistence – placing an onerous burden on his successor Air Vice-Marshal Freddie Hurrell, formerly Director-General of RAF Medical Services. With the Battle of Britain Appeal in preparation it was a challenging moment to become Appeals Director. In a year which saw a Controller's retirement it might seem impossible to match his departure in terms of service to the Fund, but such, uniquely, was the case with Jean Ashton, Deputy Director Welfare, who said goodbye after nearly forty-four years. As the Chairman noted, 'for much of that time the name of Jean Ashton has been almost synonymous with that of the Fund. Her compassion and wealth of experience endeared her to many and especially to her beloved Poles and Guinea Pig Club members'. Jean's devotion of a lifetime was earlier recognised with the award of an MBE.

Among other changes were Air Commodore D. F. Rixson's appointment as Deputy Chairman of the Main Grants Committee on the retirement of Wing Commander C. R. Griffiths after nearly eleven years on the committee. Almost as big a break with the past as Jean Ashton's retirement was occasioned by the resignation of Mrs R. E. Croome after thirty years' service as a Governor of Vanbrugh and the Duke of Kent Schools. In Edinburgh, Air Marshal Sir Richard Wakeford retired as Director of the Scottish Branch after more than ten years and from the Board of Management of Alastrean House. The Fund is indebted to him for all he did to bring about the establishment of Alastrean House. Air Vice-Marshal C. E. Simpson took his place. There was a change, too, at Princess Marina House, where Lady Kyle, widow of Air Chief Marshal Sir Wallace 'Digger' Kyle, a former chairman, joined the Board.

CHAPTER 22

THE WAY AHEAD: KENNEDY – NO SACRED COWS

When Air Chief Marshal Sir Jock Kennedy arrived at Portland Place as Controller in the summer of 1988 it was soon evident that he was very much the man for his time. Although Kennedy was not the first Controller to come from the ranks – Crowley-Milling had flown as a Volunteer Reserve sergeant pilot – his Service origins were less exalted in that he had enlisted as an AC 2 National Serviceman before being selected for the RAF College Cranwell.

Kennedy enjoys recalling how he first heard about the Fund. At his first pay parade a warrant officer directed his attention to a bucket beside the pay table and marked RAF Benevolent Fund. It was the belief that those who failed to flip a sixpence into the bucket risked being placed on a charge. National Servicemen felt especially hard done by. They were not at that time eligible for assistance.

Air Chief Marshal Sir Thomas Kennedy, Controller 1988–93.

As with his predecessor Kennedy was a Scot. He had reached Portland Place via Hawick High School and a varied career. Although he was the first post-war Controller without 1939–45 service he had flown Cyprus-based Canberras with No. 27 Squadron in the 1956 Suez campaign and commanded No. 99, a Britannia transport squadron. He had benefited from the experience of serving with wartime operational veterans and had been awarded an AFC and Bar along the way.

Finally, Kennedy's last appointment as Air Member for Personnel had prepared him well for the task ahead and set a precedent for the eventual choice of his two successors. He arrived with a reputation for being no respecter of sacred cows. As he probed much that had become routine and ritual in the Portland Place warren of offices, corners and cubby holes he noted practices more than ready for reform. In view, as will be related, of the subsequent recent change of status of the Duke of Kent School it is noteworthy that at this early stage Kennedy suggested that the time might come when the School's rationale and cost effectiveness should be reviewed. He concluded also that perceptions of the Fund among serving officers, airmen and airwomen were misconceived.

No Controller is in post long before he encounters the barrackroom myth that officers receive the lion's share of Fund money for housing and education and ignorance on stations of the Fund's overall ability and readiness to help. Each new Controller develops his own means of tackling these perennial problems and over time there is cumulative progress.

Kennedy, who had arrived at Portland Place with an appetite for change, tackled them by reversing the practice introduced by Coles and extended by Steedman of making station visits. Kennedy, while accepting routine invitations to a range of station fund-raising, cheque presentation and other occasions, preferred to sit station commanders and a variety of commissioned and non-commissioned officers around the long table in the elegant Council room. Presentation by welfare staff of individual cases and the committee's response dissolved many a misconception. Visitors returned to stations and units better informed about application procedures on a range of welfare awards and aware of the care with which applications are investigated and awards made. Such visits were of particular value to warrant officers who provide a direct link with serving men and women.

Very soon familiarity with ever increasing welfare demands on the Fund's resources alerted Kennedy, and through him the Finance and General Purposes Committee, that the Fund must immediately 'tighten ship'. His predecessor had been prone to proclaim with pride that he was liable to let his heart rule his head. Indeed, Steedman was a self-confessed big spender under whom welfare expenditure had climbed steeply. In no time Aiken, who had succeeded Lee as chairman, reined in awards although in conformity with the Fund's founding principle on the relief of distress, no approved applicant was refused or deprived.

Even so, Kennedy was confronted with the reality that calls from even a modest percentage of surviving and ageing wartime aircrew, ground-crew, others and dependants might break the Fund unless it was topped up continuously. Fearing an ever widening gap between income and expenditure he seized the opportunity of the approaching fiftieth anniversary of the Battle of Britain to prepare an epic Appeal for 1990. His aim was to enlarge the Fund's capital base by at least £20 million and enable it to meet historic commitments up to and beyond the Millennium.

Since 1989 was also an anniversary year – the seventieth birthday of the Fund – Kennedy in that year took measures to ensure the Fund's day-to-day administration, welfare work and routine fund-raising were in no way relegated. Following preliminary investigation by a steering group headed by Sir Peter Masefield, a Battle of Britain Appeal team was assembled under the chairmanship of Lord Barber whose credentials were immaculate. As a former Chancellor of the Exchequer, Spitfire photographic reconnaissance pilot, prisoner-of-war and banker, Barber was ideally placed to raise money in the City and elsewhere and to generally spearhead the Appeal.

Not since Trenchard's inspirational call fifty years earlier as the Battle of Britain obliged Germany to abandon Operation *Sealion*, the planned invasion of Britain, was there to be such a sustained reminder of the debt owed by the nation to the Royal Air Force. Trenchard's Appeal launched in 1940 while RAF Fighter Command was embattled had reaped more than £400,000. When Barber and Kennedy set their sights on an Appeal target of £20 million they were fortunate that after half a century a plethora of books, films and television programmes had produced an international legend from little more than twelve weeks of aerial fighting.

No matter that the aircrew numbers and losses of the Few were fractional compared with the overall wartime sacrifice of the RAF – predominantly in Bomber Command – the emotive pull of the Few could be expected to attract considerable support. Yet, for all such an appeal had going for it, preparation and execution would tax the Fund's organisational and creative energies and resources. Happily the planners at Portland Place enjoyed a customised promotional facility in the International Air Tattoo organisation at RAF Fairford. Certainly IAT had progressed beyond all recognition since Peake and Crowley-Milling had restored the concept of airshows as prime fund and profile raisers. Over the years IAT founding directors Paul Bowen and Tim Prince had so grown the organisation's reputation that its expertise was consulted around the world. Only the impracticability of employing key members of IAT's indispensable army of volunteers deterred Lockheed Martin, builder of the RAF's long-serving C-130 Hercules transport fleet and IAT sponsors, from hiring IAT to stage its California airshow.

In the run up to Battle of Britain fiftieth Anniversary commemoration festivities IAT had progressed beyond all recognition from its modest origins as Royal Air Forces Association-organised Air Tattoos '71 and '72 at RAF North Weald, the Embassy Air Tattoos in 1973 – the first at RAF Greenham Common – and again in 1974.

Following the 1974 display RAFA fell out of formation. IAT, based in Hut 91 at Greenham, was introduced and in 1976 the Royal Air Force Benevolent Fund went it alone with its International Air Tattoo profiting by more than £35,000. Alternating every other year with the Society of British Aerospace Companies' longer established and at that time better known Farnborough Air Show, IAT was to become the world's most prestigious military aviation event. Until the airshow settled into its current annual format it was periodically biennial. Actively productive in what Bowen and Prince termed the 'fallow years' the directors had oiled, as has been noted earlier, the organisation with contracts to stage such other events as the Bassingbourn Anglo-American Festival in 1978 and the Newbury Air Festival in 1980. Other tangential events had included the TVS Air Show South in 1986 and 1988, the Volkswagen Aerobatic Championships '86 and also in that year an International Air Show at the Army Air Corps Centre, Middle Wallop.

Meanwhile, the Fund's very own airshow was developing a distinctive character as the annual flagship event it was to become. Henceforth IATs, as with the Silver Jubilee International Air Tattoo celebrating in 1977 the Queen's twenty-five years on the throne, were generally pegged to commemorative themes. Staged in association with Nationwide Building Society the Silver Jubilee airshow was incorporated with a NATO Tiger Meet, switched from Upper Heyford, home of USAF Tiger Squadron F-111Es, to Greenham Common. On the last day the RAF Red Arrows completed their 1000th public display with a 'Jubilee Break'.

Following seven Tattoos at Greenham Common the build-up at the Berkshire base of USAF cruise missile facilities rendered it impracticable for IAT to continue there though the American base commander sought to persuade the team to remain. In the event IAT moved to RAF Fairford in Gloucestershire, itself at that time an American operational base housing KC-135 tankers on temporary duty with USAF's 11th Strategic Group.

Appropriately, the main theme of IAT '85 in association with Nationwide Building Society – first Fairford airshow – featured *Skytanker 85* displaying the largest number of air-to-air refuellers ever assembled. The second theme was the fiftieth anniversary of the DC-3/C-47. Following a fallow year Nationwide's IAT '87, enthusiastically supported by US base personnel, mounted *Skylift* and *SkyShield* featuring transport aircraft and commemorating seventy-five years of UK air defence. IAT '87 was also significant for the increasing participation of overseas aerobatic teams of which the Royal Jordanian Air Force's trio of Pitts Specials was particularly welcome.

King Hussein of Jordan was already a familiar figure at Fairford. When Bader, IAT's founding president, died in 1982 the Hashemite monarch's generous offer to succeed him was gratefully accepted, though protocol demanded Hussein's designation as patron. It was immediately evident that the king intended to involve himself as fully as home and international responsibilities permitted. Nor did he restrict his support to the annual airshow. When in 1985 RAFBE established in Bader's memory IAT's wholly sponsored Disabled Fliers' Scholarship Scheme Hussein offered to pay personally for six of the originating nine scholarships a year.

His involvement did not end here. From retirement Steedman recalled that there were times when he prayed for a little less dedication. The Controller who had flown fighters in combat confessed that he had never been more anxious than while standing on the runway when a partly trained seriously disabled woman student pilot took off with the king at her side. Wing Commander John Patterson, the scheme's administrator, shared Steedman's anxieties and also delight at such successes as the issue of an unrestricted licence to a paraplegic; in itself a fitting memorial to the legless fighter ace whose spirited refusal to surrender to disablement was to inspire so many others.

While disabled candidates were not normally high profile one of the first was Simon Weston, the Welsh Guardsman who had suffered grievous burns in the Falklands campaign. When the scheme was

As Patron of the International Air Tattoo, King Hussein flew from Jordan to attend. The occasion provides a useful opportunity to present certificates to holders of Sir Douglas Bader Flying Scholarships for the Disabled.

Pictured here at the June 1988 Tattoo, four Flying Scholarship winners (left to right): Wendy Morrell; Noel McConkey; Simon Weston; Geoffrey Schwalbe.

introduced each scholarship provided thirty-nine hours dual and solo flying during a six-week residential course.

Kennedy, as with Crowley-Milling, rated chairmanship of IAT as the most stimulating of his responsibilities. At Appeals Stanton enthusiastically encouraged Bowen and Prince's entrepreneurial drive. Fred Crawley, former deputy chairman of Lloyds Bank and now IAT's deputy chairman added this responsibility to his duties as honorary treasurer of the Fund and membership of the Council and Finance and General Purposes Committee. IAT development benefited immensely from his sage and imaginative counsel.

Since one of Fairford's annual preoccupations is to settle on a main theme for the Tattoo Kennedy, Stanton and Crawley's mix of service and business experience were much valued. Their combined connections, charm and persuasive talents contributed magnificently towards securing the co-operation of companies and overseas air forces. Yet high level arrangements are of little avail without painstaking spadework and here in this period IAT was well served, among others, by John Lightfoot, a retired local police inspector with a law degree.

Lightfoot's knowledge of the law and police background were especially useful. He was ever ready to disentangle knotty trademark and copyright problems and liaise with police on traffic and security issues. Among a wide variety of responsibilities he even found time to organise a lost children routine and a creche operated by the Women's Royal Voluntary Service.

However, the airshow should not appear to eclipse the overall contribution of many and varied station fund-raising efforts nor the RAF
Anniversary Concert at the Royal Festival Hall, which traditionally
opened the Appeals season. Jubilee years were, of course, especially
significant and the Fund was privileged with royal attendances. When the
RAF celebrated its Diamond Jubilee in 1978, the Queen Mother, Patron
since the death of her husband King George VI, was present. Sadly, it
was Peake's last appearance in the royal box. He died shortly afterwards
and the Fund expressed its appreciation of his services, noting that during
eleven years as chairman £13 million was disbursed among 100,000
beneficiaries.

In 1989 the Duke of Kent, attending a concert to mark the seventieth
anniversary of Trenchard's founding of the Fund, extended an especially
warm welcome to Peake's widow Air Commodore Dame Felicity Peake,
so long a member of the Council and the Finance and General Purposes
Committee, and also to her son, Andrew, who was later to join his mother
on them.

The Royal Philharmonic Orchestra, conducted by Louis Fremaux,
shared the occasion with the Central Band of the RAF conducted by
Wing Commander Barrie Hingley, Principal Director of Music. During
the interval the Duke of Kent presented a Wilkinson sword to Wing
Commander J. Whitston, Officer Commanding RAF Manston in recognition of this small station's donation of £20,000 from Open Day
proceeds and £13,000 reaped from sales of *The RAF Year Book.* This was
especially gratifying in a period when IAT's publishing unit at Fairford
made a promising debut. Beginning with IAT souvenir programmes the
unit, headed by Claire Lock, a former British Eagle air stewardess, went
on to supply the Farnborough Airshow programme and to produce *The
RAF Year Book* and a United States Air Force companion.

Further spreading their wings the Fairford permanent team, now
numbering thirty, organised a variety of fund-raising events which gener-
ated income and raised the profile of the Fund including a Festival of
Music at the Royal Albert Hall. They also displayed an Argentinia Bell
UH-1H helicopter *Huey* which had been seized in the Falklands and
operated a hot-air balloon on behalf of the Nationwide Anglia Building
Society. Another lucrative activity was management of company
sponsorship aviation events.

Thus, positioned to call on the complementary 'showbusiness' and
traditional fund-raising strengths of Fairford and Portland Place the Fund
was dually equipped to launch its Battle of Britain Fiftieth Anniversary
Appeal in 1990 and to meet the challenges of a changing scene which lay
ahead in the 1990s.

CHAPTER 23

INTO THE NINETIES

'The way in which the Fund conducts its relief work through its
independent Grants Committees is the envy of many similar organisations.'

Lord Catto, Chairman

At the turn of the decade, outside the bunkhouse where formerly the firemen slept, a coal-black KC-135 United States Air Force air-to-air refuelling tanker thunders off the runway and into a scowling sky; a noisy and chilling reminder that not only does RAF Fairford economically accommodate the Royal Air Force Benevolent Fund's International Air Tattoo Organisation, but that operationally it hosts the United States Tanker Task Force in Europe.

It seems appropriate that the flourishing fund-raising-through-fun business branch of the Fund should be within yards of present-day operational take-offs and landings; and at an airfield from which D-Day and Arnhem airborne operations were flown in 1944.

As the tanker climbs, Paul Bowen, IAT's director, picks off on his fingers the components of the profitable enterprise he has built in partnership with Tim Prince, the operation's director. In ten years their airshows, publishing, advertising, and radio ventures and RAF Massed Bands Festivals of Music at The Royal Albert Hall, have placed IAT in the front rank of such traditional and conventional revenue sources as donations, legacies and the serving RAF's half-a-day's-pay-a-year-scheme.

On Bowen's desk the telephone rings. King Hussein, the International Air Tattoo's Patron is calling from Amman. No royal figurehead, the King of the Hashemite Kingdom of Jordan keeps abreast of details as each event is planned and executed.

With the fiftieth anniversary of the Battle of Britain falling within what promised to be the most costly decade of its existence, the Fund challenged itself unashamedly not only to repeat but, in comparative terms, to far exceed the success of the Appeal which Marshal of the Royal Air Force Lord Trenchard urged upon it in 1940.

Trenchard, Father of the Royal Air Force, was not in current phraseology a natural communicator, and on this occasion he broke his self-imposed rule of radio silence. In a Battle of Britain broadcast he said:

It is now time to ask this country, as I feel the whole British Empire recognises all that the Royal Air Force has done, to put the Fund on a firm basis. A very large sum will be required for us to carry out our obligations to the airmen, their wives, children and dependants, so that these men may go into battle, feeling that the future of their immediate relations will, anyhow, be secured from want.

The £53,342 obtained from that appeal, together with £250,000 from Lord Nuffield and £354,530 10s from the chairman, Lord Wakefield's public appeal in the Press, plus other individual donations, provided the Fund with the financial base from which to go forward.

Fifty years on, the renewal of Trenchard's appeal at the time of the RAF's 'Finest Hour' coincided with the heaviest call ever on the Fund's resources. Survivors and widows of 1940 were elderly, as indeed was anyone who served in the 1939–45 War. Ex-service people of the post-war years do not get any younger.

If the means of money-raising and the needs of beneficiaries have changed radically since 1919 the Fund's location and basic organisational structure had remained reassuringly unchanged since it established permanent headquarters at 67 Portland Place in 1945.

Step down west London's Portland Place from the BBC and, passing the Chinese Embassy in the direction of Regent's Park, enter No. 67. It is a Tuesday morning which means that the Main Grants Committee is meeting in the spacious Adam room which serves as Council chamber and Controller's office. The chairs at the long table are upholstered in Royal Air Force blue and the walls are hung with photographic studies. Here is Lord Trenchard, who founded the Fund in 1919, and here the Duke of Kent, President since 1969, and whose father was killed on active service with the RAF in 1942 while he was chairman. Here, too, is Princess Marina, the President's mother, President in succession to her husband for twenty-five years. Sir Winston Churchill, wearing RAF wings and the uniform of an Air Commodore, is also here. He was a vice-president from 1919 until he died in 1965. 'Never in the field of human conflict was so much owed by so many to so few' – it seems almost that the phrase in which he immortalised the Few of Fighter Command in 1940 is on his lips. Or is it that memorable phrase from his radio appeal in 1951 on behalf of the Fund when he spoke of 'the debt we owe to the paladins of the Royal Air Force', extending his earlier tribute to embrace air and groundcrew of all Commands and coining a title for this book.

It is ten o'clock and, as Committee members arrive, Air Chief Marshal Sir Thomas Kennedy – Sir Jock, as he is popularly known – moves from his desk in the far corner to greet them. He is executive custodian of the Fund, whose Main Grant and sub-committees disburse its income week by week.

Over the years, inevitably, controllers, committee chairmen and members change, but the week-in-week-out work of the Grants

Committees, the heart pumping the Fund's life-blood to relieve distress, provides continuity. Air Chief Marshal Sir John Aiken takes the chair, and members of the welfare staff led by Air Commodore Robert Barcilon square off the buff folders from which they will present the day's applications.

Sir Jock's predecessors of the past twenty years, Coles, Crowley-Milling and Steedman would recognise the scene. But there familiarity fades. It is immediately apparent that, as the Fund enters its eighth decade, salaried staff and honorary Committee members are mostly of the nuclear deterrent generation, while its beneficiaries are increasingly veterans of the 1939–45 War.

Ten years earlier Air Chief Marshal Sir David Lee, Deputy Director Plans at the Air Ministry during the critical war years of 1943–44, had chaired the Main Grants Committee since 1971; Crowley-Milling, the Controller, had fought in the Battle of Britain, as had Air Commodore Roy Dutton, his welfare secretary; and Jean Ashton, Dutton's assistant had joined the Fund in wartime as a young girl. Crowley-Milling's successor, Steedman, had been a reconnaissance pilot and Dutton's successor, Air Vice-Marshal Michael Robinson, while just missing the war, flew Beaufighters in a light bomber role during the Malayan Emergency.

Kennedy personifies the change. The first Controller since that War who did not serve in it, he has inspired radical shifts in the Fund's approaches to welfare, appeal and public relations. The Fund has always been fortunate that Controllers have been men for their time. It is, therefore, no disrespect to Kennedy's predecessors that following his arrival at Portland Place in August 1988 he questioned long held concepts and doctored or excised some former practices.

Kennedy, following Steedman, was confronted with the consequences of deficit, the prospects of an ever-inflating bulge and the urgency of securing the Fund's future beyond the turn of the century. But with 1990 around the corner he entered this testing period with an exceptional advantage: the fiftieth anniversary of the Battle of Britain and the opportunity this presented to increase the Fund's capital dramatically, setting an Appeal target of £20 million.

In cold print this figure may seem unnecessarily ambitious, but placed in context with Grants Committee outgoings, an estimated overall annual expenditure for 1990 of up to £9 million and the year-by-year inflationary effects of the bulge, it was realistic.

A glimpse of the Committee in session: As the Chairman welcomes members, Barcilon, a former Lightning fighter pilot, squadron and station commander, and now presenter of the morning's list of applicants, consults foolscap sheets from the top folder. So orderly seem the files that it is easy to imagine a voice from each, offering name, rank and number, though such Service stiffness would be entirely alien to those around the table. Most – including wives of serving officers – have the relaxed approach of senior retired people to age, rank and status, but this in no way diminishes alertness and concentration as they consider cases.

The bulge of the 1939–45 War survivors supplies Barcilon and his welfare staff with all too many cases, numbers of them from Bomber Command which was the 'front line' of the RAF's war. Random selection among cases of the past ten years will turn up innumerable cases of bomber aircrew severely injured when expectation of life was as short as their Brylcreemed haircuts.

One such was that of the Wellington sergeant air-gunner who had miraculously survived heaven knows how many bomber operations over Germany and surgical operations thereafter. Suffering eighty-five per cent burns, repaired by Sir Archibald McIndoe at the Queen Victoria Hospital, East Grinstead, and revitalised through membership of the Guinea Pig Club, he sought a loan for a central heating system to make life more tolerable. As so often when burns are considered, Archie McIndoe's widow, Connie, chairman of a grants sub-committee, or Vanora Marland, also a Committee member and daughter by the plastic surgery 'Maestro's' – a Guinea Pig accolade – first wife, are present.

The Chairman turns towards Lady McIndoe. She explains that the Fund's Co-ordinating Committee for the Resettlement of Burns Cases recommends a grant of £500 and a loan of £500. The Chairman looks round the table. 'This man was badly burnt. It has been long accepted that we do everything we can for the Guinea Pig Club. A grant of £1000?' Approval is unanimous. 'Very well, agreed.'

Many applications concern housing and are regarded as fairly routine. The seventy-year-old widow of a Chief Technician who has died aged seventy four and was discharged in 1966 after twenty-nine years' service in the Engineering Branch, seeks a loan to settle a mortgage and pay outstanding house repair bills in the Isle of Man. The Committee notes that the house's value of £47,000 in 1987 had risen to £72,000 in 1988, but this does not deter a loan of £7000 of which £5000 is to clear the mortgage and £2000 for repairs.

The Committee hears that a former leading aircraftwoman with four years' service has given birth to a mentally handicapped child. The marriage has broken down. She has returned to her home town and obtained a council house which is in a deplorable condition, run down and vandalised. After investigation the Committee decides to buy a house for the benefit of mother and child.

A former leading aircraftman, who served throughout the 1939–45 War, has had two legs amputated within the past two years. The Fund purchases an electrically-propelled invalid wheelchair and makes it available on permanent loan. It also makes a grant towards winter fuel bills, general needs and comforts, and provides a weekly maintenance allowance.

The morning moves on. As successive members of the welfare director's staff present his or her share of the week's applications, it is manifest how closely each has identified with the range of domestic, social and financial problems the cases represent. Inevitably, given the nature of emotive cases, some submissions are made in terms of warm advocacy which can only come from the heart, yet each presenter manages to retain a measure of detachment sufficient to help Committee members to balance their decisions between heartfelt instincts and the written or unwritten observances of the Royal Air Force Benevolent Fund, which must rule their heads when authorising loans, grants or sympathetically refusing assistance.

Some applicants have a long history of need but, whether a folder is fat or thin, investigation of the immediate need has been thorough. Perhaps one of the Fund's voluntary welfare helpers has reported, possibly an associated ex-service welfare organisation, such as the Royal Air Forces Association, the Soldiers', Sailors' and Airmen's Families Association, or the Royal British Legion, has assisted or, as in many instances, a station commander has sought help for one of his people.

The cases are infinite in their variety: a serving airman has been let down by a fraudulent builder; a flight lieutenant who served in Korea has suffered a personality change through a rare disease; the widow of a test pilot whose death was front page news many years ago has insufficient means; the sixty-two-year-old widow of a corporal who became a Baptist minister after a medical discharge in wartime needs help.

Another folder is opened. A thirty-two-year-old corporal is dying of cancer. He has a wife, aged twenty-seven, and children of two and four. Within weeks there will be a widow and two young children. 'She would like to live near Brighton,' the Committee is told. 'She has found a suitable house, but it will be costly when one includes repairs, Value Added Tax and other expenses.' The Chairman gently makes the point that Brighton is an expensive area. 'Well, she has set her heart on it.' There is no further dissent. Agreed. A flight lieutenant has been killed in a Vulcan bomber accident and the required sum is authorised to house his family. In each case the houses will be purchased through and owned by the Royal Air Force Benevolent Fund Housing Trust.

Can this be the same Fund which in 1919 went overboard about the generosity of Mrs M. E. Salting, who presented two Ascot houses which were sold for less than £10,000. Or which felt deeply indebted to the white residents of Swaziland for their contribution of £406, and for £31 11s received from Wei-hai-wei in China? Or the Fund which in 1919 held serious reservations about accepting as a gift Vanbrugh Castle, the home in south-east London of Mr Alexander Duckham who had made a fortune in oil, and which thereafter was to accommodate the Fund's school for almost fifty-five years?

Certainly, Duke of Kent School, which emerged from Vanbrugh's coming together in September 1976 with Woolpit, a preparatory school in Ewhurst in Surrey, and upon which nearly £1 million has been spent, would astonish Trenchard and his contemporaries as would also Princess

Marina House, the Fund's convalescent and residential centre at Rustington in Sussex and Alastrean House, an equivalent care home in Scotland.

Any vestige of Vanbrugh has long since disappeared from the Duke of Kent School in the Surrey countryside. The school's gradual development to its present status as a boarding school for fee-paying pupils from service and civilian families, as well as the Fund's Foundationers, has been a feature of the past ten years. Since 1980 this transformation has taken place under the headship of Roger Wilson, who came to Duke of Kent after sixteen years at Christ's Hospital, ten of them as a housemaster of Peele A. Although it bore no influence on Wilson's appointment, unless of course it was pre-ordained, Peele A was Sir Barnes Wallis's house as a boy at the Bluecoat school So many years on, the Fund's RAF Foundationers Trust, part-funded at the start in 1951 by Wallis's £10,000 inventor's award for the bouncing bombs, which breached the Möhne and Eder dams, and for other wartime weapons, continues to educate boys and girls at Christ's Hospital. Happily, the Duke of Kent's Foundationers are particularly eligible.

There have also been marked advances in the past ten years in the Fund's convalescent and residential care arrangements. Princess Marina House at Rustington in West Sussex can now accommodate convalescent and long-stay men and women. In Scotland, Alastrean House provides residential care for elderly ex-service people from anywhere, although the north of England and Scotland are important sources. Peacefully rural in Aberdeenshire and deriving from the Fund's favoured relationship with one of its most generous benefactors, The MacRobert Trusts, Alastrean is a recent acquisition. In Scotland, too, the new Dowding House, close to the centre of Moffat, was to be a bricks-and-mortar reminder of the Fund's interdependence in so many directions with the Royal Air Forces Association. For Dowding House, a £1 million Fund and RAFA development of St Ninian's, the prep school founded by Lord Dowding's father and where the 'Leader of the Few' was born would provide sheltered housing for thirty-eight residents. The original house was restored and a wing built to provide a total of twenty-six flats, two of which are adapted for disabled people.

Princess Marina, Alastrean and Dowding Houses are prime examples of how far the Fund has come since grants of eighty years ago ran to little more than one shilling for a night's lodging, the redemption of pawning clothing, the purchase of a pair of boots in which to seek work, or provision of a hawker's licence. Comprehension of the present-day Royal Air Force Benevolent Fund's humble origins puts such awards in perspective.

CHAPTER 24

BATTLE OF BRITAIN BONANZA

Inevitably the major event of the Fund's arrangements to commemorate the fiftieth anniversary of the Battle of Britain was the International Air Tattoo. Following the scorching success – temperatures soared to ninety-four degrees Fahrenheit – of IAT '89 at RAF Fairford which attracted the biggest audience so far, Bowen and Prince knew they would be hard put to exceed it.

Ordinarily as was then customary, 1990 was a fallow Fairford year but the Ministry of Defence happily, accepting the historic importance of this anniversary, offered the Aeroplane and Armament Experimental Establishment (A&AEE) at Boscombe Down for a TVS Battle of Britain Airshow staged in association with Alliance and Leicester. Among the crowd-pullers which helped to raise some £250,000 over 9 and 10 June was a flypast by a British Airways Concorde escorted by the Red Arrows. For enthusiasts the venue was an especial attraction. It was the first time the home of the internationally acclaimed Empire Test Pilots School had been open to the public.

The choice of this alternative venue was also particularly fortunate because Boscombe's broad Wiltshire acres had hosted fighter squadrons in 1940 and it was here that Flight Lieutenant James Nicolson, piloting a No. 249 Squadron Hurricane, had been awarded Fighter Command's only Victoria Cross.

Sadly Nicolson had not survived – he was killed later in South-East Asia – to join fellow Battle of Britain pilots present to enjoy an assembly of twelve Spitfires and two Hurricanes in an aerial pageant recapturing the spirit of 1940. Some of the most spirited applause came from a party of Czechs – at IAT for the first time – honouring compatriots who fought alongside the RAF in 1940. They were harbingers of future participation by eastern European aircrew and aircraft.

On 3 September IAT, together with Philips the fine art auctioneers, organised an auction at Bentley Priory, 'leader of the Few' Air Chief Marshal Sir Hugh (later Lord) Dowding's Fighter Command Headquarters, of Battle of Britain memorabilia. It brought in £175,000.

Members of the Battle of Britain Fighter Pilots Association gallantly made themselves available for this and numerous events, not least a gentle parade on 15 September – anniversary of the climax week of London daylight raids – at Buckingham Palace while overhead their successors flew past in salute. The scene was captured in a painting commissioned from Michael Turner by Lloyds Bank (Cox & King's Branch) who made it available to the Fund. Two hundred and fifty prints were sold.

Despite being committed to their own anniversary arrangements the Royal Air Forces Association (raising £410,000), Aircrew Association and Royal Observer Corps – vital in 1940 – were among many Service-associated bodies which supported the Reach For the Sky Appeal. RAFA Sports and showbusiness personalities, especially those who, like Michael Bentine, had served in the RAF responded readily to personal appearance requests.

There was support, too, from less expected quarters. Alastair Cooke, veteran broadcaster of BBC Radio's Letter from America broke a life-time's rule of being unavailable for charity appeal broadcasts. Speaking on behalf of the RAF Benevolent Fund in The Week's Good Cause he raised £40,000. Amid multiple fund-raising activities and events the Queen and the Duke of Edinburgh attended the annual founding of the RAF commemorative concert at the Royal Festival Hall; the Queen Mother attended a Royal Gala performance of *La Traviata* at the London Coliseum; Lord Barber, supported by John Major, Chancellor of the Exchequer, launched Reach For The Sky in the City of London and Moura Lympany appeared in a Bournemouth Symphony Orchestra concert conducted by Sir Edward Heath in Canterbury Cathedral. In a spectacular moment at the London Marathon more than one million fund-raising balloons were released to represent 1.75 million members of the RAF Family who served in the 1939–45 War.

Meanwhile, in a year when he seemed to be everywhere and anywhere, Hurrell launched '. . . *so few*' an ambitious and exquisitely-produced fine art folio containing the experiences, handwritten facsimile accounts and memorabilia of twenty-five surviving members of the Few. Narrative was provided by Bill Gunston and John Golley, distinguished aviation writers. The handsome volume was illustrated by a painting of each subject commissioned from the internationally renowned silhouette artist Michael Pierce.

Bound in exquisite Moroccan-goat blue leather and printed on especially made paper guaranteed to retain its quality for hundreds of years '. . . *so few*' was published by the Fund in a limited edition of 401 copies – of which No.1 was presented to the Queen – and priced at £1600 each. The Fund profited by more than £250,000. Such sizeable sums contributed handsomely and confirmed Kennedy's wisdom in seeking to underwrite future and climbing welfare expenditure on the back of the Battle of Britain. They complemented large contributions from such conventional sources as RAF stations' £670,000, At Home Days' some £200,000 – the half-a-day's-pay-a-year scheme doubled for this anniversary year.

Service and public support had been substantial but Kennedy and the Fund's £20 million Reach For The Sky target remained elusive. Then, as miraculously as the moment in September, 1940, when the *Luftwaffe* switched its attention from Fighter Command's airfields to London – Dowding's 'miracle' – two windfalls totalling more than £15 million enabled Kennedy to exceed the target comfortably. Some while earlier the Fund had been bequeathed a parcel of land in the London suburb of Sunbury which, wedged within a triangle of roads without access, was virtually valueless. However the Fund reckoned that given access through an adjoining corridor of land in other ownership and local authority approval the Sunbury bequest was ripe for development. In time for the Battle of Britain Appeal sufficient land for an access road was acquired and Tesco paid almost £10.5 million for the land.

When out-of-the-blue legacies totalling more than £5 million from Sir Malin Sorsbie, a former RAF officer, and his wife, both of whom had died in the United States, arrived the Reach For The Sky Appeal had surpassed its target by almost £3.25 million.

Sadly, of the many who had contributed to the Appeal's successful outcome Mike Stanton, one of Reach For The Sky's most energetic and able organisers, did not live to celebrate its completion. Although Stanton had been succeeded as Appeals Director by Freddie Hurrell two years earlier he had worked devotedly for the anniversary Appeal. His knowledge of the struts and wires of IAT and working rapport with Bowen and Prince rendered him invaluable in the preparation and staging of the Battle of Britain Airshow. Moreover, Stanton's dedication was such that the day after the crowds had departed he walked the cold and windy airfield for hours and picked up the litter. After a tiring day and satisfied the airfield was tidy, he was turning out of an airfield gate and into a public road when he was killed in a motoring accident. It was a cruel fate for this former air attaché who had lobbed Viet Cong grenades out of the British Embassy compound in Saigon before they could explode.

Successful conclusion of the Battle of Britain fiftieth anniversary year offered a natural cue for change and Lord Catto retired following twelve years as chairman. Comfortable in the knowledge that he was leaving the Fund with a greatly enhanced capital base he was succeeded in the new year of 1991 by Lord Barber. For the former Spitfire photographic reconnaissance pilot, Chancellor of the Exchequer and chairman of the Chartered Bank, chairmanship of the Battle of Britain Appeal had been a tailor-made apprenticeship.

Although Barber had been approached by several charities eager to recruit him he accepted the Council of the RAF Benevolent Fund's invitation after assessing the charity as being 'efficiently and economically administered and because I knew I would enjoy it'. Barber also counted his blessings in coming through the war 'unscathed' and felt 'it seemed right I should do something to help those who were not so fortunate'.

He might have added that in 1943 he had attempted to fly an unarmed reconnaissance Spitfire home from Gibraltar, ran out of fuel near the Channel coast, baled out, been almost impaled on a French steeple and spent the rest of the war interspersing escape attempts with reading for the Bar.

Fresh from the Appeal, Barber was comfortably aware that Catto had handed over a charity that was, as he noted in the restrained tone of a banker, 'financially sound', though justifiably – even in this year of economic stagnation – he could have been more bullish. Thanks to the Appeal his first year would end with a capital base expanded by almost £27 million despite welfare expenditure of more than £7 million to assist nearly 16,000 beneficiaries. Expressing this satisfactory position in terms of charitable expectations Barber opined that providing 'the Fund could generate some £1 million a year it should have sufficient capital resources for its welfare purposes as Trenchard intended.'

But Kennedy was not a leader to rest on the Fund's laurels. Throughout 1991 there was no respite in routine fund-raising and searching for the most effective means of welfare spending, though the Gulf campaign introduced an unexpected call. Alerted following the Iraqi invasion of Kuwait to the needs of RAF families repatriated without their husbands, the Fund opened assistance with immediate payments of £500 in respect of minimal personal possessions. There followed a £5000 interest free loan to be repaid either wholly or by instalments once family circum-stances had stabilised. Subsequently, the Fund was authorised to distribute sums from the publicly subscribed Gulf Trust monies in accor-dance with its normal welfare criteria. By the end of the year £288,000 had been distributed to thirty beneficiaries. In due course the Fund was itself a beneficiary of the Emir of Kuwait who generously donated £250,000 in recognition of the RAF's role in the liberation of the city state.

Operation *Desert Storm* also threatened staging of IAT '91 at Fairford from which USAF B-52s flew round-trips to Baghdad. In the event all was well and Bowen and Prince, with their customary opportunism, announced *Gulf Salute* as a major theme in addition to a Tiger Meet of NATO squadrons and for the first time aircraft of the Czech Air Force. Thanks to the generous support of a host of sponsors, headed by Shell UK Oil and Alliance & Leicester Building Society, *Gulf Salute* contributed more than £450,000 towards welfare spending. Meanwhile, at Portland Place Hurrell crafted residual fund-raising and publicity activities which could be expected to extend the productive life of the 1990 Appeal. Coalport created a Reach For The Sky set of ten Battle of Britain theme plates. Issued by Bradford Exchange the collection benefited the Fund to the extent of £180,000. Eager to sustain sales of '. . . *so few*' Hurrell geared prestigious occasions to presentations of the fine art folio, a copy of which was presented by John Major, the prime minister, to President Bush for the Library of Congress.

Consolidation throughout 1991 in the wake of the big Appeal set the

President Bush receives a copy of the fund-raising fine art folio '. . . *so few*' from John Major.

pattern for the new year, Barber noting that fortunately the Fund, though not immune from pressures facing charities because of a 'reduction in corporate giving during the deep and prolonged recession' was well supported by friends in that sector. As the figure of more than £7.8 million demonstrates welfare work continued unabated. An extended Care Wing at Alastrean House was completed and brought into use thanks to a bequest from Mrs M. E. Barber in memory of her husband who had died as a prisoner of the Japanese.

While need assured full houses at the Fund's homes, recession and armed forces' reductions produced, at this stage, a low-level alert over the future viability of the Duke of Kent School where a small fall in pupils dropped the roll to 155, of whom fifty-six were girls. The Fund responded with a vigorous advertising programme, appearances at independent schools exhibitions and measures raising the school's profile within the Service. Amid many and habitual successes Roger Wilson, headmaster, and his staff, took especial pleasure in the news that Katherine Wade, a former Foundationer whose father was killed in a Canberra accident in Cyprus in 1972, had been elected President of the Oxford Union.

On the fund-raising front Hurrell unashamedly continued to squeeze the pips of the 1990 Appeal. A letter from Kennedy to everyone on the Appeal database produced more than £65,000 and a further £37,800 covenanted over future years. However, as might be expected in a period of recession, the airshow – where better to lift the nation's spirits – was the fund-raising flagship of the year. Organised as usual by IAT it was staged in the name of Air Tournament International at Boscombe Down.

Dab hands at producing 'firsts' Bowen and Prince excelled themselves by persuading the Russians to appear. They proved great crowd-pullers. The touchdown direct from the Lil Gromov Flight Research Institute at Zukovsky of the celebrated test pilot Anatoly Kvotchur in a Su-27P Flanker was particularly memorable. In a year marking the fiftieth anniversary of the arrival of the Eighth Air Force in the UK, United States Army Air Force, American, Russian and East European air forces competed to give of their best, producing thrilling performances.

New ground was also broken at the Royal Festival Hall when the IAT team applied their 'showbusiness' skills to an annual concert format which was beginning. In an event sponsored by British Aerospace, the BBC Concert Orchestra, conducted by Kenneth Alwyn, took part for the first time, appearing together with the RAF Central Band under Wing Commander Barrie Hingley. In the autumn all four home-based RAF bands, their concerts compèred by Tom O'Connor for the first time,

Tom O'Connor, regular concert tour compère, drums up support for the Fund throughout the country.

made another nine-venue fund-raising tour. Although the recession affected seat sales Imperial Tobacco's support assured a useful profit.

All the while the IAT organisation extended its confirming house, special events, publishing responsibilities and general commercial activities until it seemed appropriate and prudent to nail the company well and truly to the Fund's mast. It was re-entitled Royal Air Force Benevolent Fund Enterprises, retaining IAT in relation to Fairford's core aviation activities.

When Kennedy retired in the autumn Barber, true to his characteristic instinct for basics, recalled that 'Sir Jock' had joined the Fund when increasing demands on resources were of great concern. Now he left it with a heightened profile and sound financial base. The Fund, Barber added, could confidently expect the generosity it would wish well into the next century. Kennedy also left a legacy not generally known outside Portland Place. He improved staff pay and working conditions, bringing them closer to commercial standards and enabling retention and recruitment of the very best of staff. Above all he left a 'happy ship'.

Among Kennedy's many fruitful legacies was a magnificent rapport with the RAF Bands, resulting in ever improving fund-raising co-operation. Finally, Hingley played 'Sir Jock' out at the Bands' Uxbridge centre with a selection of pieces representative of his career. It was a rousing farewell for a universally popular Controller.

CHAPTER 25

PALIN STEPS UP RELIEF

When selecting Kennedy's successor the Council turned again to a former Air Member for Personnel. Fresh from meeting the challenges of a contracting Service and the 'Purple' intricacies of a Royal Air Force becoming increasingly interdependent with the Royal Navy and the Army, Air Chief Marshal Sir Roger Palin was, as was his predecessor, the Controller for his time.

Educated at Canford and St John's College, Cambridge, Palin, as with Barber, had first served in the Army where he was a subaltern in the 3rd Battalion Parachute Regiment and the 10th Parachute Battalion

Air Chief Marshal Sir Roger Palin, Controller 1993–98.

(Territorial Army). After transferring to the RAF Palin had later combined the natural qualities of a successful fighter leader with the intellectual requirements of a succession of staff appointments leading penultimately to command of the RAF in Germany and of the 2nd Tactical Air Force. *En route* a sabbatical year as guest scholar at the Woodrow Wilson International Centre for Scholars in Washington had helped to fine-tune him for the more cerebral demands of high command.

In the aftermath of the Battle of Britain bonanza national recession continued to cast a shadow over charity fund-raising as Palin considered his options. Since he had arrived at Portland Place in the Fund's seventy-fifth anniversary year, fate had handed him a helpful peg on which to hang commemorative fund-raising in and out of the Service. At the same time, conscious of the addition of the Battle of Britain millions and a statutorily watchful Charity Commission, Palin moved to loosen the purse-strings and spend more generously on welfare. Where possible, welfare committees were encouraged to make outright grants rather than repayable loans, especially where assistance would improve the quality of life of aged widows.

As he settled in to the weekly routine of the Main Grants Committee Palin noted for his own guidance: 'Is the Fund as benevolent as it could be and should be? Is sufficient help being given, say, to disabled spouses, is housing help appropriately provided and is it not time to welcome national servicemen as beneficiaries?' Palin further asked himself: 'Should the Fund seek to fly wing-tip to wing-tip with its sister organisation, The Royal Air Forces Association?'

In planning a way forward Palin was much assisted by Kennedy and Barcilon's recent welfare review and study with RAFA of homes. But Palin decided to go further and, at the request of the Trustees, set in hand a wide-ranging strategy review of all aspects of Fund business including Appeals Administration, links with RAFA and Care in the Community.

At the heart of the review lay one imperative. The Fund must move closer to RAFA. After noting that dual welfare facilities covering a range of required residential care were broadly complementary, the review concluded that each organisation should continue to manage its own homes while developing ever closer co-operation to ensure mutual best practice, at the same time seeking harmonisation where practicable.

Implementation of the review fell to Barcilon's successor, Air Vice-Marshal Bob Peters, who had joined the Fund from the prestigious appointment of Commandant of the RAF Staff College, Bracknell. As with Palin the new welfare director brought recent and entirely post-war experience of the Service and its needs. He was particularly aware of the incidence of chronic or remedial difficulties – often resulting from ill-health in Service families.

Conscious that a historic public and Service tendency to associate

Benevolent Fund relief of distress primarily with wartime and peacetime
campaigns, death and disablement had long shrouded such family need,
Hurrell took measures to correct this understandable misconception.
Since the Service through the voluntary pay deduction scheme and fund-
raising events contributed so handsomely towards annual Fund income
he considered it vital to let members know just how *their* Fund was
looking after its own.

Posters graphically illustrating individual serving cases were distributed to stations and units and an arrangement was made with *RAF
News*, the Service's fortnightly newspaper, to carry a page devoted exclusively to the Royal Air Force Benevolent Fund in each issue. Edward
Bishop, author of this and previous editions of *The Debt We Owe*, who had
recently joined Hurrell's team as press and public relations consultant,
was tasked to compile the page. As a long-experienced journalist and
author, Bishop was soon very much in his stride and a flow of stories and
pictures began to reflect the Fund in action.

An early example of the Fund's help for serving people – with of course
the subject's agreement – was a combined poster and *RAF News*
presentation of the plight and assistance of Paul Airey, a junior technician
working on Victor tankers at RAF Marham. Under the heading *Help Top
Up Your Fund* the poster showed a Victor refuelling a Hercules and
carried a picture and story describing how, following a motorcycle accident in which he was paralysed from the waist down, the Fund had
helped him.

Paul's story appeared simultaneously in *RAF News* where he told how
the Fund helped him to regain his independence and replaced a heavy
National Health Service wheelchair with a light one on permanent loan.
In addition to a grant to cover a deposit for a car through the Motability
Scheme, modification of its controls and access for his wheelchair, the
Fund also contributed towards computer equipment to develop chair-
borne work skills. Accompanying pictures showed Paul's activities as a
paraplegic sportsman in which he skis, water-skis, makes free-fall parachute descents and swims competitively.

Publication of Paul's and other such experiences also helps to satisfy
the imperative of countering the persistent perception of the Fund priori-
tising officers and their families. In the same period *RAF News* carried the
story and picture of Senior Aircraftman Stephen Pritchard who had also
been crippled as the result of a motorcycle accident.

Stephen was a Movements Operator with Air Movement Squadron,
RAF Bruggen, when he gave a lift to a friend. On the way to the base he
hit a steel post and was thrown into a ditch, receiving multiple injuries.
His friend's fractures were not so serious. Paralysed from the waist down
and his right arm partially paralysed Stephen can expect to be in a wheelchair for the rest of his life. Following prolonged and specialist treatment,
Fund grants helped to equip him with a personal computer and powered
wheelchair. Through the Housing Trust it also provided him with a new

bungalow at Rhostyllen, Wrexham in Clwyd where he wished to live. As further needs became apparent Stephen received a deposit on an Astra car, the costs of adaptations and furniture including the price of a special medical bed. Previously Stephen had been a keen sportsman and had water-skied and rowed for the RAF. In time, thanks to his own determination and the Fund's support, he began to take part in paraplegic rugby and football before joining the *Birmingham Bandits*, a rugby team for tetraplegics.

In addition to increasing awareness throughout the RAF of how the Fund is always there to assist serving personnel Stephen's story stimulated immediate interest in the Housing Trust which had been established as far back as 1972 and was currently operating 250 homes. In response to letters to *RAF News*, readers learned through the Fund page how the Trust can provide a home for a widow and dependent children where a serving husband has died while the family was living in married quarters which have to be vacated.

Generally, it was explained, although in relevant cases houses are rent free, Housing Trust homes are rented, rents being based on ability to pay. Should beneficiaries at any time require warden care the Housing Trust can arrange transfer to sheltered accommodation.

Issue by issue the Fund's page developed as a valuable link between the Fund and the Service in which fund-raising ventures began to complement how-your-money-pays-for-welfare news and pictures. Under the heading *French raid Biggin Hill to honour Spitfire pilot and raise Fund cash*, Edward Bishop described how two microlight and five light aircraft of the René Mouchotte Flying Club of Paris raided Biggin on behalf of the Fund. Mouchotte had fought in the Battle of Britain with Nos 245 and 615 Hurricane squadrons before receiving command of No. 615 Squadron. Lord Barber, a busy and ubiquitous chairman, accepted a handsome donation. Bob Ogley, generous donor of his *Biggin on the Bump* and other book royalties, was also present to explain Biggin's wartime role.

Another developing benefit of the introduction of the *RAF News* page was the opportunity it offered to keep the Service briefed on the broad and sometimes unusual public support of the Fund. News of the presentation of a cheque in 1993 for £11,500 from the Pigeon Keepers' Wings Appeal commemorating wartime pigeon services was accompanied by a feature on the exploits of birds supplied by pigeon breeders, some of whom enlisted as pigeoneers. Apart from pigeons carried in operational aircraft, birds speeding intelligence, and photographs and diagrams from enemy-occupied Europe – including V1 and V2 details – gave valiant service. Eighty-two-year-old former Corporal J. Tucker of the RAF Pigeon Service who had served with Lord Cheshire VC and who had initiated the appeal asked for the proceeds to be devoted to improvements to the South Wing lounge at Princess Marina House.

Meanwhile, and shortly before Kennedy handed over to Palin, the fund-raising event of 1993 was the International Air Tattoo, its ever-rising status further heightened by recognition as the official public celebration of the RAF's seventy-fifth anniversary. After miserable weather had washed out a 1 April Anniversary Royal Review by the Queen at RAF Marham – for which Palin had been responsible as AMP and Fairford had been consulted – the July staging of IAT '93 at RAF Fairford attracted especial attention. The Fund's airshow went some way towards compensating for the disappointment.

A spectacular figure seventy-five skywriting anniversary formation carried over from the weather-aborted Royal Review and composed of twenty Hawks led the modern section of the celebratory aerial pageant. Nor was there any shortage of royalty at this almost alternative Royal Review. Palin welcomed the Dukes of Edinburgh and Kent and Prince Michael; and from Jordan, King Hussein, Queen Noor and their son Prince Faisal.

Supported in view of the occasion by a larger than usual RAF presence and by substantial sponsorship led by British Aerospace, Bowen and Prince set out to surpass all previous airshows. IAT assembled more foreign participants and a greater range of aircraft types than ever, among them an exciting variety from Russia and East Europe.

In the event the Russians, inviting visitor inspection of a Tu-95 Bear making its first appearance in the West and mounting a breathtaking aerobatic display, were great crowd-pullers. Unfortunately, however, Russian enthusiasm got the better of the pilots of a pair of MiG-29s which collided towards the end of their duo display. Spectators, safely positioned as always away from the action, saw the pilots eject and their Fulcrum aircraft crash in flames. That no-one was seriously injured or static aircraft badly damaged in IAT's first serious accident owed much to its Emergency Services Plan which serves as model for airshow organisers around the world.

The entire episode was captured by BBC Television which had acquired rights to make a ninety-minute programme for home and overseas. Accorded a record 'gate' IAT produced a better than ever £400,000 for the Fund and was assured of an annual Fairford airshow henceforth. Thus, IAT '93 was the crowning feature of a bustling year during which RAF Gatow raised £50,000 through a *Salute to Berlin* airshow staged – with some assistance from RAFBE – to mark the RAF's departure from the station.

The year also marked the publication of Enterprises' first book *Brace By Wire to Fly By Wire*, addition of an annual *USAF Year Book*, launch of *Skywords* containing *Skyhigh* merchandise offers and a *Skyhigh* trailer. Fairford's year also saw a major development of the Fund's concert tradition. Having kicked off the seventy-fifth commemoration with a combined Central Band of the RAF and BBC Concert Orchestra broadcast concert sponsored in the early spring by Marshalls of Cambridge at the Royal Festival Hall, it ended the year with the launch of a Superkings-sponsored inaugural Massed Bands Christmas concert tour compèred by Tom O'Connor.

At the close of Palin's first year Barber reflected that although the Fund had been spared the worst effects of recession it had not escaped entirely. If it had received less corporate support, old friends remained faithful despite their own problems and the Fund had benefited from prudent investment. Further on the scale of that true barometer of Fund achievement, welfare spending of £8.325 million on 17,620 beneficiaries was evidence of Palin's encouragement of more liberal assistance.

Hard on the heels of the RAF's seventy-fifth birthday the Fund was confronted at the outset of 1994 with the need to organise a suitable programme on which to base commemoration of its own seventy-fifth anniversary. Concluding that in the wake of the comparatively recent Battle of Britain fiftieth Anniversary Appeal it should adopt a less aggressive approach to its seventy-fifth birthday the Fund refrained from issuing a specifically linked call for financial support. Even so the anniversary of a year in which welfare spending would for the first time top £9 million was not to pass unrecognised. An autumn Royal Gala Evening at the Royal Albert Hall in the presence of the President, the Duke of Kent, was planned for the Royal Albert Hall and a special service at St Clement Danes, the RAF Central Church, leaving IAT to provide the outdoor sparkle.

As the year progressed, national statistics reinforced the wisdom of the Fund's policy of maintaining a strong financial base while not shrinking from ever-rising welfare demands. Social trends identified by the Government confirmed what Portland Place Grants Committees had known for some time. In the committees' experience people were ceasing work sooner and living longer, leaving society to support and care for larger numbers of the elderly.

Given that statistics indicated that more than one-fifth of the population was over sixty and that numbers of old people were expected to rise for the next forty years there were clear implications for the Fund. For the present, however, welfare outgoings increased during the year by no more than ten per cent, but Peters was concerned that too many of his case folders reflected the national experience of marital breakdown and debt.

Although applications from serving families were occurring at the rate of about one in twenty and costing some £2 million a year it was reassuring that serving families continued to seek protection offered by the Fund's Insurance Advisory Service (IAS) and Dependants Fund and Dependants Income Trust (DINCOME). Membership of the Dependants Fund continued to run at the satisfactory level of ninety-five per cent of serving people. DINCOME was buoyant and stood at 54.8 per cent of the Dependants Fund. Interest in the Insurance Advisory Service, now a member of the recently created Personal Investment Authority, was sharpened by press reflection of poor advice received from some insurance and pension firms.

Among Palin's earliest initiatives was to improve sources of welfare intelligence. He acted to strengthen the network of the Fund's voluntary Helpers in the field, inviting old hands and younger recruits to refresher courses for which RAFA generously offered expertise and facilities. The value of Palin's 'wing-tip to wing-tip' urge was especially evident in Edinburgh where the Fund accommodated RAFA in its 20 Queen Street building. Rapport between Group Captain Dan Needham, the Fund's Scotland director, and the Association was correspondingly close. Palin also led development and improvement of operational links with other associated charitable bodies which regularly help to investigate, prepare and present cases. Notably, these are the British Legion and the Soldiers', Sailors' and Airmen's Families Association (SSAFA).

The Anno Domini escalator of ageing veterans had become an especial factor in the notebooks of the Fund's Helpers, RAFA branch members, Portland Place welfare staff and others assessing their needs and recommending means of relief. One of Welfare's more difficult tasks, remains the selection of residents for Princess Marina House and Alastrean House. In this period Care in the Community regulations began to add to the difficulties. Generally, experience told welfare workers which candidates merited consideration and would benefit from admission but, as they discovered, human considerations and membership of the RAF Family did not always match criteria of local authorities. Where differences occurred, as Barber emphasised in his annual statement for 1994, the Fund would continue to use its own criteria for offering permanent residence. Indeed, it had accepted a number of people who had been refused local authority support.

The Chairman also found comfort in the homes' good standing with the registration authorities among which the Fund's care of the elderly and disabled was acknowledged to be of the very highest quality. He reported that the residential wing of Princess Marina House was full and the waiting list such that the home could be filled twice over. Alastrean House was also full and for the first time in many years there was a growing list of potential applicants. As Alastrean's Board of Management faced new challenges Air Vice-Marshal George Chesworth succeeded Air Marshal Sir Peter Bairsto who had served as chairman since Steedman's time.

Although there was evidence on the Homes' front that full fees might be deterring some people from applying, Barber reported that seventy per cent of residents were currently subsidised. He noted too that ageing veterans were increasing the need for nursing as opposed to residential care and dual registration of some or all rooms was being considered. This would increase the Fund's ability to care for those who could no longer help themselves.

While the needs of people older in years than the Fund were necessarily placing an increasing call on resources, the seventy-fifth anniversary of the Fund's founding served also to recall that its school continued to flourish as its oldest establishment. Led by the headmaster, Roger Wilson, Duke of Kent School began the academic year with 156 pupils of whom 59 were girls. Vastly changed since its Vanbrugh Castle days the school, since its move and change of name, had accepted ever increasing numbers of fee-paying Service and civilian children. However, Foundationers, though much outnumbered, continued to receive absolute priority of admission and in this anniversary year accounted for thirteen boys and five girls who could expect to join thirty-seven former pupils being assisted at reputable senior schools. Transition to the status of a more broadly based preparatory school, hastened by changing Service conditions, had been greatly assisted by Air Marshal Sir Charles Ness during his years as chairman of the governors and the Fund's Education Committee until his untimely death in 1994 aged seventy. Air Marshal Sir Michael Simmons took his place at very short notice.

On the fund-raising front the absence of a focused seventy-fifth birthday appeal offered Hurrell an added incentive to stimulate routine measures and, beginning with the *RAF News* page and poster campaign, introduce initiatives. Following publication of '. . . *so few*' in 1990 members of the Battle of Britain Fighter Pilots Association, had urged consideration of a companion volume in honour of Bomber Command aircrew. Hurrell reinvigorated the '. . . *so few*' team and during the art folio's preparation organised advance publicity to test the water and obtain pre-publication orders.

Eight-hour bomber sorties and sometimes even longer, the fighter boys insisted, had called for qualities, which while different, were even more testing than brief but frequent 1940 combat in the aerial tiltyard over Britain. However, Bomber Command, despite almost 56,000 losses, did not share equal honours with Fighter Command in public memory. Hurrell moved to level the balance of public perception. Setting out to select twenty-five surviving bomber aircrew the Fund, while obtaining the wholehearted support and co-operation of Bomber Command VCs, eschewed the temptation to present their stories with Pierce's silhouettes of wartime household names. In the event the experiences of most of the hitherto unsung heroes were so publishable that Hurrell obtained the assistance of a Halifax wireless operation/air-gunner to help promote the project at a national press, radio and television conference at Birmingham Airport, followed by lunch in the Lord Mayor's parlour.

After both his legs had been shot away over Germany in 1944 Dennis Salt had parachuted into a snowdrift and been saved by two young German girls in the face of villagers who wanted to shoot him or leave him to die. The Fund had found the girls, now elderly ladies, and brought them to Birmingham to tell their stories. The result was massive coverage obtained by Bishop in *The Daily Telegraph* and *Daily Mail,* among nationals, the provincial press, radio and television. The Fund coupled this initiative with a presentation of '. . . *so few*' to the Lord Mayor of London for the City's archives as a promotional trailer for '. . . *so many*'. Subsequently, in a move which opened up war-occupied Jersey as a fruitful fund-raising source Bishop spearheaded a promotion in the Channel Islands. With the permission and assistance of Warwick Blench of the Perspective Eye gallery in St Helier, Air Marshal Sir John Sutton, the Lieutenant Governor, accompanied by Lord Barber, opened an exhibition of '. . . *so few*', a dummy copy of the future '. . . *so many*', the James Butler Battle of Britain *Scramble* sculpture and Fund promotional material. Attended by 150 of the island's wealthiest residents the event produced instant and subsequent sales, sowed the seeds of future legacies and was followed later by the receipt of a single donation for £250,000.

In a climate in which RAF closures and reductions reminded the Fund of the importance of creating and nourishing new sources of charitable income, Palin strove to maintain a high level of Service revenue. He was never too busy to collect a cheque as, for example, when in the new year of 1994 he visited Leeming to receive £20,000 raised there. The cheque, presented by the station commander, Group Captain Phil Roser, equalled the amount currently spent daily to relieve distress within the RAF family. The total was impressive, but Palin was also conscious that small sums raised by ingenious individual efforts contributed handsomely to annual fund-raising revenue; for instance the air commodore who collected £34 from golfers recovering stray balls from his garden.

Further evidence that while overall Service income might be diminishing it was not disappearing was the presentation at Portland Place by Air Marshal Sir Andrew Wilson, AMP, of a cheque for £272,715 representing At Home Day proceeds and £60,000 from the RAF Central Fund. This brought the most recent annual contribution from serving personnel to £2.435 million, accounting for 22.95 per cent of the Fund's Ordinary income – satisfactory figures on which Wing Commander Jack Connell could comfortably bow out after eleven years as Director Finance. Barber noted: 'He helped to navigate the Fund's finances through a difficult period and it is a measure of his dedicated service that the Accumulated Fund increased from £21 million to £86 million during his stewardship.' In the context of continually-rising welfare expenditure Connell's achievement was all the more creditable.

Although there was no specific Fund seventy-fifth birthday appeal, IAT and the various constituents of RAF Benevolent Fund Enterprises did not allow the anniversary opportunity to pass without an all-the-fun-of-the-fair 'circus' airshow with the showmanship of ringmasters Bowen and Prince written all over it. The fortieth birthday of the C-130 Hercules,

attended by generous Lockheed participation and sponsorship, provided
an additional anniversary peg. Forty US Air Force and Air National
Guard *Fat Alberts* were supplemented by C-130s flown in by air forces
around the world, bringing the total of visiting aircraft to more than
350 representing fifty national air arms.

Surprises are the oxygen of IAT events and '94 was no exception. After
landing a Slovak MiG-21 the pilot said that his government wished to
present the aircraft to the Benevolent Fund. A suitable if somewhat ad
hoc ceremony was swiftly arranged at which Prince Michael of Kent
accepted the MiG from Pavos Kanis, Slovak Defence Minister. At
another ceremony King Hussein, accompanied by Queen Noor,
presented flying certificates to the year's nine disabled winners of Bader
flying scholarships, of which Hussein had paid for six. At the post-
airshow wash-up it was noted that there had been some alleviation of
Fairford's notoriously difficult traffic conditions. This was in part due to
traffic advice from Superintendent Wong, on secondment from Hong
Kong to the Wiltshire and Gloucestershire police.

While the airshow was the cream layer of IAT's seventy-fifth anniversary cake, Fairford iced it by staging a flypast at the opening of the
Channel Tunnel by the Queen and President Mitterand, and handling
VIP and public ticketing for D-Day fiftieth anniversary events at home
and in Normandy. Towards the end of the year the Gala Evening at
the Royal Albert Hall and autumn and Christmas concert tours by the
Massed Bands of the RAF were again reminders that IAT does not hiber-
nate after the airshow. It had been a busy year throughout the Fund. In
no way had progress been impeded by the absence of a seventy-fifth
anniversary appeal. Indeed, Barber summed up: 'Our anniversary year
was one in which many other charities had to struggle hard just to maintain their status quo. Yet despite a ten per cent increase in welfare
expenditure the Fund ended the year in sound financial health.'

But he warned that for the next ten years at least, demands on the
Fund's resources would increase and it could not afford to be complacent.

> Over that same period our traditional sources of revenue will diminish and
> we must face the probability that with the passing of the generations that
> remembered the War the numbers of bequests to the Fund will fall. With
> the financial base of the Fund secure we can face the challenges that lie
> ahead with confidence. We work for a good cause and I have no doubt
> that, properly presented it will continue, as it must, to be well supported.

There could have been no more appropriate sentiment with which to
close a year during which Wing Commander Jack Connell retired as
Director Finance and Dame Felicity Peake, retaining her seat on the
Council, retired from the Finance and General Purposes Committee
(F&GP) after sixteen years service.

With the departure from the F&GP power-house of Dame Felicity, widow of Sir Harald Peake, a former chairman, the Fund lost the inspired and devoted counsel of a former Director Women's Royal Air Force who had first joined the Council in 1946. Sad though she was to leave Dame Felicity was much consoled and heartened that her banker son, Andrew, had recently followed his father and mother on to the Council and F&GP.

CHAPTER 26

BONUS YEARS OVER

T he new year of 1995 ushered in the last remaining major 1939–45 War anniversary before the dawn of the new Millennium. Since few veterans were likely to survive to commemorate another major anniversary year, there was an awesome sense of finality about the parades and events commemorating the fiftieth anniversary of Victory in Europe and Victory over Japan. No doubt the ending of the War *will be* remembered at future suitable intervals but as Barber, ever the realist, opined, the bonus years of fiftieth anniversaries were over and the generous flow of legacy income, in part inspired by them, was likely to decline.

At the Fund, media recall of VE and VJ Day scenes in 1945 and plans to link and theme IAT with the anniversary were salutary reminders that ageing veterans and dependants were likely to continue to make heavy demands on its resources. Seizing the moment, the F&GP Committee called for an overall strategic review aimed at assessing welfare, spending and policy expectations over the next fifteen to twenty years. Action, though it would inevitably require increased welfare spending, was swift.

An early measure entitled national servicemen to assistance should their circumstances justify it. Another recognised – ahead of the state – the plight of war widows who had remarried but whose second marriages had ended in divorce. Other innovations and reforms prompted by the review included the addition of assistance with pre-prep and tertiary education for Foundationer children and the abandonment of loans, a decision to make all maintenance awards as grants.

The opportunity was also taken to move yet closer to RAFA, in partnership with whom contract care beds at the point of need were to be provided for beneficiaries unable to enter either of the Fund's homes. As Barber reported: 'Partnership with the Association grows increasingly close and combines the advantages of their numerous and widespread membership who can identify and investigate cases of need with the Fund's ability to raise the means to pay for whatever welfare expenditure is approved.'

It was clear that implementation of the consequences of the Strategic Review would require further improvement of welfare intelligence links with sister ex-service organisations and the Fund's own Helpers. To this end, Palin conducted six meetings of Helpers spread through England,

Scotland and Wales and invited representatives of RAFA, SSAFA, the Royal British Legion and the War Pensions Welfare Society to attend. The Controller updated participants on Fund policy and stimulated mutually beneficial discussions.

An ongoing benefit of this initiative is the assembly of relief packages resulting from a combination of investigative and award sources as with the case in the early 1990s of SAC Rob Linge, an RAF chef who had lost an arm when a petrol-fuelled cooker exploded in the Gulf. Alerted by the War Pensions Welfare Society the Fund sanctioned an interest free loan of £50,000 to buy a flat. Subsequently, the Fund made a further loan of £60,000 for a more suitable home, the Gulf Trust made a grant of £4430 and the Ministry of Defence, accepting liability for Rob's injuries, made an initial payment of £50,000. Rob rebuilt his life. He became one-armed golf champion of England and Wales, played squash and badminton, excelled at tenpin bowling and drove with a false arm.

If, unusually, RAFA was not involved in this particular case, Palin, shortly to offer RAFA a half-share of the Fund's page in *RAF News*, placed great importance on continuously reminding the Service of the virtues of an ever improving Fund-RAFA axis. An all-stations explanatory poster was issued and *RAF News* carried an article by Edward Bishop, headed *Fund and Association depend on each other*. He wrote:

> The workaday warm and productive welfare partnership between the sisters is not always apparent to beneficiaries – and even less to Service and public contributors to both organisations. Put together, the individual strengths of Fund and Association combine to provide a remarkable welfare package. A large proportion of the cases financed by the Fund are prepared and put forward by the Association.
>
> While RAFA, by virtue of its big membership, is well placed to carry out caring and supportive casework, the Fund's Grants Committees are the more able to authorise frequently heavy expenditure for the relief of distress. Expressed simply, the efforts of the Fund on behalf of the RAF Family and its sister organisation are complementary. As a membership organisation RAFA is in pole position to alert the Benevolent Fund to need and to commend cases. As a charity of seventy-five years standing the Fund is better placed to pay for them.
>
> The figures speak for themselves. RAFA's welfare spend is currently £1.8 million while the Fund is disbursing more than £8 million a year on RAFA-originated and other cases. This figure could not be supported without support of the Service through the half-a-day's-pay scheme and the warm-hearted generosity of RAFA branches.

The article went on to cite examples of interdependence in practice, notably joint development of Dowding House at Moffat on the Scottish borders, the Fund's contribution of £25,000 to enable the Association's contract care scheme to be extended to cover twenty-six nursing care, convalescent and respite places and endowment of beds at Sussexdown, a RAFA Home.

Meanwhile, the Fund reviewed policy on its own residential homes. Although Princes Marina House and Alastrean House continued to offer short-term nursing care, and respite and recuperative breaks a previously suspected need for nursing as opposed to residential care had become a reality. Alastrean was modified to meet local authority guidelines and all rooms were registered for dual residential and nursing use.

A conservatory extension was built to allow the frailest of veterans to sit in a bright, sunny room and, weather permitting, observe the Scottish scenery. While the Alastrean board did not envisage an early change of status to a nursing home it had so ordered accommodation that, excepting those in an advanced stage of mental illness, the home could accept or keep residents requiring care.

Hale and hearty though he was as the nation commemorated the fiftieth anniversary of the end of the War, Squadron Leader S. G. – known to all as John – Betty, an Alastrean resident, exemplified the ranks of elderly veterans in the Fund's care. When war came in 1939 John was already a veteran. He had enlisted in 1922 as a boy mechanic and been awarded the DFM in the 1930s while serving in India as a sergeant pilot. After being commissioned he received the AFC while instructing Polish Battle of Britain pilots. When John retired in 1972 he had served fifty years and twenty-four days in RAF uniform.

Changes at Alastrean were paralleled at Princess Marina House where the North and South Wings were re-named Burton and Kyle respectively, in memory of Air Marshal Sir Harry Burton and Air Chief Marshal Sir Wallace 'Digger' Kyle, former Chairmen of the Board of Management. Their widows unveiled plaques to mark the occasion. Here, too, provision of nursing care seemed likely to become a priority. The F&GP committee directed that Kyle Wing be surveyed to identify means of arranging for more extensive nursing care.

Fund-raising, as might be expected given the VE and VJ anniversaries and the last opportunity, excepting the Korean War and brief campaigns, for a fiftieth anniversary bonus, held up well. Members of the RAFBE team at Fairford, staging a Victory Airshow at IAT '95 surpassed themselves. Never complacent about previous successes, Bowen and Prince, aware of increasing competition from other weekend attractions, restructured the flying programme and included emotive, themed tableaux. Many thousands of 1939–45 War veterans were present and there was scarcely a dry eye when in a spectacular commemorative finale Harrier, Tornado and other contemporary aircraft formed up in salute along the flight-line runway as a Blenheim, Lancaster, Fortress, Mosquito, Spitfire and Hurricane flew past.

Mainly devised by Sean Maffet, IAT's chief commentator, and narrated by Peter Donaldson of BBC Radio 4 an astonishing piece of aerial theatre had opened with a flypast by twelve Tiger Moths – the type in which so many veterans had first gone solo – and ended with a Spitfire, Mustang and Me 109 flying through a smoke 'V' created by the Red Arrows.

Earlier, amid eight continuous hours of flying, vintage aircraft, current when the Fund staged air pageants in the 1920s, vied for applause with Eurofighter 2000, making its maiden appearance at an airshow. Among other 1990s attractions *Skytanker 95* provided an eyecatching centrepiece in which an immaculate South African 60 Squadron Boeing 707-344C was its nation's first military representative at a UK event. Organisers of a military airshow to celebrate the seventy-fifth anniversary of the founding of the South African Air Force, who had arrived aboard the tanker, were impressed. They invited Bowen and Prince and members of their RAFBE team to help stage their airshow at Waterkloof Air Force Base in October. IAT '95 also marked the gift of a Hunter which was accepted on behalf of the Fund by Prince Michael of Kent. At another ceremony Prince Faisal of Jordan, deputising for his father, presented flying certificates to ten disabled fliers.

However, Fairford is not a one-week-end fund-raising wonder, a fact of which RAFBE's publishing, direct mail and concert activities are fruitful reminders. Eight new book titles were published while *Skyhigh*, the Fund's gift and leisure wear business, prospered, its Christmas catalogue achieving record sales. Collaboration with the Air Training Corps produced a new range of outdoor clothing. In addition to its routine ticketing for IAT and other airshows it assisted with arrangements for the Victory celebrations in London, including a major event in Hyde Park. Concerts conformed to the developing pattern of an autumn and a Christmas tour. Additionally, thanks to the beyond-the-call-of-duty and ever-cheerful co-operation of RAF Music Services, a VE Night Concert performed by the Massed Bands of the RAF was a sell-out at the Birmingham Symphony Hall.

It was half-way through this year that Hurrell, Appeals Director and also a director of RAFBE, handed over his responsibilities to Air Commodore Colin Reineck. Freddie, as Hurrell was universally known, had in his unobtrusive yet effective style involving the minimum of paperwork, helped fashion Fairford's flagship contribution to fund-raising. Yet his part in IAT '95 was but a fraction of his portfolio in his final months. Among other activities Hurrell finalised the production and initial sales of the fine art folio '. . . *so many*', the companion volume to the brilliantly successful '. . . *so few*' and masterminded a magnificent and profitable dinner at RAF Bentley Priory to commemorate the seventy-fifth anniversary of the South African Air Force.

With retirement imminent it pleased Hurrell that, assisted by the VE and VJ anniversaries, his last year was his most successful. At the close of the dinner at which an auction conducted by Lord Tebbitt, former fighter pilot and cabinet minister, had augmented bucket donations and pledges with £11,000, Air Chief Marshal Sir Michael Graydon, Chief of

Air Staff, paid Hurrell warm tribute. 'Indefatigable Freddie', CAS said, had raised millions of pounds in the past seven years.

Barber, who was also retiring, noted: 'We will miss the imaginative and innovative fund-raising efforts of Air Vice-Marshal Freddie Hurrell. A hard act to follow but in Air Commodore Colin Reineck, who served in both the Fleet Air Arm and the RAF, we know we have a worthy successor.' Reineck immediately found himself organising the Fund's first Battle of Britain Golf Classic sponsored by ServiceTec Ltd. Now an annual event, it has accrued more than £40,000 and much goodwill for the Fund. In his early days Reineck also had the pleasure of receiving a donation of £6000 from Group Captain Chris Burwell, station commander at Scampton, who had raised the money by completing the 192 mile Wainwright coast-to-coast walk in memory of his wife Jill who had died of cancer.

If this was a modest amount in the totality of fund-raising income it contributed to Barber's sense of immense satisfaction that in his last year the Fund had the wherewithal to spend more than £10.25 million on 18,358 welfare and general assistance awards. He was also comforted that beyond individual and family beneficiaries it maintained its tradition of making substantial donations – totalling more than £575,000 in 1995 – to outside organisations and schools in recognition of help given to past and present members of the RAF Family.

In the course of a valedictory letter Barber noted:

> As I look back at the work of the Fund over these recent years and the many activities and events with which my wife and I have been involved, my abiding recollection is one of satisfaction at having been associated with a charity which brings relief from hardship suffered not only by those who fought in the war but, as time passes, by more and more of those who have served in the RAF since 1945.

In the new year of 1996 Lord Barber was succeeded as Chairman of the Council by Sir Adrian Swire who had served in the Royal Air Force Volunteer Reserve and the Royal Hong Kong Auxiliary Air Force and was an Honorary Air Commodore in the Royal Auxiliary Air Force. A former trustee of the RAF Museum, Swire shared with his predecessor a great affection for the Spitfire and had owned and flown a Mark IX. Happy coincidence though this was, it was not, of course, an essential credential for a chairman. When Swire took over he had been chairman since 1987 of John Swire and Sons, London, parent company of the Swire Group. He was also a director of Swire Pacific, Hong Kong; Cathay Pacific Airways, Hong Kong; and bankers HSBC. In every respect Swire's business and Service background was superb for a chairman who was faced with guiding the Fund through a period of ever-increasing welfare expenditure, fund-raising and investment to

Successive Chairmen with their Spitfires. Sir Adrian Swire (left), a peacetime enthusiast, and Flight Lieutenant Tony Barber (below) in wartime.

meet it, and explaining the continuing requirement for a substantial capital base.

While the needs of ageing 1939–45 War members of the RAF Family remained the core current and future financial responsibility, for which the Fund must attempt to anticipate and prepare, government draw-down of the armed forces produced more immediate and short-term need among a younger generation. Peters, Director Welfare, noted there was 'a significant increase of requests from those still serving or who have recently left the Service'. Some of this he attributed to the numbers of men and women who were being invalided, medically discharged or denied the extensions of service they had anticipated. Peters emphasised: 'As RAF manpower reduces further over the coming years we must expect this trend to continue.'

Sadly, all too many medical cases serve as reminders that young, previously healthy service people suffer misfortune. Corporal David Cawthorn of 12 Squadron thanked the Fund: 'The system does work and is there for people who need it. Thank you for the assistance to my parents and myself during my recent chemotherapy treatment in Aberdeen. Your decision was not only a great benefit to me but also gave great peace of mind to my parents.'

The wonder of the Welfare department is that from its warren of offices and cubbyholes at Portland Place it can offer a helping hand to a casual caller, a corporal in Scotland, a Polish veteran in Bolivia or a member of the Royal Flying Corps who encountered Lawrence of Arabia in the desert. Alerted that, aged seventy-six, former Sergeant Piotr Graia of the Polish Air Force and RAF was eking out a precarious existence panning for gold and seeking employment in remote mining camps, Welfare tracked him down and arranged a regular allowance.

Through the good offices of the Air Bridge Association which it supports, the Fund in 1996 helped 190 former members of the wartime RAF who had returned to Poland, Ukraine and the Czech and Slovak Republics and suffered years of persecution and deprivation under Communist rule; relief which is ongoing. Harold Eager, who had known Lawrence, was one of the Fund's oldest beneficiaries. Full of memories of the Sopwith Snipe he remained mobile, if grounded, on a powered scooter provided by the Fund. He has since died aged almost 100.

Although Eager took pride in maintaining his independence, generally provision of facilities for the ever-more elderly continued to be an increasingly important aspect of welfare work. New Wing nursing accommodation at Alastrean made possible the admission of new or existing residents who, previously, would have had to receive specialist care elsewhere. At Princess Marina House steps were taken to upgrade Kyle Wing to accommodate more residents dependent upon heavier nursing care. Some *en suite* rooms were created from office accom-modation which was re-located to the adjacent and recently improved

Newton Driver House, the 1970 bequest from which Princess Marina House had evolved.

Consideration on the part of the Fund that its new nursing facilities would help to cater for excess demand for short-term care at RAFA's neighbouring home at Sussexdown, represented a further closing of the gap with the Association. At the time residence at Princess Marina of Bill Hooper, creator of the brilliant wartime cartoon *Tee-Emm* training manual character Pilot Officer Prune and former illustrator for RAFA, spoke of the bond. Wearing his RAFA-badged blazer and extravagant moustache Bill worked on in his studio room until he died aged eighty.

In the year's outstanding example of co-operation with RAFA the Fund paid for the restoration and adaptation of Rothbury House. Purchased by RAFA, this former and imposing Victorian-built hotel was officially opened by Princess Margaret in November for short-stay respite-care visitors. In a further measure of co-operation and in recognition of another need identified by RAFA, the Fund participated in a joint scheme to provide short-term nursing contract care for those unable to use the sister organisations' homes.

Deep in John Buchan country at Moffat in Dumfriesshire, Dowding House – formerly St Ninians preparatory school where the Leader of the Few was born – continued to bear further witness to Fund-RAFA co-operation. In an act of faith the sister organisations raised £1.6 million between them – £11,000 was donated by King Hussein – to restore the dilapidated building and open a complex of twenty-six sheltered flats for the elderly.

In a year remarkable for 'jointery', as Palin frequently expressed it, the Fund contributed handsomely to a £1.2 million modernisation programme at RAFA's Sussexdown, Storrington, nursing home. At the time it was noted that in the past ten years the Fund, in addition to its initial Rothbury share of £300,000, had made more than £825,000 available for RAFA home developments.

Meanwhile, all such moves continued to be facilitated by attendance of Fund Helpers at RAFA casework courses and Palin's conduct of regional inter-related charity meetings. Nowhere is the Fund-RAFA relationship stronger and more effective than in Scotland where, enabling daily exchanges, the sister organisations share a headquarters building in Edinburgh. Cross fertilisation is further enhanced by Group Captain Dan Needham, Director Scotland's membership of RAFA's Scotland Council while the Association's Director Scotland sits on the Fund's Scottish Grants Committee.

At Appeals, as Reineck, former fighter, bomber and helicopter pilot, squadron and station commander and air attaché in Bonn, took over from Hurrell a change of style was evident. If fund-raising activities had flourished under the spell of Hurrell's bedside manner and creative inspiration they were – if lower keyed – no less effective in response to Reineck's Staff College and command qualities.

Reineck reorganised the directorate. Wing Commander Pat Gallanders specialised in legacies – currently running at some £4 million a year – while Flight Lieutenant Ann Dewar, formerly in the Finance Directorate, moved across as Assistant Director Appeals with responsibility for all public relations. Her move brought an immediate raising of the Fund's profile in the eyes of the RAF and the public. Among other staff changes and additions John Hatwell, who had followed Stanton from Saigon, retired as personal assistant to the Director and was replaced by Sam Limb, a fellow warrant officer with embassy experience.

Among Reineck's early enterprises was the organisation, with the blessing of Strike Command, of a dinner at Strike's High Wycombe Mess to honour twenty-three survivors of 25 Bomber Command aircrew profiled in '. . . *so many*'. Although some aspects were sponsored by Messier-Dowty and Sun Alliance, the dinner's fund-raising success owed much to the efforts of businessman Alan Curtis. Veterans lined a top table which included the Duke of Edinburgh, the Duke of Kent, four Marshals of the Royal Air Force, Air Chief Marshal Sir Michael Graydon, Chief of Air Staff, and Air Chief Marshal Sir William Wratten, Strike Commander-in-Chief. Towards the end of the dinner the Duke of Edinburgh, accepted on behalf of the Queen, copy number one of 401 '. . . *so many*' fine art folios. Subsequently, at a Clarence House ceremony, Tony Edwards, chairman of Messier-Dowty and whose company paid £1600 for the volume presented copy number two to the Queen Mother on the occasion of her ninety-fifth birthday.

At Fairford, lacking a major war anniversary, it dawned that somewhat unbelievably IAT had been in business for twenty-five years. Bowen, Prince and their team, supported by their more than 4000 volunteers, seized the opportunity to stage a Silver Jubilee airshow. It had been a considerable achievement to develop and sustain the world's premier military air display from the comparatively primitive Embassy Air Tattoo, organised on behalf of RAF charities in 1971 by Bowen and Prince at North Weald. It did not go unrecognised. Twenty-five years after the Air Tattoo's modest introduction the Queen honoured IAT with the privilege of Royal status. Marking the beginning of a close and warm relationship with RIAT, the actor David Jason – he is now a vice-president – arrived in a Harrier to open the event.

While the Jubilee – title sponsor Rover Group – was the overall theme of RIAT '96 characteristically the display included supporting attractions, notably SeaSearch '96 – a Russian Navy Il-38 made its overseas debut – celebration of the thirtieth birthday of the Harrier and twenty years of British Airways supersonic Concorde services. Tribute was also paid to the Spitfire and its designer, R. J. Mitchell, on the sixtieth anniversary of the fighter's first flight. In a sentimental link with the 1971 display Ray Hanna, who had piloted a Spitfire that day, led a flypast of the Red Arrows and gave a dazzling Spitfire performance. Later in the year the celebrated fighter was further remembered when the Massed Bands played *Fanfare for the Spitfire* composed specially for the Superkings-sponsored concert tour by Wing Commander Rob Wilkinson, Principal Director of RAF Music.

Throughout RIAT '96 there was an especially happy twenty-fifth birthday atmosphere, the spirit of which was visibly caught by the Fund's distinguished royal guests headed by the Duke of York and Prince

Fund supporter David Jason flew into RIAT '96 aboard an RAF Harrier.

Michael of Kent. Michael Portillo, Minister of Defence, also caught the mood when he addressed the annual hangar-staged Gala Dinner. Unhappily, ill health prevented King Hussein's attendance at the air tattoo but his son Prince Faisal was accompanied by Queen Noor. While

Not quite the Andrews Sisters, but the USAF Europe band brought the house down on the 1997 concert tours.

Joyce Tribe, who served as a carpenter, enthuses about her Fund-provided scooter to the Duke of Edinburgh at a Royal International Air Tattoo.

the Queen talked with the year's group of disabled fliers, the Prince, surrounded by past and present tattoo volunteers, joined Bowen, Prince and Crowley-Milling at a ceremony to cut a Silver Jubilee cake. Sadly the air marshal, who was terminally ill and but for whom and its founder directors there would have been no RIAT, did not survive the year.

One of 'Crow's' final acts on behalf of the Fund was to contribute a foreword to a glossy and profusely illustrated souvenir Silver Jubilee account of the air tattoo. He wrote: 'Over the years there are some things which have never changed – the commitment and energy of the ever-growing team of splendid volunteers . . . a dedication to the safety and enjoyment of our spectators and the aim of meeting Trenchard's mandate of promoting the Royal Air Force and raising money for the Fund's much needed welfare work.' Crowley-Milling concluded by thanking Imperial Tobacco for so many years of generous support.

The Silver Jubilee history was but one of six titles among which *Mighty Hercules, Hawks Come Of Age* and *Royal Air Force Yearbook 1996* featured strongly. On the merchandising side *Skyhigh* introduced an *AvIATion Premier Video Collection*, which is especially reputed for its quality and impressive air-to-air sequences. Business continued to progress at the Direct Mail and Response Handling Unit, the Fund's ticketing and fulfilment operation. Nor were there any doubts about the quality of Hospitality International, the Fund's catering enterprise, particularly in RIAT's annually sponsored Patron's Pavilion.

Sitting at the centre of the money spider's web at Portland Place, Wing Commander David Bailey, who had succeeded Connell as Finance Director in 1994, was much exercised by the task of reconciling charity accounting with the entrepreneurial instincts and activities of RAFBE, currently contributing some £400,000 to welfare resources. Happily, however, it was a task in which he was wisely, if unobtrusively, counselled by Fred Crawley, long serving Honorary Treasurer of the Fund and also a director of RAFBE. Since retiring from the chair of Alliance & Leicester the ever-affable and approachable Crawley, camera at the ready and as at home among the press and bobble-hat photographers at RIAT as in a City boardroom, had become even more available – if that were possible.

Bailey was also confronted by the fallout of the Charities Act of 1993 which introduced far reaching changes in the style and standards of annual reports and accounts. Two years afterwards Charity Accounting Regulations prescribed rigorous disclosure requirements, known as the Statement of Recommended Practice (SORP), and changed the format of annual accounts. Although these regulations were not mandatory until 1 March 1996, the Fund decided to adopt them for its financial year ending on 31 December 1995. In conformity and in a masterly manner Bailey assembled a financial portrait of the Fund and presented it at the rear of the Annual Report for 1995 which appeared as the regulations came into force in the next year.

In practice, Bailey began by describing the Fund's three Trusts and the limited company Royal Air Force Benevolent Fund Enterprises. He also listed unconnected charities for which the Fund provides an accounting service – The Royal Observer Corps, The Royal Air Force Escaping Society, and the Royal Air Force and Dependants Disabled Holiday Trust. There followed a subject by subject breakdown of income and expenditure, details of which are available in the appendices.

At this time of breaks with the past, the departures from the Council of Dame Felicity Peake and Marshal of the RAF Sir John Grandy, deputy chairman, saddened the Chairman and fellow members. There was consolation, however, in the maintenance of the family tradition by Dame Felicity's son, Andrew, and the election of Marshal of the RAF Lord Craig in Grandy's place. Dame Felicity and Sir John were also afforded the comfort of leaving in the knowledge that the Fund was sufficiently resourced to increase its welfare expenditure by £2 million to £12 million in their final year.

Fortunately, as Swire declared in his annual statement, an anticipated reduction in Service revenue and less public income in the aftermath of the 1995 VE and VJ celebrations was in some measure balanced by an encouraging number of legacies and successful investment.

CHAPTER 27

NEW TIMES, NEW DIRECTIONS

Clean breaks with tradition and long-standing practice are alien to the Benevolent Fund's conservative ethos. Generally, it edges almost imperceptibly towards change. Consequently, the decision in 1997 on the advice of the Charity Commissioners to make The Duke of Kent School an independent charity with all that the change implied, was as Swire noted in his annual chairman's statement, 'a milestone in the Fund's history'.

While the School's priority of admission to Fund Foundationers remained inviolate, an important advantage of its new status was that henceforth the governors would enjoy the freedom to generate income from a variety of sources. Meanwhile, the Fund would retain historic and sentimental links – long nurtured since the school's origination at Vanbrugh Castle – through a Trustee and member of the Board of Governors.

Indeed the very title of the new charity, The Alexander Duckham Memorial Schools Trust (ADMST) perpetuated the memory of the donor of Vanbrugh Castle at Blackheath. Air Vice-Marshal Michael Adams, father of a former Duke of Kent School pupil, was appointed chairman of ADMST and the Board of Governors, the Fund's presence being further strengthened through the membership of the Controller and a departmental director.

Freed from previous restrictions when it was part of the Fund, the school was now able to market itself more effectively and broaden its recruitment in ways which were not open to it as an integral part of the Benevolent Fund. Enrolment for the 1997 autumn term of three new Foundationer girls bringing the Foundationers' total to thirteen – five boys and eight girls – reinforced the school's declared intent to maintain priority of admission for Foundationers and other children of Service families. The recently announced practice of allowing parents of Foundationers choice of preparatory school other than Duke of Kent was also continued. During the year the Fund continued to support seventy-one Foundationers in various stages of their education at a wide range of educational establishments.

As with the alteration of the school's status, another move by Welfare evidenced the Fund's readiness to react, as with the recent eligibility of national servicemen, to broaden its criteria, was to take into account the presence of reserve personnel serving alongside regulars. With the introduction of the Reserve Forces Act 1996 Peters, in concert with Headquarters Personnel and Training Command, had identified this potential area of need before he left Portland Place to become Clerk to the Guild of Air Pilots and Air Navigators. His successor, Air Vice-Marshal Terry Sherrington, who had replaced him after a brief period as Director Administration, followed through.

Previously Air Officer Administration, RAF Strike Command, Sherrington, who had joined the Fund as Administration Director following Group Captain George Lucas's retirement, brought the advantages of recent and varied Service experience to Welfare. Certainly his first year – in which welfare spending rose to £14.4 million – was challenging. Serving cases began to show a significant increase due to an unusually large number of people being medically discharged or invalided. Palin noted in his half-yearly internal *Newsletter*: 'This probably arises from the Service's inability as in previous years to retain a serviceman who is less than fully fit by remustering to another trade or holding a less arduous appointment'. The Controller also cited the incidence of applications for help from personnel 'whose expectations of extension have been dashed for help with their earlier than expected translation to civilian life'.

Due to force reduction this new source of need was, of course, additional to the customary run of serving cases which, while fractional overall, individually cost very much above the average. This, as Sherrington reiterated in his annual Welfare review, is because such cases generally arise from a fatal accident or other tragedy, often leading to costly housing and education needs and possibly help for life. Every such case, as he noted, brings home the wisdom of Service families joining the Dependants' Fund and Dependants' Income Trust and heeding the advice of the Insurance Advisory Service – since re-entitled the Financial Planning Service.

Sherrington also updated the availability of assistance with housing. Assistance, he announced, will be considered for those who have been medically discharged with a severe disability which excludes them from normal civilian employment. He explained that if a beneficiary can find fifty-one per cent of the purchase price the Fund will consider lending the balance secured as a mortgage against the property. Alternatively, where capital is not available, the Housing Trust may buy a suitable home for a beneficiary and let it at a rent appropriate in the circumstances. In 1997 the Housing Trust bought eighteen houses bringing its ownership to a total of 248 properties. Where members of the RAF Family already own houses but find themselves in financial distress and cannot meet the cost of repairs, the Fund can assist with a low interest loan secured against the property.

On the homes' front, infirmity and disability, often compounded by financial hardship, continued to confront the elderly and place great pressure on Princess Marina House, Alastrean House and the joint

Fund-RAFA Rothbury House. Alastrean, where the majority of residents needed nursing support, experienced its busiest year and had a waiting list. Similarly, Princess Marina, whose long-serving manager, Group Captain Eric Goodman was appointed OBE, could not accommodate all long-term applicants. Consequently the Fund continued to work closely with RAFA to make greater use of private residential homes and to extend a service of advice to those seeking to make arrangements with local authorities. Further, buoyed by the success of Rothbury, the first joint Fund-RAFA venture, Flowerdown House, a sea front property at Weston-super-Mare, was purchased for joint ownership and management by RAFA.

The Controller and Director Welfare take especial pleasure in meeting veterans, and attend reunions when their busy diaries permit. Of these the Guinea Pig Club dinner, chaired since Tom Gleave's death by former Fairey Battle pilot Bill Simpson, is an annual early autumn fixture at its East Grinstead birthplace. Although the Fund's special relationship with aircrew survivors of wartime surgery under Sir Archibald McIndoe is perpetuated by regular meetings at headquarters of the Co-ordinating Committee for the Resettlement of Burns Cases, Guinea Pigs are reassured by Fund representation at the reunion. For Palin and Sherrington, making his first appearance in 1997, mixing with some sixty Guinea Pigs was particularly moving. Of a worldwide total of 197 surviving club members – they numbered 650 in wartime – the presence of the elderly Czech Major-General Alois Siska, who had qualified for membership as a Wellington bomber sergeant pilot, was an eloquent reminder of the Fund's far-reaching assistance.

In a year in which celebration of the fiftieth anniversary of the formation of the United States Air Force was to provide the main theme of RIAT, Appeals at Portland Place supported Fairford's tribute to USAF and in particular the annual Massed Bands concerts. Closer co-operation with the entrepreneurial activities of RAFBE did not, however, diminish Appeals' customary fund-raising efforts. Reineck reported: 'Donations from the public rose markedly . . . and legacy income was particularly buoyant, again exceeding expectations'. He attributed this in part to the use of modernised promotional material and, where suitable, the use of colour.

It was also encouraging that despite a more than thirty per cent reduction in serving people, income from the RAF was only twenty per cent down and voluntary subscription income had dropped just ten per cent. As the Appeals Director declared, the figures demonstrated a magnificent display of Service loyalty to the Fund despite closing stations and shrinking numbers. On the fringe of mainstream fund-raising a promotional stimulus was given to the sale of remaining volumes of the fine art folios '. . . so few' and '. . . so many'. It was particularly gratifying that matching pairs were purchased by Zafar Malik, an international businessman, who presented them to the RAF Club and RAF Museum.

During the 1939–45 War the United States Army Air Force had been much impressed by the RAF's independent status. Thus it welcomed the change in 1947 from USAAF to USAF. Fifty years on, USAF's birthday celebration at RIAT '97 provided a memorable centrepiece and gate money crowd-puller – more than 200,000 attended – for the airshow. Perhaps the biggest attraction was the arrival from New Mexico of Squadron Leader Mark 'Sooty' Sutton at the controls of an F117-A Nighthawk. Reminder of an Anglo-US military aviation relationship returning to the 1914–18 War this exciting programme novelty also symbolised USAF's ever-readiness to contribute to the success of RIAT and indirectly to welfare fund-raising.

A touchdown visit by *Spirit of Kansas*, a B-2 Stealth bomber making its first visit to Britain, was further evidence of USAF's support of RIAT and the US Chief of Staff, General Ronald R. Fogleman, was himself on hand to show the top secret bomber to the Duke of Kent before it took off for home almost immediately. Earlier the general had contributed a fore-word to the anniversary-inspired *From Sabre to Stealth*, a tribute to USAF and one of four titles published by RAFBE during the year. Continuing to spread its wings the Fund's trading company expanded its *Skyhigh* mail order business and introduced a briskly selling *Skyhigh Village* at the airshow. As ever, the Fund was indebted to members of the Royal Family for their support. The Duke of York was guest of honour at the annual Gala Dinner, while the Duke of Gloucester and Prince Michael of Kent were present at the air display.

Flying in from Jordan, King Hussein's daughter Princess Alia met the year's batch of ten successful disabled fliers and presented their flying certificates. Martin Abbott, Principal of the re-entitled RIAT Flying Scholarships for the Disabled in memory of Sir Douglas Bader, announced the number of scholarships was to be increased to twelve. Somewhat unusually two successful applicants had become disabled while serving in the RAF.

Paul Davies was a navigator when a cliff fall during jungle survival resulted in paralysis from the waist down. Thanks to the scheme and Sun Alliance's sponsorship, wheelchair-bound Paul, who had become a solicitor, could now learn to fly in Atlanta. Stewart McQuillan, one of King Hussein's personally sponsored students, was a mechanic when he fell from a Tornado wing and was similarly paralysed. The Fund cared for his children as Duke of Kent Foundationers and at one time he occu-pied a Housing Trust. Stewart, who is also a glider pilot and director of a charity for rescuing birds of prey, said: 'If other disabled people can see that I have achieved what many able-bodied people believe to be un-obtainable then perhaps they will also chase their dreams'.

As ever no RIAT would be possible without an umbrella of generous sponsorship by many companies. Headed in 1997 by Lockheed Martin, British Aerospace, Marshall of Cambridge and Breitling of Switzerland, they assured an exhilarating weekend of flying and fun which was especially enhanced by Breitling's Top Guns competition and Fighter '97 and Tiger themes. Bowen and Prince were delighted when subsequently Breitling engaged RAFBE to provide technical support for its *Breitling Orbiter* hot-air balloon round the world challenge.

If, as always, life was more down to earth at Portland Place, the usual annual evolution took place. Retained because of the good fortune since 1945 of a 973-year lease and peppercorn rent which far outweighed the necessity of a somewhat tight squeeze, the elegant headquarters building welcomed new faces and new technology. Wing Commander Mike Vearncombe who, fresh from the Service, had succeeded Lucas, Administration Director, in the new appointment of Head of Administration Services, oversaw the first stage of a programme to improve the Fund's Information Technology. This involved the installation of networked personal computers. The second stage was planned to follow a business practices review to ensure that IT is closely and cost-effectively matched to future needs.

On the general financial front and at the end of a year of heavy capital expenditure – principally on residential homes – and in which Fred Crawley, long serving Honorary Treasurer, was appointed CBE, Bailey reported: 'Before making adjustment for capital gains on investments and transfer of the Duke of Kent School's assets, the Charity's direct charitable expenditure totalled £14.4 million. Income totalled £14.2 million. However, after adjustments for capital expenditure on assets an operating surplus of £556,555 was achieved and transferred to reserves.'

The founding of the Royal Air Force in 1918 followed by that of the Fund in the next year afforded the Fund the convenience of anniversaries in 1998 and 1999 upon which to look back and to look forward. In retrospect a shilling (five pence) for a night's lodging, the price of boot repairs to walk to work, purchase of a tool of a trade, godsends in Lloyd George's 'land fit for heroes', contrast staggeringly with expenditure, say, of more than £100,000 on an airman crippled in a motorcycle accident.

But the world and social expectations have moved on. Not even the far-seeing Trenchard, father of the RAF and its Charity, could have dreamed that a grandson, as a member of the Council and Finance and General Purposes Committee, would help to counsel a Fund bolstered by assets in the region of £150 million. Nor could he have foreseen that the very success of its fund-raising and Morgan Grenfell's astute investment raise questions about current and future need for such reserves.

The anniversaries re-activated accusations of hoarding. Two world wars were so distant and the RAF so reduced, the argument ran, that the Fund could provide for all future need. For all Palin's liberalisation of assistance and qualification for it, suspicion of unnecessary hoarding

lingered among the donating public and to some extent within the RAF
Family.

Not, fortunately, that this misconceived concern currently diminished
fund-raising income. Swire noted in his 1998 Statement:

> The traditional sources of income held up well and it is gratifying to note
> that serving members of the RAF continued to support the Fund magnifi-
> cently. This support is particularly praiseworthy considering that overall
> numbers continued to decrease while overseas commitments grew,
> resulting in fewer personnel having less time available in which to under-
> take voluntary fund-raising activities.

The Chairman also noted that, although donations from the public were
not greatly changed from the previous year, overall voluntary income
was boosted significantly by legacies totalling almost £5 million.

Naturally, the RAF's eightieth was a gift to RAFBE which based the
year's activities on it. In the tradition of the former annual Royal Festival
Hall concerts celebrating the 1 April 1918, founding of the RAF, the
trading company packed the Barbican Centre for a gala, attended by
the Duke of Kent. Sponsored by British Aerospace and performed by the
Central and RAF Regiment Bands the concert blended a rousing musical
programme with readings and film clips surveying the Service's first
eighty years.

Customarily supported by a host of sponsors headed by Lockheed
Martin, British Aerospace and Marshall of Cambridge, RIAT '98
coupled commemoration of the eightieth anniversary with that of the
fiftieth of the Berlin Airlift. More than 150,000 people enjoyed the flying
display staged over the last weekend in July. On the Sunday the Duke of
Edinburgh, making an extended walkabout, met men and women whose
periods of service ranged from 1918 to the present day – including Airlift
veterans. Music, much in evidence throughout the anniversary year,
made an innovative airshow debut when the Band of the RAF College,
Cranwell, performed an Airshow Proms Concert accompanied by the
launch of forty hot-air balloons.

Under the spur of the eightieth anniversary year there was lift-off too
for the trading companies and publishing ventures re-branded as
AvIATion Trading (formerly *Skyhigh*) and the AvIATion Book
Collection. While sales from new spring and Christmas catalogues
improved impressively, a partnership formed with Orion Publishing
Group brought RAFBE's publishing ventures the benefits of professional
counsel and market access. The advantages of the Orion link were soon
evident in the production and sale of new titles, especially *Airshow*
novelist and television documentary writer Graham Hurley's fly-on-the-
wall account of RIAT '98.

Meanwhile AvIATion Trading's partnership with MBNA affinity
cards further re-enforced the advantages of RAFBE's policy of making

commercial links. In these circumstances director Bowen and Prince's company appointments were re-designated as chief executive and operations director. The by now almost 'traditional' autumn Superkings-sponsored fund-raising tour by the Central Band and Christmas tour by the Massed Bands, highlighted by a rousing concert – it also marked the twenty-first anniversary of the Aircrew Association – at the Royal Albert Hall, rounded off the Fund's Fairford team's exceptionally busy and successful year.

While, despite trading, publishing and concert excursions, Fairford's fund-raising function remained centred on the airshow 'big bang', Appeals at Portland Place ploughed on steadily with an essential, if less glamorous, week-in week-out public relations and fund-raising programme. Reineck strengthened the practice of increasing Fund awareness by personally briefing station and squadron commanders, and officers selected for middle or senior command and management training. Moreover, more than 120 illustrated talks were delivered, mostly by Ann Dewar, to all RAF recruits and senior NCOs attending specialist training courses. Members of Reineck's staff also made less formal presentations on stations and in crewrooms. In support, six articles illustrated by the cartoonist Bill Tidy on various aspects of the Fund's work – shades of Bill Hooper in *Tee Em* – were targeted at station magazines. So much of such efforts, loosely termed public – or in this case Service – relations is difficult to quantify, but the Fund was encouraged that, as Reineck reported: 'Despite decreasing numbers, subscription

Hail a cab and help the Fund. Charlie Figgures, a BBC television presenter, did just that.

income from the half-day's-pay arrangement remained bouyant and we benefited financially from events such as At Home and Open Days as well as from a number of individual and group fund-raising activities.' Legacies totalling £4 million and donations from the public also held up well. As with public relations the harvest from advertising cannot be quantified, but it is reasonable to claim that on-the-news advertisements pegged to specific RAF exploits when they occur contributed to it. Preparations were made to extend this practice to television with the purpose of linking a Fund advertisement to such classic films as *The Dam Busters* and *The Battle of Britain*.

In order to encourage each and every benefactor to feel fully appreciated, Reineck introduced the practice that every donation, no matter how modest, is acknowledged by a personal letter from himself or his deputy, Pat Gallanders. These letters are invariably accompanied by a leaflet

The Fund raised £20,000 by selling this donated number plate.

The London Marathon 1999. Annually RAF and other runners take part
in the marathon on behalf of the Fund.

describing the Fund's work and, as a result, many heartening examples
of the affection in which the Fund is held drop into the in-trays. Enclosing
a 1914–18 War uniformed photograph of herself with rifle, Alice Baker,
aged 100, wrote: 'I have everything I need and I know the Benevolent
Fund does a lot of good work. One of my friends received help . . . so I
thought instead of receiving presents for my 100th birthday I would ask
friends and family to make a donation'.

Viewed in relation to Sherrington's disclosure at the end of 1998 that the
Fund was opening more than 300 new cases a month and still spending
some £14 million a year on welfare, the thoughtfulness and generosity
of Alice and so many other 'Alices' are as warmly appreciated as substantial sums from, say, the RAF Central Fund and major donors.
    During the year particular attention was paid to reaching out to
members of the RAF Family in the care of some 100 other associated
charitable organisations. Noting that the Fund already awarded grants of
little short of £1 million to such bodies as the Royal Star & Garter Home
(£135,000), Air Bridge Association (£108,000), St Dunstan's (£100,000)
and RAFA (£50,000), the Finance & General Purposes Committee
suggested Welfare be more proactive in this direction. Sherrington
reported: 'We are now engaged in widening our net to help other organisations who, through many different avenues, help the extended RAF
Family.' Measures were taken in tandem to broaden criteria for eligibility

Then: Alice Baker
defended Dover in the
1914–18 War.

Now: Alice Baker
requested Fund donations
on her 100th birthday in
lieu of presents.

with the result that, as previously with national servicemen, members of the Royal Air Force Reserve and Royal Auxiliary Air Force became eligible for assistance.

However, while policy changes at Portland Place ebb and flow with the tide of social and other changes, the satisfaction of attaching a beneficiary's thank-you letter to a case folder is constant. On the eve of the Fund's eightieth anniversary the contents of many such letters illuminated the wisdom of conserving resources and topping them up with fresh fund-raising income. Patricia Watkins, whose husband Ted was a sergeant armourer from 1938 to 1951 and relies on a constant supply of

Former SAC Tim Harrald was invalided aged twenty-five in 1997 following a massive heart attack. Now Tim, Coleen and little Jack live in a Fund property.

Corporal Clive Williams's son suffers from muscular dystrophy. The Fund helped to make Martin mobile.

Ladybird group children with special needs are supported by the Fund in
the area of RAF Lossiemouth.

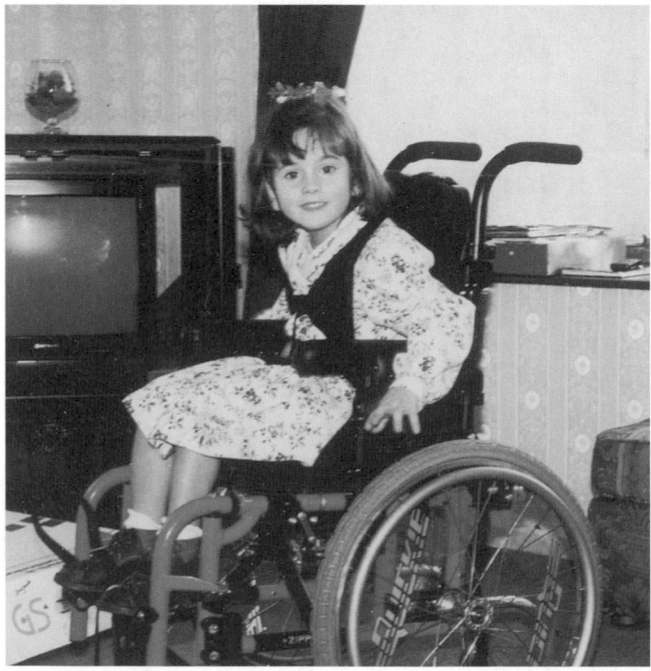

'The care and help
Louise has received
from the Fund has
made all the
difference' – Mrs
Anne Jones, mother
of Louise. Her
daughter suffers from
cerebral palsy.
Louise's father is a
former SAC.

For Brian Alldis, aged eleven, a sports wheelchair seemed unattainable until the Fund responded to the plea of his father, a former flight sergeant. Brian proudly displays his gold medal.

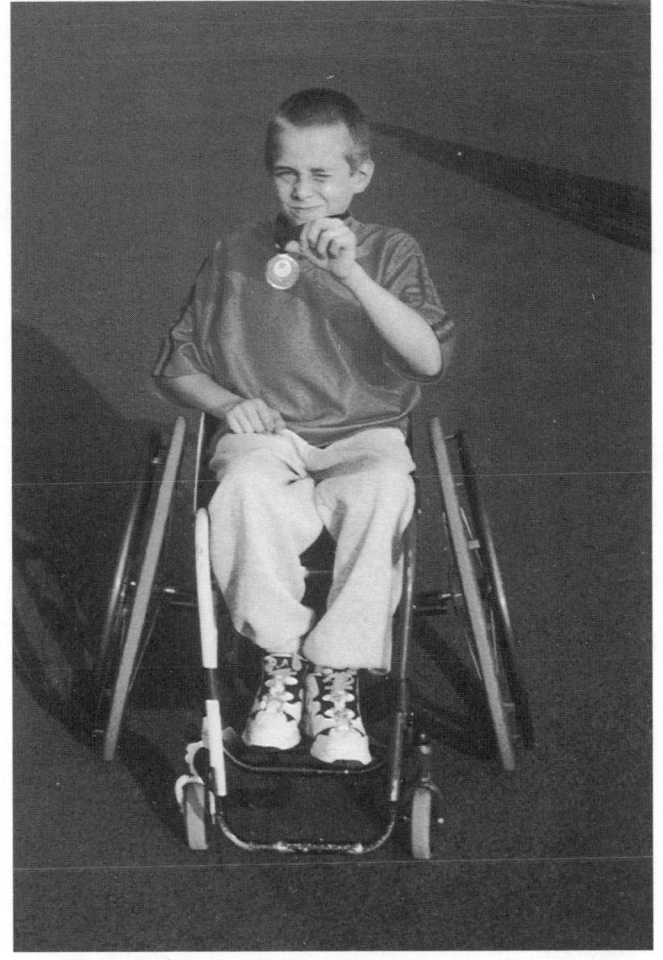

piped oxygen, wrote: 'The stairlift will be a tremendous boon as . . . going upstairs is like climbing Everest. It also means we can remain in our home'.

John Hickinbottom, who served in the RAF Police from 1948 to 1950 and who had been paralysed down one side since 1977, had persevered with using a bath until finally he could not climb out of it. He wrote: 'It was freezing, but the more I tried to get out of the bath the more tired I became. I was there for nearly twelve hours and I didn't know what to do'. The Fund provided John with an easy-access shower. SAC Tim Harrald was only twenty-five when he had a heart attack and was invalided from the Service. After the Fund had provided John, his wife Coleen and their son, Jack, with a home for as long as they need it John wrote: 'You have provided security for my family and for that I am ever grateful'.

Rupert Pemsell, aged fourteen, member of 2433 (Ramsgate) Squadron Air Training Corps, raised money on an expedition.

In the course of his annual review of housing Sherrington reported: 'Help with house purchase was given where the family's breadwinner had to leave the RAF because of his or her spouse's severe disablement and to the families of those who died in the Service and left widows with dependent children'. He noted that in 1998 the Housing Trust had bought sixteen properties. Each was selected by the beneficiaries to be close to their families and support systems. The sale of fourteen homes brought the Housing Trust's total to 250 properties.

For those no longer able to live in their own homes, the ceaseless quest to attain a required balance of respite, residential and residential nursing care facilities continued. As the Queen and the Duke of Edinburgh learned during a visit to Alastrean House, developments there enable the home to meet residential and nursing needs for up to fifty-two people with *en suite* facilities in each residential room. The rooms are dual registered to offer nursing care in addition to nursing arrangement for high dependency residents in the new wing.

Former SAC Carol Blood helps her husband, Peter, learn to walk again. One day the Fund's lightweight wheelchair may be redundant.

When wartime LAC Frank Hope was burgled in 1998 the Fund replaced stolen savings and helped with house repairs.

Terry Sharp, who served in the 1950s and 1960s, relied on his wife Josephine to push him around until the Fund provided a dual-control electric wheelchair.

When the Queen visited Alastrean House, the Fund's home in Scotland, she met Mabel Gordon, formerly a corporal cook and housekeeper to the Queen Mother.

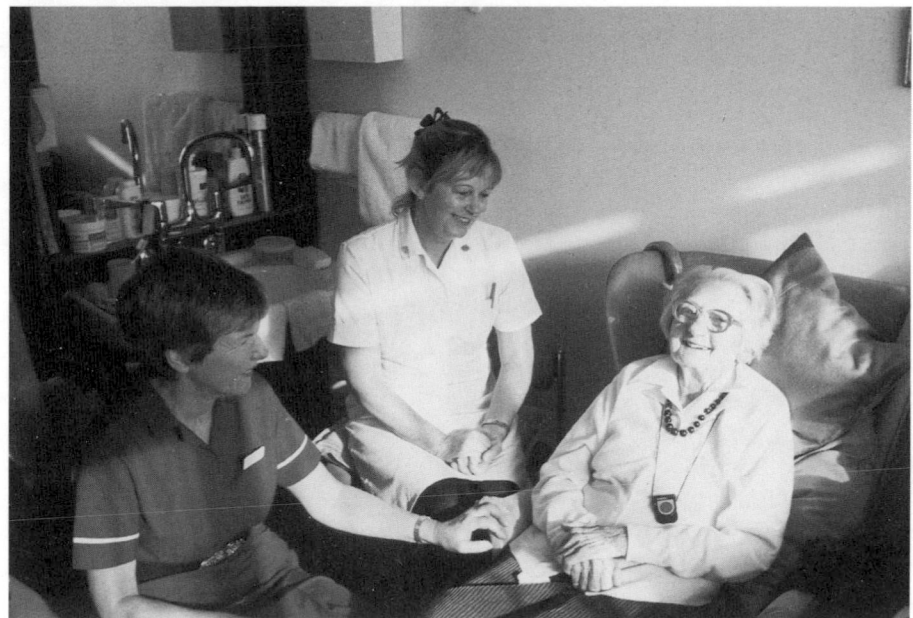

In good hands. A resident at Alastrean House, the Fund's home in
Scotland.

Although royal attention was centred on Alastrean the visit served, as
devolution develops, as a timely reminder of the Fund's Scottish Branch
and of its director Needham's correctly independent style and stewardship. Queen Street, Edinburgh, if similarly elegant, is a world away from
Portland Place yet fortunately so at a time when devolution may, as
Needham suggests, accentuate differences in law, social attitudes and
approaches to charity giving. A particular advantage of the Fund's
foothold north of the border is the opportunity for close liaison with
Scottish branches of other national charities and establishments such
as Scottish Veterans Residences (£26,500 in 1998) which the Fund
assists. During the year the branch processed 730 cases involving welfare
payments totalling more than £407,000; figures which should reassure
8000 members of the RAF and their families serving in Scotland.

In the south at Princess Marina House, fresh challenges faced Wing
Commander Phil Bush as he succeeded Goodman as general manager.
It was deemed prudent for Care Services, as the Homes Department had
been re-designated, to examine the feasibility of accommodating those
who are more dependent on help and of detaching nursing cases to
Sussexdown, RAFA's nearby home.

Other moves further developed the Fund's welfare interdependence
with RAFA. Officially opened by the Duke of Gloucester, Flowerdown
House joined Rothbury House, as a second joint Fund-RAFA short-term

recuperative and respite care home. Innovatively, Rothbury also began to offer recuperative breaks for young families in four two-bedroomed flats named the Malcolm Apartments. For older people six one-bedroomed flats became available in Tedder Court. Veteran beneficiaries were pleased that Lord Tedder, who with his wife, the irrepressible 'Toppy', had launched the RAF Malcolm Clubs in North Africa during the 1939–45 War, were suitably remembered and honoured.

For all the co-operation and cross-fertilisation between the Fund and RAFA their combined resources remain unable to meet overall need. Consequently, the Fund contributes towards the costs of caring for more than 400 beneficiaries in other charitable and private homes around the country; external support which rose by twelve per cent in 1998. Fortunately, as Swire reported at the close of the year, 'traditional sources of income held up well', overall voluntary income being boosted significantly by legacies totalling almost £5 million. Moreover, market turbulence late in the year failed to disturb returns.

This healthy position and consequent broadening and increasing of welfare spending owed much to the leadership and inspiration of Palin, upon whose retirement in October the Chairman stated: 'Sir Roger steered the Fund through a particularly challenging period during which spending on welfare almost doubled . . .' Between them Swire and Palin had laid down a firm runway and bright flarepath from which Palin's successor Air Chief Marshal Sir David Cousins, a former fighter pilot, could take off into the blue of the new Millennium and beyond. Swire, while congratulating newcomer Dame Helena Shovelton on being appointed DBE, also bade farewell to Aiken, so long a distinguished member of Council and the Finance & General Purposes Committee.

CHAPTER 28

TOWARDS THE BLUE MILLENNIUM

With the appointment of Cousins as Controller the Fund turned yet again to the most recent Air Member for Personnel. Kennedy and Palin had been Controllers for their time and now Cousins, fresh from the painful manpower problems of a continually contracting Service, was the most suitable candidate to pilot the Fund into the new century.

In one respect Cousins was particularly fortunate. There were no forseeable money problems on the horizon. With a capital base of almost £150 million earning income and healthy current fund-raising, legacy and other revenue there was no immediate difficulty in the Fund's eightieth anniversary year in meeting its expected charitable responsibilities.

Rather the need for imaginative proposals to enlarge the Fund's charitable scope while never losing sight of core and historic welfare objectives exercised the new Controller and his staff. Looking towards the Millennium the moment was right to introduce a radical policy and departmental review.

Very soon after moving from Headquarters Personnel and Training Command at RAF Innsworth to Portland Place, Cousins asked himself

Air Chief Marshal Sir David Cousins, Controller 1998 to date.

Controller and Directors welcome Air Chief Marshal Sir David Cousins,
Air Member for Personnel (second right), in 1996. Right to left: Air
Commodore Colin Reineck, Appeals; Cousins; Air Vice-Marshal Bob
Peters; Group Captain George Lucas; Air Chief Marshal Sir Roger Palin;
Wing Commander David Bailey.

– much as had Palin five years earlier – are we doing enough to help?
Are we making the best possible use of our people and our resources and
what do others think of us? At the behest of the F&GP Committee
Cousins and Sherrington began to investigate the prospects of building
on Palin's charitable initiatives and developing Fund capital projects,
solo, or dual with RAFA. Preferably, they believed such new directions
as seemed meritable should also give promise of enhancing Service and
public conceptions of the Fund and to combat negative opinion. Especial
consideration was given to the possibility of Fund participation in
provision of family facilities on stations where a pressing need for
nurseries had been identified.

Yet, as ever and as particularly the RAF role in NATO's Balkans inter-
vention demonstrated, the Fund was conscious that while seeking to
spend more widely and liberally it must always be ready to respond to the
demands of unpredictable and costly catastrophe. In any period a welfare
director's recurring nightmare is the loss, say, of just one transport aircraft
filled with RAF personnel or in other circumstances up to 500 personnel
at a cost to the Fund of many hundreds of thousands of pounds.

Balancing the fear of such catastrophes against a desire to spend more generously on serving and veteran beneficiaries and on appropriate accommodation at Fund or joint Fund and RAFA homes calls for judgement, not to say a little luck. Such exigencies as the Falklands, Gulf and Balkan campaigns occur in a world supposedly at peace and limit the peace dividend for Service charities.

It would be tempting fate to increase welfare spending and capital expenditure while at the same time easing fund-raising measures. Eighty years on from 1919 Sherrington and his staff, while ministering to existing cases, were opening 300 new individual files a month. True, as the century drew to a close a previously predicted annual welfare spending peak of £20 million seemed less likely. Yet there could be no certainty that a ceiling had been reached at the current two-year average of around £14m a year.

For eighty years the Fund had learned to expect the unexpected. Cousins, a tall man for the Lightning cockpit of his fighter days, had hardly stretched his legs beneath the Controller's desk when an *unexpected* blow fell. Preparations were well advanced at Fairford to stage the annual fund-raising summer airshow when air attacks on targets in Belgrade and Kosovo involved operational use of the Fairford airfield. Over the years there was always the risk that Fairford, in title an RAF station but in practice currently accommodating USAF's 424th Air Base Squadron, would become unavailable for an airshow.

RIAT had already invited the air arms of the world to celebrate NATO's fiftieth birthday, the Royal Auxiliary Air Force's seventy-fifth, Fund's eightieth and Red Arrows' thirty-fifth before the US, Britain and seventeen NATO allies became committed to air operations in the Balkans. As Bowen, Prince and their staff continued to assemble the late July airshow, their office windows rattled with the thunder of B-52 and B-1 bombers making round trips to targets in Belgrade and Kosovo. The expected short, sharp bombing assault lengthened into weeks and months and ticket sales mounted as RIAT '99 neared.

It was a considerable act of faith. Although the Fund was insured in some respects against cancellation there was no possibility of recouping loss of profits, the essential fund-raising-for-welfare element of the airshow. Moreover, another act of faith was taking place beyond the airfield's main gate and perimeter boundary. Following a symbolic and publicised ground-breaking dig of the first turf by all Fund directors, Barnwood Construction of Gloucester had started to build Douglas Bader House to house RAFBE and RIAT which were scheduled to release base accommodation to USAF before the end of the year.

Fortunately, as the Fairford team reached the airshow cancellation point of no return bombing ceased. Generously, USAF flashed green for RIAT '99. It was a decision for which the Fund is indebted. At much the same time as the directors broke ground for Douglas Bader House, King Hussein died. Staging of RIAT '99 seemed inconceivable without Bader's successor as President, albeit in the title of Patron. Although Queen Noor and their son Prince Faisal were ever-ready to deputise in Hussein's unavoidable absence the king's cheery arrival and departure at his TriStar's controls had endeared him over the years to hundreds of thousands of spectators. Sadly, RIAT crowds will not hear again Hussein's ritual loud-speakered farewell on take off for Jordan: 'This is King Hussein leaving and saying goodbye'.

At RIAT '99 the Fund paid the diminutive desert ruler and honorary RAF air chief marshal the airshow's ultimate tribute. A memorial flypast in *Missing Man* formation was flown by the Falcons aerobatic team of the Royal Jordanian Air Force, four RAF Jaguars from No. 6 Squadron – historically associated with Jordan – and a Dove presented by the RAF to the king in the 1950s. Happily, however, the incomparable RIAT-Jordan relationship remains. Queen Noor has graciously accepted her late husband's mantle as Patron and disabled people sponsored from Jordan are still taught to fly after qualifying for places under the Bader memorial scheme.

With RIAT's future use of the Fairford base pledged by USAF, Douglas Bader House under construction to accommodate seasoned RAFBE and RIAT press, public relations, marketing and business executives and staff, Cousins deemed it prudent to examine the feasibility of employing so much promotional experience and expertise in more general support of the Fund.

Following the 24–25 July airshow the Controller, after reviewing the comparative fund-raising and publicity activities of the Appeals directorate, switched almost all Appeals responsibilities to Fairford. Reineck, whose administrative talents had greatly assisted a smooth transition, retired and Dewar left the Fund to marry a serving officer in the RAF Regiment.

Henceforth, Fairford assumed overall responsibility for fund-raising, promotional and commercial activities. It was a challenging task, but Fairford's seasoned team was ready and willing to meet it. Working to directors Bowen and Prince the principals were Wing Commander Amanda Butcher, Deputy Director Airshows; Caroline Rogers, Deputy Director Business Development; Wing Commander Gordon Harris, Deputy Director Admin & Finance; Wing Commander Tony Webb, Deputy Director Public Affairs; Patti Heady, Press and Public Relations Officer; Heidi Standfast, Marketing Manager; David Higham, Deputy Director Trading and Peter R. March, Year books' managing editor. March's *Freedom of the Skies*, a handsome, colour illustrated hardback published by Cassell, part of Orion, in association with the Fund to mark the NATO anniversary, was an especially enterprising element in Fairford's bounteously repaid act of faith.

Thanks largely to the combined experience and efforts of RIAT's talented team, staff and more than 4000 volunteers RIAT '99 was staged despite disruptive conditions, and disbelief that in the immediate wake of NATO's Balkan operations it could not possibly take place.

Rekindling memories of 1949, NATO's inaugural year, the Battle of Britain Memorial Flight Dakota introduced a four-hour aerial reprise of the Alliance and its Iron Curtain opponents in the air. Spitfire paired with Soviet Yak 3, Sabre with MiG-21 and, covering the present, F-15 with Ukrainian Air Force Su27. Looking towards the future the top-secret bat-winged B-2 flew and joined the static display.

From the Lancaster, a hardy annual of the airshow, Dakota, Spitfire and Hurricane to B-2. How the years had rolled by since 1949 when the founding of the Fund lay but thirty years in the past and the Battle of Britain only nine years before the birth of NATO. Eighty years ago when a plan for a Royal Air Force Memorial on the Embankment gave rise to the RAF Benevolent Fund it seemed inconceivable that European issues would ignite another war. Fifty-one years ago they did. Hostilities were resumed and it seemed possible in 1940 that Germany would reverse its 1918 defeat. But in that fateful summer the RAF saved Britain from invasion, occupation and perhaps from national oblivion.

At the time Winston Churchill, Britain's wartime prime minister, said: 'Never in the field of human conflict was so much owed by so many to so few.' He repeated the phrase when he broadcast an appeal on behalf of the Fund and added that by 1945, the few had become the many. Churchill concluded: 'The Royal Air Force Benevolent Fund is part of the conscience of the British nation. A nation without a conscience is a nation without a soul. A nation without a soul is a nation that cannot live.'

The future was not for Trenchard, Churchill or any of the Fund's benefactors and servants to see but one thing *is* certain. Past legacies, donations and fund-raising efforts together with future Service, public and corporate support will ensure that the Fund will be there for members of the extended RAF Family so long as eligibility and need remains.

APPENDIX A

PATRONS, PRESIDENTS, FOUNDER, LIFE VICE-PRESIDENTS, CHAIRMEN AND CONTROLLERS

Patrons

6 May 1936 to 6 February 1952	His Majesty King George VI
3 June 1952 to date	Her Majesty Queen Elizabeth II

Presidents

6 November 1919 to 5 May 1936	His Royal Highness The Duke of York
25 February 1937 to 6 October 1941	His Royal Highness The Duke of Gloucester
11 March 1943 to 27 August 1968	Her Royal Highness Princess Marina, Duchess of Kent
January 1969 to date	His Royal Highness The Duke of Kent

Founder
Marshal of the Royal Air Force the Rt. Hon. The Viscount Trenchard GCB, OM, GCVO, DSO, DCL, LLD

Life Vice-Presidents
The Rt. Hon. Julian Amery MP
The Rt. Hon. The Lord Amulree PC, GBE, KC
The Rt. Hon. The Lord Ashfield PC, TD
The Duke of Atholl KT, GCVO, CB, DSO
Air Chief Marshal Sir John Aiken KCB

The Rt. Hon. The Lord Barber of Wentbridge
His Excellency The Rt. Hon. J. A. Beasley PC
Marshal of the Royal Air Force Sir Michael Beetham GCB, CBE, DFC, AFC
Admiral of the Fleet The Earl Beatty OM, PC, GCB, GCVO, DSO

Wyndham Birch Esq. DSO, MBE
The Hon. Sir Reginald Andrew Blankenburg
The Hon. Sir Edgar Rennie Bowring KCMG
Marshal of the Royal Air Force Sir Dermot Boyle GCB, KCVO, KBE, AFC
Lieutenant-Colonel The Rt. Hon. Lord Brabazon of Tara GBE, MC, PC
The Rt. Hon. The Viscount Brentford PC, DL
The Rt. Hon. S. M. Bruce CH, MC
The Viscount Burnham CH, GCMG, LLD, DLITT, MA, JP

Marshal of the Royal Air Force The Lord Cameron of Balhousie GCB, CBE, DSO,
   DFC
The Lord Catto of Cairncatto
The Most Hon. The Marquess of Cholmondeley GCVO
The Rt. Hon. Sir Winston Churchill KG, OM, CH, FRS
The Rt. Hon. Sir Joseph Cook GCMG
Air Vice-Marshal Sir John W. Cordingley KCB, KCVO, CBE
The Viscount Cowdray PC, GCVO, DL
Marshal of the Royal Air Force The Lord Craig of Radley GCB, OBE, DSC, MA,
   FRAeS

The Rt. Hon. The Viscount De L'Isle VC, KG, GCMG, GCVO, PC, FCA, FRIBA, LLD
Marshal of the Royal Air Force Sir William Dickson GCB, KBE, DSO, AFC

Marshal of the Royal Air Force Sir Edward Ellington GCB, CMG, CBE
Marshal of the Royal Air Force The Lord Elworthy KG, GCB, CBE, DSO, MVO,
   DFC, AFC, MA

The Hon. George Howard Ferguson KC, LLD, BA
The Rt. Hon. Andrew Fisher PC
The Rt. Hon. Hugh Fraser MBE, MP

Marshal of the Royal Air Force Sir John Grandy GCB, GCVO, KBE, DSO
Air Chief Marshal Sir Michael Graydon GCB CBE FRAeS
The Rt. Hon. Frederick Guest CBE, DSO, MP
Dame Helen Gwynne-Vaughan CBE, LLD, DSC, FLS

Air Chief Marshal Sir Lewis Hodges KCB, CBE, DSO, DFC
Marshal of the Royal Air Force Sir Andrew Humphrey GCB, OBE, DFC, AFC
Lady Humphrey OBE

Air Chief Marshal Sir Richard Johns GCB, CBE, LVO, ADC, FRAeS
His Excellency The Rt. Hon. Sir William Joseph Jordan KCMG, PC, LLD, LP (NZ)

Air Chief Marshal Sir Thomas Kennedy GCB, AFC
The Rt. Hon. The Viscount Knollys GCMG, MBE, DFC

The Hon. Peter Charles Larkin
Air Chief Marshal Sir David Lee GBE, CB
The Most Hon. The Marquess of Londonderry KG, MVO

The Hon. Sir Thomas Mackenzie GCMG, JP, FRGS, MLC, LLD
The Rt. Hon. Harold Macmillan OM, FRS, DCL, LLD
The Rt. Hon. Vincent Massey CH
Sir Charles McLeod, Bt.
The Lord Montagu of Beaulieu KCIE, CSI, CC, JP, VD, DL
The Rt. Hon. The Lord Mottistone PC, CB, CMG, DSO

Marshal of the Royal Air Force The Rt. Hon. The Lord Newall GCB, OM, GCMG,
  CBE, AM
The Rt. Hon. George Heaton Nicholls
The Viscount Northcliffe

Air Chief Marshal Sir Roger Palin KCB, OBE, MA, FRAeS
Air Commodore Dame Felicity Peake DBE, JP, AE
The Hon. Sir James Parr KCMG
The Hon. Sir Charles Parsons OM, KCB, MA, LLD, DSC, FRS, JP
Sir Geoffrey Pattie MP
The Rt. Hon. Sir George Perley GCMG
Marshal of the Royal Air Force Sir Thomas Pike CGB, CBE, DFC
Marshal of the Royal Air Force The Rt. Hon. The Viscount Portal of Hungerford
  KC, CGB, OM, DSO, MC, DL, DCL, LLD
Joan, Viscountess Portal of Hungerford

The Rt. Hon. The Lord Quickswood PC, DL, LLD

Colonel The Hon. Deneys Reitz
The Rt. Hon. The Lord Rhyl OBE, PC
The Lord Riddell
The Rt. Hon. The Lord Riverdale CBE, LLD, JP
N. Robertson Esq.
The Viscount Rothermere PC
The Rt. Hon. The Lord Rowley QC, PC, MA, LLB
Major-General The Hon. Sir Granville Ryrie KCMG, CB, VD

Marshal of the Royal Air Force Sir John Salmond GCB, CMG, CVO, DSO, DCL,
  LLD
The Rt. Hon. The Lord Shackleton of Burley KG, PC, OBE, LLD, DSC, FBIM
Marshal of the Royal Air Force Sir John Slessor GCB, DSO, MC, DL, JP, CC
Marshal of the Royal Air Force Sir Denis Spotswood GCB, CBE, DFC
The Rt. Hon. The Viscount Stansgate PC, DSO, DFC
Rear-Admiral Sir Murray Sueter CB
His Grace The Duke of Sutherland KT
The Rt. Hon. The Earl of Swinton GBE, CH, MC, DL, LLD, PC
The Lord Sydenham GCMG, GCIE, GCSI, GBE, FRS
Air Vice-Marshal The Rt. Hon. Sir Frederick Sykes CBE, GCSI, GCIE, KCB, CMG,
  PC

Marshal of the Royal Air Force The Rt. Hon. The Lord Tedder GCB, DCL, LLD
The Rt. Hon. The Viscount Templewood PC, GCSI, GBE, CMG, DCL, LLD, DL, JP
Brigadier-General The Lord Thomson PC, CBE, DSO

The Rt. Hon. The Viscount Thurso KT, CMG, PC, LLD, JP
Marshal of the Royal Air Force The Rt. Hon. The Viscount Trenchard GCB, OM,
    GCVO, DSO, DCL, LLD
The Rt. Hon. The Viscount Trenchard MC

Air Chief Marshal Sir Augustus Walker GCB, CBE, DSO, DFC, AFC, MA
The Hon. Sir Edgar Walton KCMG
The Rt. Hon. The Viscount Ward of Witley PC
C. T. te Water Esq.
The Hon. Sidney Frank Waterson
The Rt. Hon. The Viscount Weir PC, GCB, DL
Sir Thomas Wilford KCMG, KC
The Rt. Hon. Sir Kingsley Wood MP
Marshal of the Royal Air Force Sir Keith Williamson GCB, AFC

Chairmen

The Rt. Hon. Lord Hugh Cecil PC, MP	1919–1929
Sir Charles C. McLeod Bt.	1929-1934
The Viscount Wakefield of Hythe GCVO, CBE	1934–1940
His Royal Highness Prince George,	
Duke of Kent KG, KT, GCMG, GCVO	1941–1942
The Rt. Hon. The Lord Riverdale GBE, LLD, JP	1942–1952
The Rt. Hon. The Viscount Knollys GCMG, MBE, DFC	1953–1966
Sir Harald Peake AE	1967–1978
The Lord Catto of Cairncatto	1978–1991
The Lord Barber of Wentbridge	1991–1995
Sir Adrian Swire	1996 to date

Controllers

Air Vice-Marshal Sir Hazelton Nicholl KBE, CB	1944–1947
Air Vice-Marshal Sir John W. Cordingley KCB, KCVO, CBE	1947–1962
Air Marshal Sir John Whitley KBE, CB, DSO, AFC	1962–1968
Air Marshal Sir William Coles KBE, CB, DSO, DFC, AFC	1968–1975
Air Marshal Sir Denis Crowley-Milling KCB, CBE, DSO, DFC, AE	1975–1981
Air Chief Marshal Sir Alasdair Steedman GCB, CBE, DFC,	
FRAeS, CBIM	1981–1988
Air Chief Marshal Sir Thomas Kennedy GCB, AFC, DL	1988–1993
Air Chief Marshal Sir Roger Palin KGB, OBE, MA, FRAeS	1993–1998
Air Chief Marshal Sir David Cousins KCB, AFC, BA	1998 to date

APPENDIX B

THE FUND'S WORK, 1919–1998

	Awards	Relief expenditure £		Awards	Relief expenditure £
1919	---	919	1960	12,585	527,979
1920	---	---	1961	12,157	580,087
1921	---	6,569	1962	12,727	593,717
1922	320	5,868	1963	13,570	634,667
1923	539	9,861	1964	12,389	675,024
1924	750	8,380	1965	11,635	859,392
1925	1,022	8,636	1966	11,590	890,272
1926	1,180	10,451	1967	11,368	803,885
1927	1,406	10,461	1968	10,240	845,155
1928	1,699	12,538	1969	9,552	905,199
1929	1,812	14,498	1970	10,302	935,441
1930	1,812	14,450	1971	10,038	1,005,598
1931	1,966	15,581	1972	9,557	1,071,380
1932	2,189	15,167	1973	8,190	1,293,264
1933	2,529	17,759	1974	7,663	1,619,738
1934	2,174	16,189	1975	7,368	1,494,033
1935	2,134	18,785	1976	7,859	1,759,626
1936	1,928	18,817	1977	6,916	1,486,402
1937	1,849	20,292	1978	7,852	2,023,322
1938	2,132	22,290	1979	7,088	2,048,078
1939	2,477	22,921	1980	8,128	2,709,005
1940	3,709	27,766	1981	8,906	3,041,828
1941	5,596	38,352	1982	9,480	3,973,847
1942	8,354	55,610	1983	10,778	4,063,643
1943	12,824	89,495	1984	12,138	5,340,060
1944	17,780	163,679	1985	13,044	7,135,469
1945	28,591	326,697	1986	14,742	8,164,663
1946	31,134	507,615	1987	14,777	8,556,972
1947	28,546	529,735	1988	15,880	8,641,262
1948	32,541	668,656	1989	15,168	7,486,955
1949	30,362	711,829	1990	15,856	7,993,519
1950	27,044	608,816	1991	15,822	7,015,978
1951	24,143	640,466	1992	18,430	7,834,584
1952	25,659	681,474	1993	17,620	8,325,423
1953	22,752	588,364	1994	17,882	9,105,542
1954	20,240	557,316	1995	18,358	10,252,911
1955	17,465	523,916	1996	24,692	12,427,606
1956	17,199	568,564	1997	26,746	13,131,393
1957	16,475	579,118	1998	29,534	12,487,919
1958	15,912	520,478			
1959	14,986	495,500	Totals	937,878	178,894,711

APPENDIX C

HONOURS AND AWARDS FOR SERVICES TO THE FUND

Year	Name	Award
1944	Squadron Leader V. S. Erskine-Lindop	OBE
1945	Sir Bertram Rumble	Kt
1947	F. C. Hawkes Esq.	OBE
1947	Mrs F. Vesey Holt	OBE
1948	J. F. Linney Esq.	CBE
1951	F. Wilkins Esq.	OBE
1952	W. Wallace Withers Esq.	CBE
1956	Major (formerly Sqn. Ldr.) H. G. Vyse	OBE
1959	E. de Rougemont Esq.	CBE
1961	Mrs R. J. Sanceau	MBE
1962	Air Vice-Marshal Sir John W. Cordingley	KCVO
1964	P. F. du Sautoy Esq.	OBE
1965	Mrs G. Inglis	MBE
1968	Flight Lieutenant J. A. B. Cairns	MBE
1972	Mrs E. A. Page	MBE
1973	Harald Peake Esq.	Kt
1973	Flight Lieutenant G. C. Sykes	MBE
1974	John H. Corner	OBE
1975	Mrs K. R. Masters	MBE
1975	Lady Drummond	MBE
1976	Miss Helen McDougal	MBE
1980	Miss Jean Ashton	MBE
1983	Miss W. Sheerin	MBE
1985	P. M. Cutting Esq. DFC	OBE
1998	F. W. Crawley Esq. FCIB, CIMgt	CBE
1998	Group Captain E. J. Goodman	OBE
1999	G. Hayhoe Esq.	MBE

SOME OF THE ORGANISATIONS AND SCHOOLS WITH WHICH THE FUND HAS CO-OPERATED

Abbeyfield Society
Air Bridge Association
Alexandra and Albert School, Reigate
Alexandra House, Newquay
Alzheimer's Disease Society
Army Benevolent Fund
Ashwellthorpe Hall Association
Association of Jewish Ex-Servicemen and Women
Association to Combat Huntington's Chorea
ATS and WRAC Benevolent Funds

Badger House (The Cornelius Trust)
Barnardo's
Bedfordshire War Pensions
Birmingham & Midland Limbless Ex-Servicemen Association
Birmingham War Pensions Association
Blond McIndoe Centre for Medical Research
Bournemouth War Memorial Homes
British Commonwealth Ex-Services League
British Hospital and Home for Incurables, Streatham
British Limbless Ex-Servicemen's Association
Broughton House

Calibre, Cassette Library
Care for Mentally Handicapped
Chaseley Trust for Disabled Ex-Servicemen, Eastbourne
Cheshire Foundation Homes for the Sick
Chest, Heart and Stroke Association
Children with Leukaemia
Christ's Hospital
Church Army
Churchill Centre for Rehabilitation
Church of England Children's Society
Clifton College, Bristol
College of St Barnabas
Compton House

Confederation of British Service & Ex-Services Organisations (COBSEO)
Coningsby Special Needs Group
Counsel and Care for the Elderly
Cranleigh School
Crohn's in Childhood Appeal
CRUSE Bereavement Care
Cumbria & Lancashire War Pensions Association
Curphey Home, Jamaica

Danson Clinic of the Incorporated Liverpool School of Tropical Medicine
David Tolkien Trust for Stoke Mandeville
Dean Close School, Cheltenham
Disabled Drivers' Association
Dolphin School, Newark
Douglas Haig Memorial Homes
Dresden House, Hove

Earl Haig Fund (Scotland)
East Grinstead Medical Research Team
East Lancashire Homes for Disabled Sailors, Soldiers and Airmen (Broughton
     House, Salford)
Ellesmere College
Enham Trust
Ex-Royal Air Force Dependants' Severely Disabled Holiday Trust
Ex-Service Fellowship Centres
Ex-Services Mental Welfare Society
Ex-Services War Disabled Help Department of the Order of St John and the
     British Red Cross Society
Eventide Homes, Brixham

Family Welfare Association
Far East Prisoners of War and Internees Fund
Finchale Training College for the Disabled, Durham
Forces Help Society and Lord Roberts Workshops

Gordon's School, Woking
Guild of Air Pilots' Benevolent Fund
Guinea Pig Club
Gwennili Trust

Hanover Housing Association
Harcourt School, Andover
Help the Aged
Help the Hospices
Holiday Care Service
Home Farm Trust, Bristol
Hospice of St Francis
House Association for Officers' Families
Hurstpierpoint School, Hassocks

Invalid Children's Aid Association

King Alfred School, Somerset
King Edward VII's Hospital for Officers (Sister Agnes Foundation)
King Edward VII Convalescent Home for Officers, Isle of Wight
King George's Fund for Sailors
Kingham Hill School, Oxford
Kitchener Scholarships – The Lord Kitchener National Memorial Fund

Ladybird School, Lossiemouth
Laurel Court
League of Remembrance
'Lest We Forget' Association
Lilian Faithful Homes, Cheltenham
Lord Wandsworth College, Basingstoke

Malvern College
Marie Curie Memorial Foundation
Marlborough College
Mental After Care Association
Mill Hill School
Morden College Home, Blackheath
Motor Neurone Disease Association
Multiple Sclerosis Society

National Association for Mental Health
National Council for One-Parent Families
National Gulf Veterans
National Music for the Blind
National Organisation for the Widowed and their Children (CRUSE)
National Society for Cancer Relief
Noah's Ark Development Group
Northam Lodge & Rose Hill
'Not Forgotten' Association
NSPCC

Officers' Association
Officers Pensions Society
One Parent Families

Papworth and Enham Foundation
Park House Preparatory School, Paignton
Paul Bevan Cancer Foundation
Phyllis Tuckwell Memorial Hospice
Pilgrims Hospice
Polish Air Force Benevolent Fund
Portland Training College for the Disabled, Mansfield
Princess Louise Scottish Hospital for Limbless Sailors, Soldiers and Airmen

Queen Alexandra Hospital Home, Gifford House, Worthing

Queen Elizabeth's Foundation for the Disabled, Leatherhead
Queen Victoria School, Dunblane

RAF Widows Association
Reed's School, Cobham
Regular Forces Employment Association
Relate
Royal Air Force and Dependants Disabled Holiday Trust
Royal Air Forces Association, Richard Peck House, St Annes-on-Sea;
    Sussexdown, Storrington; Dowding House, Moffat
Royal Association for Disability and Rehabilitation (RADAR)
Royal British Legion
Royal British Legion Industries
Royal Caledonian Schools
Royal Homes for Officers' Widows and Daughters
Royal Hospital and Home, Putney
Royal Hospital for Neuro-disability
Royal National Institute for the Blind
Royal Naval Benevolent Society
Royal Naval Benevolent Trust
Royal Patriotic Fund Corporation
Royal Star and Garter Home, Richmond
Royal Surgical Aid Society, Homes for the Elderly
Royal United Kingdom Beneficient Association (RUKBA)
Royal Wanstead School
Royal Wolverhampton School

Salvation Army
Scottish Bobath Centre
Scottish National Institution for the War Blinded
Scottish Naval, Military and Air Force Veterans' Residences
Scottish Veterans' Garden City Association
Scottish Veterans Residences
Shaftesbury Homes and 'Arethusa'
Sir Beachcroft Towse Ex-Service Fund for the Blind
Sir Oswald Stoll Foundation
SOS Society
Soldiers', Sailors' and Airmen's Families Association (SSAFA)
SOUNDAROUND
Spinal Injuries Association
SSAFA Forces Help
SSAFA Officers' Widows' Branch
SSAFA Royal Homes for Officers' Widows & Daughters
St David's Home for Disabled Ex-Servicemen
St Dunstan's
St Edward's School, Oxford
St Luke's Hospice
St Loye's College for the Disabled, Exeter
Sue Ryder Home, Nettlebed

Talking Books for the Handicapped
Talking Newspapers
Tape Programmes for the Blind
Thames Valley Hospice (Pine Lodge)
Thistle Foundation, Edinburgh
Treloar Trust, Alton
Turning Point

Viscountess Barrington Homes

Wellington College, Crowthorne
Whitefoord House and Rosendale, Edinburgh
Winged Fellowship Trust
William Simpson's Home
Women's Royal Naval Service Benevolent Trust

INDEX